WORK REDESIGN

J. RICHARD HACKMAN
Yale University

GREG R. OLDHAM
University of Illinois

Addison-Wesley Publishing Company
Reading, Massachusetts • Menlo Park, California
London • Amsterdam • Don Mills, Ontario • Sydney

This book is in the Addison-Wesley series:

ORGANIZATION DEVELOPMENT

Editors:
Edgar H. Schein
Richard Beckhard

Library of Congress Cataloging in Publication D ta

Hackman, J   Richard.
    Work redesign.

    (Addison-Wesley's organization development
series)
    Bibliography: p.

    1. Division of labor. 2. Industrial
organization. 3. Work design. 4. Personnel
management. I. Oldham, Greg R., joint author.
II. Title.
HD51.H32   658.3   79-8918
ISBN 0-201-02779-8

ISBN 0-201-02779-8
DEFGHIJK-DO-898765

If only it weren't for the people, the goddamned people," said Finnerty, "always getting tangled up in the machinery. If it weren't for them, earth would be an engineer's paradise "

—from *Player Piano* by Kurt Vonnegut, Jr.

FOREWORD

It has been five years since the Addison-Wesley series on organization development published the books by Roeber, Galbraith, and Steele, and it is almost ten years since the series itself was launched in an effort to define the then-emerging field of organization development. Almost from its inception the series enjoyed a great success and helped to define what was then only a budding field of inquiry. Much has happened in the last ten years. There are now dozens of textbooks and readers on OD; research results are beginning to accumulate on what kinds of OD approaches have what effects; educational programs on planned change and OD are growing; and there are regional, national, and even international associations of practitioners of planned change and OD. All of these trends suggest that this area of practice has taken hold and found an important niche for itself in the applied social sciences and that its intellectual underpinnings are increasingly solidifying.

One of the most important trends we have observed in the last five years is the connecting of the field of planned change and OD to the mainstream of organization theory, organizational psychology, and organizational sociology. Although the field has its roots primarily in these underlying disciplines, it is only in recent years that basic textbooks in "organization behavior" have begun routinely referring to organization development as an applied area that students and managers alike must be aware of.

The editors of this series have attempted to keep an open mind on the question of when the series has fulfilled its function and should be allowed to die. The series should be kept alive only as long as new areas of knowledge and practice central to organization development are emerging. During the last year or so, several such areas have been defined, leading to the decision to continue the series.

On the applied side, it is clear that information is a basic nutrient for any kind of valid change process. Hence, a book on data gathering, surveys, and feedback methods is very timely. Nadler has done an especially important service in this area in focusing on the variety of methods which can be used in gathering information and feeding it back to clients. The book is eclectic in its approach, reflecting the fact that there are many ways to gather information, many kinds to be gathered, and many approaches to the feedback process to reflect the particular goals of the change program.

Team building and the appropriate use of groups continues to be a second key ingredient of most change programs. So far no single book in the field has dealt explicitly enough with this important process. Dyer's approach will help the manager to diagnose when to use and not use groups and, most important, how to carry out team building when that kind of intervention is appropriate.

One of the most important new developments in the area of planned change is the conceptualizing of how to work with large systems to initiate and sustain change over time. The key to this success is "transition management," a stage or process frequently referred to in change theories, but never explored systematically from both a theoretical and practical point of view. Beckhard and Harris present a model which will help the manager to think about this crucial area. In addition, they provide a set of diagnostic and action tools which will enable the change manager in large systems to get a concrete handle on transition management.

The area of organization design has grown in importance as organizations have become more complex. Davis and Lawrence provide a concise and definitive analysis of that particularly elusive organization design—the matrix organization—and elucidate clearly its forms, functions, and modes of operation.

Problems of organization design and organization development are especially important in the rapidly growing form of organization known as the "multinational." Heenan and Perlmutter have worked in a variety of such organizations and review some fascinating cases as well as provide relevant theory for how to think about the design and development of such vastly more complex systems.

As organizations become more complex, managers need help in diagnosing what is going on both internally and externally. Most OD books put a heavy emphasis on diagnosing, but few have provided workable schemes for the manager to think through the multiple diagnostic issues which face him or her. Kotter has presented a simple and workable model that can lead the manager through a systematic diagnostic process while revealing the inherent complexity of organizations and the multiple interdependencies that exist within them.

Human resource planning and career development has become an increasingly important element in the total planning of organization improvement programs. Schein's book provides a broad overview of this field from the points of view of the individual and the total life cycle, the interaction between the career and other aspects of life such as the family, and the manager attempting to design a total human resource planning and development system.

The study of human resources in organizations has revealed the variety of new life-styles and value patterns which employees of today display, forcing organizations to rethink carefully how they structure work and what they consider to be "normal" work patterns. Cohen and Gadon provide an excellent review of various alternate work patterns that have sprung up in the last decade and are revolutionizing the whole concept of a normal work week.

Finally, one of the most significant ways to develop organizations is to redesign the work itself. It has been widely recognized that a key to improving life in organizations is to find ways of making work meaningful and challenging. Hackman and Oldham have spent a decade developing ways of analyzing work situations and developing diagnostic tools and guidelines for work redesign, which are presented in concise form in their book for this series.

Edgar H. Schein

PREFACE

Writing this book was work. But it was a nice kind of work. We found ourselves stretched beyond what we thought we knew when we tried to write it down, and we learned a lot. We did the book in our own way and on our own schedule, as several frustrated editors at Addison-Wesley will confirm without even being asked. And we got a little queasy from the ups and downs of the roller-coaster as we discovered, on rereading first drafts of chapters a month after writing them, that they were terrible—or, occasionally, pretty good. It has been an intensely involving experience; it gave us almost as much pleasure as frustration, and it feels awfully good to be done.

At least according to the criteria we set forth in this book, the task we have had for the last couple of years was well designed. Writing the book was something we found personally meaningful; we felt shared responsibility for the product, and we received plenty of feedback as we worked—from each other and from many helpful colleagues and students.

Lots of jobs are not so well designed. They demotivate people rather than turn them on. They undermine rather than encourage productivity and work quality. They aren't any fun.

This book is about ways that jobs can be set up so that work and fun are not so often at opposite poles of people's experiences, and so that productivity does not have to be at the expense of the satisfaction and growth of the people who do the producing.

While we believe that there are many people and many organizations that would be better off if jobs and work systems were redesigned along the lines suggested in our book, we have not written an evangelical tract touting the saviorlike qualities of work redesign. Indeed, as will be seen in the last chapter, we see some reasons for pessimism about the potency of work redesign as a device for planned, developmental changes in organizations. And we are uneasy about the future directions that work and organizational design may take in this country.

We probably are not as balanced and objective in our reporting and interpreting as we could have been. When we have opinions about the material, we state them. And we have been quite free in offering new ideas about the design and management of work systems—ideas that have not been tested by research and that may well turn out to be wrong when they are. We have, however, tried very hard to label our opinions and untested ideas as such, so that each reader can make his or her own assessment of their merit.

In Part One of the book we review a number of different approaches to managing the relationship between people and the work they do. We conclude that review with a summary of the main features of our own approach to set the stage for the remainder of the book. Here are some extracts from that summary, to provide prospective readers with an idea of what is in store.

• Our approach focuses squarely on the actual work that people perform in organizations. We assume that problems stemming from unsatisfactory relationships between people and their jobs can, in many instances, be remedied by restructuring the jobs that are performed, rather than by continued efforts to select, train, direct, and motivate people so that they fit better with the requirements of fixed jobs.

• We deal separately with the design of work for individuals (in Part Two of the book) and the design of work for groups (in Part Three). We believe that the choice between individual and group designs is one of the most important that is made when work systems are restructured, and that the conditions required for individual work effectiveness are rather different from those needed for effective team performance.

- We deal explicitly both with individual differences in how people react to their work, and with aspects of the organizational context that affect the feasibility, potency, and persistence of work redesign activities. While our approach is neither an "individual differences" theory nor a "systems" model, we recognize the importance of both in affecting what happens when people perform work in organizations and when jobs are redesigned.

- Throughout the book, we emphasize the importance of collecting diagnostic data about a work system before it is redesigned. There are, we believe, few universals regarding work redesign: what is appropriate in one set of organizational circumstances will wholly miss the mark in another. And what changes intuitively seem right when one first looks at a work system often turn out later to be wrong or irrelevant. For these reasons, pre-change diagnostic work seems to us critical to competent work redesign, and our change models explicitly incorporate diagnostic activities.

- Finally, our approach highlights the links between basic theory about behavior in organizations and practical technologies for the design and redesign of jobs. If a theoretical proposition has no implications for action, we are likely to suffice by noting it as a matter of passing scholarly interest. And if a particular technique for change has no conceptual basis, we are unlikely to mention it at all. We share with Lewin the view that there is nothing so practical as a good theory, and we have tried very hard to keep the conceptual and practical threads of our approach woven together.

In sum, we have attempted here to bring together our own work and that of many others to provide some realistic alternatives to traditional wisdom about how jobs and work systems should be designed. And, in Part Four of the book, we have placed these alternatives in organizational and societal context—where it becomes clear just how difficult it is to implement nontraditional ideas about the design and management of work in traditional organizations.

We hope our book will be useful to managers and consultants who are personally involved in deciding how to structure and manage jobs and work systems. We hope students will find the book enlightening and interesting. And, of course, we very much hope that our professional and scholarly colleagues will find here a new idea or two worthy of their attention. We have tried to write the book so that the ideas and views presented will be accessible to all of these audiences, and we apologize for those occasions when our resolve fails and we lapse into jargon to make a point that could be better said in English.

We have had many helpers and critics in writing the book, and we are grateful to them all. Support from the Office of Naval Research (through Contract N00014-75C-0269, NR 170-744, of the Organizational Effectiveness Research Program to Yale University) provided time for writing and the wherewithall to carry out much of the research that gave rise to the book.[1] Special thanks are due Dr. Bert T. King, our scientific officer at ONR. His high standards of excellence, his commitment to the scholarly autonomy of principal investigators, and his personal support provide for us a model of what a scientific officer should be.

Some of the ideas here really belong to Edward E. Lawler. We would like to give him credit in the appropriate places, but we simply do not know which ideas are his: our involvement with Ed over the years has been so rich and stimulating that it is no longer possible for us to sort out who thought of what first. So we apologize to Ed for any unintended thefts, and we thank him for being such a close and generous friend and colleague.

We also have benefitted from the ideas and perspectives of many other colleagues, only a few of whom can be named here. Bob Janson and Ken Purdy of Roy Walters and Associates provided access to many organizations for our research, taught us a great deal about how work systems *really* operate, and helped us see what is required to create conditions for constructive change in messy organizations. Richard Beckhard, Eliza Collins, Terry Mitchell, and Edgar Schein reviewed the first draft of the manuscript, and this final version is much improved over what they read because of what they said. Marie Avitable, Naomi Buchanan, and Brenda Mullins provided prompt and expert typing, and were most understanding of our erratic writing schedules. And our heartfelt thanks go to the graduate students with whom we have worked over the last four or five years. They shared with us their ideas, commented helpfully on bits and pieces of the book as we wrote them, and altogether taught us a great deal.

---

1   The United States Government has a royalty-free license throughout the world in all copyrightable material contained herein.

We needed more than the usual doses of patience and support while writing this book, as everyone who has had anything to do with us recently knows all too well. Our spouses, Judith and Linda, gave us that in good measure. More important, however, is the context they provide for us as persons: how they live their lives enriches ours immeasurably, and the dedication of this book to them is but a token expression of how we feel about them and how they help us feel about ourselves.

New Haven, Connecticut   J.R.H.
Urbana, Illinois   G.R.O.
November 1979

CONTENTS

**PART ONE
INTRODUCTION**

1
PEOPLE AND THEIR WORK

Ralph Chattick is a 44-year-old worker in a metal fabrication shop on the south side of Chicago.[1] He grew up in the same neighborhood where he now lives, and has worked for the same company since graduating from high school many years ago. His job is to cut sheets of metal according to specification, with good accuracy and little waste. Ralph's work goes to another section, where various types of metal assemblies are constructed.

Ralph doesn't work very hard at his job, and he doesn't have to. He knows how to get through a workday without getting too tired and without attracting any special attention from his foreman. Indeed, one might infer from observing Ralph at work that he and his foreman have an agreement of sorts—perhaps best characterized as a truce—which specifies that if Ralph does a reasonable amount of work of reasonable accuracy, the foreman will leave him alone. The pay Ralph gets is adequate, and if asked on a survey whether or not he was "satisfied with his job," Ralph would say, without much thought, "yes." He is not angry, he's not looking for a better job (although he'd like more pay), and he's not much interested in how

---

[1] The name of the person described and numerous other identifying details have been changed.

well the company does. Ralph gets along. He knows his place, it's reasonably comfortable, and he stays there.

The top management of the company where Ralph works is concerned. Productivity is down, customers are complaining about the quality of the products, and the organization seems to be stagnating. An organization development consultant has been contacted, and the president of the company is considering contracting with the consultant for a program to improve the quality of organizational management. The program being contemplated will involve a thorough diagnosis of the managerial styles of all top- and middle-level managers, a study of interlevel and interdepartmental relationships, and an analysis of how the design of the organization itself fits with the imperatives of its technology and its environment. Based on the results of this diagnostic work, a change program may be undertaken to revitalize the management of the organization and, it is hoped, eventually to improve the productivity and profitability of the company.

Will the program, if undertaken with vigor and commitment, achieve its goals? Perhaps. But if improved productivity is among the goals of the program, it will at some time have to touch Ralph and his co-workers—because they are the ones *who do the productive work of the company.* Many organizational change programs deal with Ralph "later," after important issues in organizational design and management have been addressed and dealt with. And, unfortunately, it often turns out that "later" means "never."

This book explores the possibility that one of the major influences on organizational productivity is *the quality of the relationship between people who do the work and the jobs they perform.* If there is a good "fit" between people and their jobs, such that productive work is a personally rewarding experience, then there may be little for management to do to foster high motivation and satisfaction—other than support the healthy person-job relationship that exists. But if that fit is faulty, such that hard and productive work leads mainly to personal discomfort and distress, then there may be little that management *can* do to engender high productivity and satisfying work experiences. For this reason, we believe it is advantageous to address person-job relationships first, rather than later, if improved productivity and quality of worklife are among the goals of an organization.

A CRISIS IN PERSON-JOB RELATIONSHIPS?

Just how satisfactory are person-job relationships in contemporary organizations? Are most people prospering in their work, or at least as comfortable with their jobs as Ralph seems to be? Or are most employees chafing in jobs that are grossly inappropriate for their personal needs, skills, and aspirations?

There is a good deal of controversy about the matter. Some commentators argue with vigor that we are currently in the midst of a major "work ethic crisis" that portends revolutionary changes in how work will be designed and managed in the future. Others respond that the purported "crisis" is much more in the minds of those who herald its arrival than in the hearts of those who perform the productive work of society. That there is a great deal of commentary and controversy about the quality of person-job relationships is clear. But *is* there a crisis?

Yes

Consider the following statement, which opens a book by Harold Sheppard and Neal Herrick titled *Where Have All the Robots Gone?*

> In today's highly regimented, increasingly automated, and deeply impersonal industrial society, the human being who has found fulfilling work is indeed among the blessed. But more and more workers—and every day this is more apparent—are becoming disenchanted with the boring, repetitive tasks set by a merciless assembly line or by bureaucracy. They feel they have been herded into economic and social cul-de-sacs (Sheppard and Herrick, 1972, p. xi).

A similar theme is used by Studs Terkel to introduce his book *Working,* in which the thoughts and feelings of workers from many occupations and classes are reflected:

> This book, being about work, is, by its very nature, about violence—to the spirit as well as to the body. It is about ulcers as well as accidents, about shouting matches as well as fistfights, about nervous breakdowns as well as kicking the dog around. It is, above all (or beneath all), about daily humiliations. To survive the day is triumph enough for the walking wounded among the great many of us. . . .

For the many, there is a hardly concealed discontent. The blue-collar blues is no more bitterly sung than the white-collar moan. "I'm a machine," says the spot-welder. "I'm caged," says the bank teller, and echoes the hotel clerk. "I'm a mule," says the steelworker. "A monkey can do what I do," says the receptionist. "I'm less than a farm implement," says the migrant worker. "I'm an object," says the high-fashion model. Blue collar and white call upon the identical phrase: "I'm a robot" (Terkel, 1974, pp. xi-xii).[2]

These themes have been echoed throughout the 1970s—from the popular press (such as Barbara Garson's article in the June 1972 *Harper's* titled "Luddites in Lordstown") to statements prepared by government task forces (such as the book *Work in America* published in 1973 by a special task force created by the Secretary of Health, Education, and Welfare). By the mid-1970s, numerous statistical data had accumulated to support the expressed concerns. In 1976, for example, roughly 80 million hours *per week* were lost to absenteeism (Hedges, 1977). Productive output per employee hour decreased in two-thirds of the industries included in the Bureau of Labor Statistics's 1974 report on industrial productivity (Herman, 1975). Turnover rates, averaging 1.2 percent per month in the early 1960s, more than doubled by the end of the decade (Bureau of Labor Statistics, 1976).

A vivid account of the impact of these changing statistics in one industry is provided by Gooding (1970):

Absenteeism has risen sharply; in fact it has doubled over the past ten years at General Motors and at Ford, with the sharpest climb in the past year. It has reached the point where an average of 5 percent of G.M.'s hourly workers are missing from work without explanation every day.... On some days, notably Fridays and Mondays, the figure goes as high as 10 percent. Tardiness has increased, making it even more difficult to start up the production lines promptly when a shift begins—after the foreman has scrambled around to replace missing workers. Complaints about quality are up sharply. There are more arguments with the foreman, more complaints about discipline and overtime, more

---

2   ©   Pantheon Books, a division of Random House, Inc. Reprinted by permission.

grievances. There is more turnover. The quit rate at Ford last year was 25.2 percent (p. 70).

How are we to account for such changes in employee behavior and attitude? Those who perceive that we are in the midst of a work ethic crisis tend to argue along the following lines. No less than a revolution in the way productive work is done in the United States has occurred in this century, they suggest. In the last several decades, organizations have increased the role of technology and automation in attaining organizational objectives, and have dramatically expanded the number of jobs that are specialized, simplified, standardized, and routinized. Moreover, organizations themselves have become larger and more bureaucratic in how they function. As a consequence there have been great increases in the use of managerial and statistical controls to guide and enforce the day-to-day activities of organization members.

The efficiencies of advanced technology, the economies of scale, and the benefits of increased managerial control also have generated substantial increases in the productive efficiency of organizations—and substantial economic benefits to the owners of organizations and to the society as a whole. These economic benefits, it is argued, have been responsible for a general increase in the affluence, education, and personal level of aspiration of individuals in American society.

Specifically, as organizations increased in efficiency early in this century, workers demanded (and, through unionization, got) an increased share of the economic benefits that were being generated. Moreover, through taxation, another portion of these benefits was channeled into programs and activities aimed at increasing the personal and social welfare of the populace. People become more affluent, the number of years of schooling obtained by young people dramatically increased, and the hopes and expectations of the present generation of workers about what life—and work—would hold for them took a quantum jump upwards. As George Strauss summarizes:

> During the 1940s and 1950s workers called *steady work* the most important thing they wanted from their jobs. A comprehensive 1957 study that summarized the extensive literature to date listed job factors influencing satisfaction in roughly this order: job security, opportunities for advancement, company and manage-

ment, wages, and intrinsic work—with intrinsic work coming fifth. By sharp contrast, in a 1969 survey *interesting work* came first and job security was rated seventh, and six of the eight most desired aspects of work related to job content (Strauss, 1974, p. 63.)[3]

In sum, even as work organizations have continued to get bigger, more mechanistic, more controlling of individual behavior, and more task-specialized, the people who work in those organizations have become more highly educated, more desirous of "intrinsic" work satisfactions, and perhaps less willing to accept routine and monotonous work as their legitimate lot in life. According to this line of reasoning, we may now have arrived at a point where the way most organizations function is in severe conflict with the talents and aspirations of most of the people who work in them. Such conflict manifests itself in increased alienation from work and in decreased organizational effectiveness, as evidenced in the sagging attendance and productivity figures noted earlier. Ways of structuring jobs and managing organizations that worked early in this century, it is argued, cannot work now because the people who populate contemporary organizations simply will not put up with them.

Ralph Chattick? A temporary causality of poorly designed work. Living evidence that simplified, routinized work is neither effective nor humane. Yet while work stamped out the spark of Ralph's humanity, reversal is possible. Expand Ralph's job, make it challenging, manage him as a person rather than a machine part, and he will surprise management (and, perhaps, himself) with a level of motivated, productive work of which he now seems incapable. And he will move from a state of personal stagnation to growth in the bargain.

Yes, profound alterations in the design and management of work are required. And the benefits of those changes will be well worth the cost and effort required to bring them about.

No

Other observers argue that there is no real "crisis" in the world of work—that instead the reports of worker discontent and demands for

---

3   © The American Assembly, Columbia University. Reprinted by permission.

personally fulfilling work activities have been wildly exaggerated by journalists and social scientists. The work ethic crisis, it is argued, is more manufactured than real, and represents a serious misapprehension of the needs and satisfactions of those individuals who are seen as most troubled by dissatisfying work.

Considerable evidence can be marshalled in support of this view—some anecdotal, some systematic and scientific. Perhaps most widely publicized is the project sponsored by the Ford Foundation to test whether or not U.S. automobile workers would find satisfaction and fulfillment working on highly complex and challenging team assembly jobs in a Swedish automobile plant. Six Detroit auto workers spent a month working as engine assemblers in a Saab plant—and at the end of the month five of the six reported that they preferred the traditional U.S. assembly line. As one worker put it: "If I've got to bust my ass to be meaningful, forget it; I'd rather be monotonous" (Goldmann, 1976, p. 31). Summing up the negative reactions, Arthur Weinberg, a Cornell labor relations expert who accompanied the six workers to Sweden, reported:

> They felt it was a deprivation of their freedom and it was a more burdensome task which required more effort which was more tedious and stressful. They preferred the freedom the assembly line allowed them, the ability to think their own thoughts, to talk to other workers, sing or dance on the assembly line, which you can't do at Saab. There is a freedom allowed on the assembly line not possible in more complex work. The simplified task allows a different kind of freedom. The American workers generally reacted negatively to doing more than one task. They were not accustomed to it and they didn't like it (Gainor, 1975).

The results of this transatlantic experiment are paralleled by the findings of Siassi, Crocetti, and Spiro (1974), who found that automobile workers holding production line jobs did not show heightened levels of depression, dissatisfaction with work or with life, boredom, loneliness, or "unrelatedness." These researchers concluded that psychiatrists should be very careful about attributing the emotional complaints of assembly line workers to "blue-collar blues" caused by the stress of assembly line work. More generally, they suggested that "to impute boredom, alienation, anomie, or the seeds of mental illness to another man's work or existence is a hazardous thing. To some blue collar workers, the social scientists' preoccupation with books, dry articles, tables of statistics, and obsessive academic discourse must seem more boring, more alienating, more fraught with anomie, than his own existence. That worker might provide excellent evidence that the lonely, dissatisfied social scientist has a much higher rate of surveyed mental illness, psychiatric utilizations, and suicides than any UAW population" (p. 264).

Other researchers and critics also have cast doubt on the popular notion that people who work on routine and repetitive tasks inevitably experience psychological or emotional distress as a consequence (e.g., Hulin and Blood, 1968; Strauss, 1974). Perhaps most supportive of the "no crisis" view is a U.S. Department of Labor Monograph titled *Job Satisfaction: Is There a Trend?* (Quinn, Staines, and McCullough, 1974). This report reviews findings from major national surveys of job satisfaction extending from 1958-73 to determine if, as is sometimes argued by those who perceive a work ethic crisis, the level of satisfaction has been dropping.

The results are clear: not only has there been no significant decline in job satisfaction over the last two decades, but the *level* of satisfaction is—as it has been—quite high: better than 80 percent of the work force consistently report being "satisfied" with their jobs.

It is true that younger workers are more dissatisfied with work than older workers (slightly more than 80 percent of workers under 30 report being satisfied with their jobs, while about 95 percent of workers over 40 report job satisfaction). Yet younger workers were more dissatisfied than their older colleagues 25 years ago, just as they are at present, casting doubt on the hypothesis that contemporary young workers are at the cutting edge of a trend toward increasing job alienation and dissatisfaction.

Those who doubt the existence of a crisis in job satisfaction conclude, on the basis of data such as these, that the "crisis" can be observed only if one looks through the eyes of journalists and behavioral scientists who have a vested interest in seeing it. Indeed, it has been suggested that those who argue for the existence of a crisis in work satisfaction are guilty of one of the gravest sins of a social scientist: attributing the motives and aspirations of the scientist to the people being studied, rather than hearing and reporting accurately what those people actually are saying.

Data from a 1973 survey by the Survey Research Center of the

University of Michigan would seem to support this position.[4] While blue-collar workers reported less overall job satisfaction than did white-collar workers, questions about what was most *important* to blue- versus white-collar workers suggested that "interesting work" is not nearly as important to the blue-collar workers as more bread-and-butter matters such as job security and pay. Specifically, the five "most important" aspects of the job, in order, were as follows for blue- and white-collar workers (Quinn, Staines, and McCullough, 1974, p. 16):

Blue-collar Workers

1. The pay is good

2. I receive enough help and equipment to get the job done

3. The job security is good

4. I have enough information to get the job done

5. The work is interesting

White-Collar Workers

1. The work is interesting

2. I have an opportunity to develop my special abilities

3. I have enough information to get the work done

4. I have enough authority to do do my job

5. I receive enough help and equipment to get the job done

While all aspects of the job listed above are generally viewed as important (no item in either list is endorsed by fewer than half the workers surveyed), it is clear that interesting and skill-enhancing work is a higher priority for white-collar workers (who also tend to be better educated), while pay and job security are more important to the less well educated blue-collar sample.

So if blue-collar workers are dissatisfied, perhaps the major reasons have to do with their pay, with roadblocks that interfere with getting the job done, and with job security. If these items were taken care of, then job satisfaction would be expected to be high. And, by

---

4   The results of the most recent Survey Research Center survey, however, provides some evidence of a decline in job satisfaction. See Staines and Quinn, 1979.

implication, when changes are contemplated to improve the quality of worklife of blue-collar workers, perhaps they should focus on the items highest on the "importance" list of these workers—rather than on changes intended to make jobs more interesting and challenging.

A crisis in job satisfaction? An explosion of blue-collar blues? No. Most people are satisfied with their work. And when they are not, the reasons have more to do with basic issues such as pay and job security than with any unfilled aspirations for interesting and challenging work assignments. Ralph Chattick is a perfect example: he is paid well, his supervisor treats him fairly, and (most importantly) he is not asking to have his job changed. When he says he is satisfied we should believe him. If we really want to be helpful to Ralph and improve his "quality of worklife," then let's focus our changes on the things *he* wants (like a higher salary) rather than on something that journalists or behavioral scientists *think* he should want.

SOME FACTS ABOUT PEOPLE AND WORK

Both the argument for and the argument against a crisis in job satisfaction can be persuasive, and one can argue either side of the question forcefully and with ample supporting data. How can we understand the seeming conflict in the evidence, and how should we come to terms with it in planning and carrying out organizational change?

There are no neat answers to such questions. Yet there are certain facts about people and about work which, if understood, would make discussions about the "crisis" a little less polemic and a little more thoughtful than typically has been the case. These facts, moreover, offer some guidance about how person-job relationships might best be managed in contemporary organizations. Discussed below, these four facts form the basis for the approach to personal and organizational change that is developed in this book.

Fact One: Many People Are Underutilized and Underchallenged at Work

These people, whom O'Toole (1975) calls the "reserve army of the underemployed," have more to offer their employers than those employers seek, and they have personal needs and aspirations that cannot be satisfied by the work they do. It seems to us indisputable that numerous jobs in the bowels of organizations have become increasingly simplified and routinized in the course of the last century, even as the workers who populate those jobs have become generally better educated and more ambitious in their expectations about what life will hold for them.

The result is a poor fit between large numbers of people and the work they do. And, the Peter Principle notwithstanding, this misfit usually has developed because the person is too much for the job rather than because the job is too much for the person. Whether these individuals represent a fifth of the work force or four-fifths is not the question. The fact is that there are millions of individuals in this society for whom work is neither a challenge nor a personally fulfilling part of life.[5]

Fact Two: People Are More Adaptable Than We Realize

When they absolutely must do so, people show an enormous capacity to adapt to their environments. Almost whatever happens to them, people survive and make do: gradually going blind, winning the lottery, losing the home to fire or flood, gaining a spouse and children—or losing them. The same is true for work.

This plasticity often goes unrecognized by those who argue loudly on one or the other side of the "work ethic" debate. Part of the reason is that it is very hard to see adaptation happening, except when the environment changes dramatically and suddenly. When change is gradual, as it is when a person adjusts to a job and an organization, it is almost invisible unless you look at exactly the right time. In studies of work and workers, we tend to catch people after they have adapted to their work situation, or before they have done so, rather than right in the middle of it. It is very hard to figure out what is happening (or what has happened) to a person at work if you look only once.

---

5   A conservative estimate made by one prominent advocate of the "no crisis" view is that approximately 20 percent of all employees are inappropriately matched to their jobs (Fein, 1976b). Given that there are roughly 90 million people in the United States labor force, this suggests that at least *18 million people* have jobs that are poor fits with their needs or skills.

With this in mind, let us review the case of Ralph Chattick, but this time with some additional information about how his life and career developed. We will discover that Ralph, like the rest of us, is a pretty adaptable person.

Ralph did very well in high school, and thought seriously about the possibility of going on to college (although he didn't know exactly what he would *do* with a college degree; no one in his immediate family had ever had one). His teachers were encouraging, but ultimately the limitations of family finances, and Ralph's inability to obtain a large enough scholarship, decreed that he would go to work directly after graduation.

When he took up employment in the metal fabrication shop (where he still works) he retained his dream of saving money and of applying once again to college in a few years. His first job was as a helper to a metal cutter, and he rather enjoyed it. There were some skills involved in metal cutting that he found challenging to learn, and the man he was helping was a good teacher. After two years he was promoted to a position in a cutting department where he worked mostly without supervision, and from what he heard from his foreman he was performing quite well.

But soon he mastered the job, and work became a fairly predictable routine. Ralph began to get bored. He had some money saved, and he once again raised in his mind the possibility of applying to college. However, he also wanted to get married and start a family, and it was clear to Ralph that doing one precluded doing the other. He eventually decided to go ahead with marriage (it was not a hard choice), to use his modest savings to set up house, and after his personal life settled down to do something to improve his situation at work.

Ralph's initial attempts to better his life at work took place within his own company. When he asked about the possibility of promotion, he was told that he might eventually become a foreman (indeed, people were rather encouraging about his prospects), but that promotion would be some years down the road and would depend on whether a position opened up—and who else was applying. A career in higher management was unlikely because he did not have any college work. A transfer to another department was possible, he learned, but he would have to wait his turn. Besides, the jobs that were mentioned to him sounded no better than the one he now held. The one job on the repair and maintenance crew that did sound interesting (and offered the chance to gain some new skills) had such a long waiting list that Ralph did not even put in a bid.

As his restlessness and frustration increased, Ralph looked around for a job in a different company. Unfortunately, unemployment was high at the time, and there were few good jobs open. The only ones that struck him as really attractive required college, experience, or technical skills that Ralph did not have.

At about this point in Ralph's life, in his mid-twenties, he faced a choice of lifetime significance. On the one hand, he could keep looking for a job that he would find fulfilling, and keep fighting the constraints he experienced at work. Or he could accept his job and his organization as his lot in life, and begin the process of adjusting to it. It was a major choice, one of the most important Ralph would make about his work career. But he did not experience it that way. Instead, it was a series of smaller choices, none of which seemed monumental at the time: not to borrow money to go to school; to quit looking at the want ads in the paper; not to spend so much time with those of his workmates who were always complaining about the job and scheming about how to make things different for themselves.

Gradually, the summed effects of those small choices began to show themselves. Ralph's feelings of restlessness dropped. He developed an "understanding" with his supervisor, and devised ways of getting through a typical workday without being bothered too much by the monotony of the work. His productivity settled into a predictable pattern: not too little, not too much, and not to worry too much about quality and waste. Ralph's expectations about what work should mean to a person changed from what they were when he started with the company, and his aspirations about his work career became less ambitious. Increasingly, he became more interested in his wages and what they could buy, and (for the first time) he began to notice how his retirement plan funds were accumulating. Had the possibility of changing organizations come up in later years (it never did), Ralph probably would have decided against such a move because he would have lost substantial retirement benefits.

Others who started work about the time Ralph did took other routes. Some left the organization and succeeded in finding jobs they liked better; some left and later wished they hadn't. Others stayed but were unable or unwilling to adjust as Ralph did: there are some alcoholics in Ralph's section, and one individual who is a moderately heavy user of drugs. A few have defined the company as the "enemy," and fight that enemy whenever and however they can, through sabotage, theft, fraudulent absences, and deliberately low productivity or work quality. But the great majority took the same route Ralph did, and adapted to what they experienced as the inevitability of it all.

When we have to, most of us do. Not to do so would open us to continual feelings of dissatisfaction and distress, which we're well-motivated to avoid. So we adapt: some of us to challenging, exciting jobs, others of us to a pretty routine state of affairs.

When someone, be it a manager or a social scientist, observes us working comfortably at our job, the temptation is to attribute our attitudes and our behavior to "the way we are" as individuals. More often, however, what the observer sees and hears is the way we have *become*. Our work experiences, what happens to us day in and day out over the years, change us in profound ways (Brousseau, 1978; Kohn and Schooler, 1978; Kornhauser, 1965; Sarason, 1977; Seligman, 1975). We may become more rebellious, or more complacent; more oriented toward personal growth and learning, or more security conscious; more neurotic, or healthier. But we are changed. Those who would take what we say and how we act on the job today as reflecting fixed traits of "personality" severely underestimate the profound long-term effects of adaptation processes.

Fact Three: Self-Reports of Job Satisfaction Are Suspect

Precisely because we adapt to our work environment, it is hard to interpret self-reports of how "satisfied" people are with their work, or how "motivated" they feel to perform well. If we had asked Ralph if he was satisfied with his job when he first started to work, his answer would have been a clear "yes." He was involved, he was learning new and interesting things, and he had a vision of an attractive future. If we had asked him a few years later, as he was trying to find ways to get out of a job he experienced as nonchallenging and monotonous, his answer would have been a resounding "no." And hear him now:

Are you satisfied with your work?

Yes, I guess so.

Would you keep working if you won a million dollars in the lottery?

Sure. *(Why?)* Well, you have to do something to fill the day, don't you? I don't know what I'd do if I didn't work.

Do you work hard on your job?

I do my job. You can ask them if I work hard enough.

Is it important to you to do a good job?

Like I said, I do my job.

But is it important to you personally?

Look, I earn what I'm paid, okay? Some here don't, but I do. They pay me to cut metal, and I cut it. If they don't like the way I do it, they can tell me and I'll change. But it's their ball game, not mine.

Ralph is telling us that he is basically satisfied with his work. But how are we to interpret that? Take it at face value and conclude that he is a "satisfied worker"? No, obviously all is not well with Ralph; some signs are present in the above interview excerpt, and our knowledge of Ralph's personal and job history make us even more dubious about the validity of his "yes" to our question.

Yet it also would be inappropriate to assume that Ralph doesn't know what he is talking about, that his "yes" is not an honest response. Ralph is not lying. All things considered, he does find his present work situation basically satisfactory.

The phenomenon of job satisfaction becomes clearer, and the diagnostic task more difficult, when we put ourselves in Ralph's person and consider the alternatives he has in responding. In fact, things are not awful, which is part of the reason for responding affirmatively. But perhaps more important, to answer other than affirmatively would raise for Ralph the specter that *he has been a bad chooser in his life:* "If I'm dissatisfied with this job, then what the hell have I been doing here for the last twenty-five years? Why haven't I done something about it?" This is an anxiety-arousing issue for most of us to face, and (given our penchant for avoiding anxiety) not an issue that we would readily choose to engage. So the easiest response, and also one that seems honest, is to say "sure, I guess I'm satisfied with my job."

For these and other (more methodological) reasons, short-answer responses to job satisfaction questions, especially among people who have some tenure in their jobs, are suspect. To understand more completely how a person feels about his or her work, one would have to get beneath the surface of the response, as we have done by exploring Ralph's personal history, and as Terkel did in his revealing interviews for the book *Working*. Alternatively, we might look beyond questions of satisfaction for other indicators that all is (or is not) well in the person-job relationship. Productivity, work quality, absence and turnover rates, degree of utilization of employee talent, and overt signs of high commitment to (or alienation from) the work may be useful in this regard. Simple self-reports of job satisfaction are not a sturdy enough base on which to build plans for organizational change, let alone national policy about quality of worklife issues.

Fact Four: Change Often Will be Resisted, Even When It Is a Good Idea

Listen again to Ralph, as the possibility of change is raised:

Is there any way in which you'd like to see your job changed?

Sure, more money.

Any other ways?

Sometimes the boss gets on my back, but I guess that's not too much of a hassle. The tools are okay. Sometimes they tell you to do things one way and then bitch that you didn't do it a different way; that's bad. (Pause) The job itself is a bore, that's for sure.

What if they gave you a job where instead of just cutting metal you did the whole assembly. Would you like that?

They'd never do that.

But what if they did?

(Pause) No, that wouldn't really make sense. It's set up pretty good now. Things are okay the way they are. I come in here, do my job, and go home with my skin still on. You start rocking the boat, no telling what's going to develop.

Would you like to be a foreman?

(Laugh) That's a hassle I don't need. Leave that to the other guys. There's a couple of them I'd like to see canned, though.

Why should Ralph resist change—indeed, resist the very *thought* of change? There are at least three good reasons. First, even opening the question resurrects the anxieties that were long ago put away when Ralph made his peace with the job. Second, change raises the possibility that Ralph will have to learn some new ropes, when no new ropes have been learned for years. And third, Ralph may have a very real and understandable concern about change wrecking the rather comfortable style of work he has developed. As he says, he knows how to get through the day with his "skin still on," and if things were different who knows what might happen to his well-learned and effective strategies for dealing with his job and his supervisor?

Is change worth such risk and possible pain? To Ralph at age 20, yes, without question. Now, no, also without question.

If change agents are genuinely interested in Ralph's well-being and have genuine respect for his feelings and beliefs, should they leave him in peace and search for an organization where the employees are more eager for what they have to offer? Or should they work intensively with Ralph (and others of similar views), in hopes of helping him work through his concerns and anxieties and eventually alter his views about the desirability of more complex and challenging work? Or, perhaps, should the agents charge ahead with change in any case, on the grounds that Ralph feels the way he does largely because of what the organization did to him by keeping him on a routine, monotonous job—and that the change can reverse what has been an unfortunate set of organizational experiences?

Such questions have no easy answers, and they will appear more than once in this book as we delve into strategies and options for personal and organizational change through the redesign of work. In any application of work redesign there will be differences among people in their readiness for job change and in their desire for it. Sometimes it will be a 20-year-old who will be as uncomfortable with the prospect of change as Ralph is, and sometimes it will be the 44-year-old who is ready and eager for change. But there will always be individual differences among people in their attitude toward change, and a well-designed change program will always have to deal with them.

ONE MORE TIME: IS THERE A CRISIS?

The question has no clear answer, given the degree to which people adapt to their work, the caution with which answers to job satisfaction surveys must be interpreted, and the variation among people in their readiness for and attitudes toward change. What *is* clear is that the person-job relationship is key in understanding both organizational productivity and the quality of employees' work experiences. Moreover, there appears to be plenty of room for improving the fit between people and their jobs: there are literally millions of people in tens of thousands of organizations who are neither giving as much to their work as they might, nor getting as much from it as they need.

Jobs that underutilize people are just as inefficient as computers that underutilize their memories or assembly lines that run too slowly. And jobs that provide people with insufficient opportunities to satisfy important personal needs at work can be just as debilitating as a marriage that goes sour or a school that fails to educate. That some people adapt to a bad job (as they adapt to a bad marriage) by emotionally withdrawing from it and seeking need satisfactions elsewhere is no consolation.

Is there a national crisis in job satisfaction? It is probably the wrong question. A better question, perhaps, is how organizations can be designed, staffed, and managed so that employees are simultaneously utilized and satisfied to the fullest extent possible, with neither the goals of the organization nor the personal needs of the employees dominating the other. In other words, how can we achieve a "fit" between persons and their jobs that fosters *both* high work productivity and a high-quality organizational experience for the people who do the work?

In the next two chapters we examine theories and prescriptions for change that have been offered to answer this question. Chapter 2 reviews approaches that attempt to improve person-job relationships by altering the people themselves or the context in which they work. We find these approaches wanting. Then, in Chapter 3, we turn to the design of work as a change strategy. We review several quite different models for work design, ranging from industrial engineering principles to the prescriptions of contemporary psychological theories, and we assess the strengths and weaknesses of each. That chapter ends with a summary of the "hybrid" model of work design that characterizes our thinking about the matter, and that guides the ideas for work redesign and organizational change that are developed throughout the rest of this book.

FOR ADDITIONAL READING

Terkel, S. *Working.* New York: Pantheon, 1974. Chock full of interviews with all kinds of people working on all kinds of jobs, this book provides insights about the role of work in the lives of contemporary Americans that are far richer than most social science research findings on the topic. Witty, moving, and humane.

O'Toole, J. *Work, learning and the American future.* San Francisco: Jossey-Bass, 1977. O'Toole addresses a number of major questions about the utilization of human resources in U.S. organizations, probes the interdependencies between work and education, and analyzes how changes can be wrought in a technology-dependent capitalist society. The book takes up where the classic *Work in America* left of, but on a grander scale—and perhaps more thoughtfully.

Gyllenhammar, P.G. *People at work.* Reading, MA: Addison-Wesley, 1977. This book by the president of Volvo provides a detailed description of what was done in one of the major European innovations in work redesign, and what the learnings have been thus far.

Fein, M. Job enrichment: A reevaluation. *Sloan Management Review,* Winter 1974, 69-88. Here is the case *against* work redesign as a strategy for personal and organizational change. The author suggests that few benefits will be obtained by increasing worker autonomy and job complexity in blue-collar settings—in part because intrinsic aspects of the work such as these are of secondary importance to the people who work there.

2
APPROACHES TO CHANGE: THE PEOPLE AND THE WORK CONTEXT

We suggested in the previous chapter that many people in contemporary organizations are underchallenged and underutilized in their jobs. As a consequence, some such individuals are neither as productive nor as satisfied at work as they might be; others gradually adapt to this unsatisfactory state of affairs and accept it as their lot in life.

What might be done to improve the match between people and their work, and thereby improve both organizational productivity and the quality of employee work experiences? How can we achieve a better fit between what people want from work and what they get from it? How can we increase the congruence between what people are asked to do on the job and what they are willing and able to do?

Behavioral scientists, over the last several decades, have generated a buffet of ideas and techniques for dealing with these questions. We review a number of these devices in Chapters 2 and 3. In this chapter we focus on four widely used approaches that have to do with changing either people or the setting in which they work. They are:

1. Changing the *people* who do the work, through improved selection, placement, and training procedures.

2. Changing *other people*, specifically supervisors, by improving supervisory selection and training practices.

3. Changing the *context* in which the work is performed by adding workplace amenities and improving the scheduling of working time.

4. Changing the *consequences* of work by altering the contingencies that determine the benefits (and costs) to employees of hard and effective work.

Each of these approaches is, in its own right, critical to the competent management of people at work. It is hard to imagine an effective work organization in which managers do not give serious attention to selection and training, to supervision, to the work context, and to the contingencies that link what employees do and what they receive. Moreover, we will argue later in this book (Chapters 6 and 8) that the success and persistence of work redesign is profoundly affected by some of these organizational practices. Managed poorly, they can render impotent even well-conceived and well-executed changes in jobs; managed well, they can reinforce and amplify the beneficial effects of well-designed work.

This chapter, however, deals with the *direct effects* on work productivity and employee satisfaction of changes in the people and the work context. As will be seen below, attempts to improve organizational functioning that rely solely on these approaches often fail, and none of them appear useful as a general "fix" for organizational problems. This chapter explores some of the reasons why this is so, and sets the stage for Chapter 3, in which we examine the redesign of jobs as an alternative strategy for improving the match between people and their work.

CHANGING PEOPLE: SELECTION AND TRAINING

Selection and training are among the most popular devices for dealing with people in organizations and are among the approaches to change about which we know the most. Moreover, selection and training have the advantage of dealing directly with the person-job relationship, rather than with the organizational context in which that relationship exists.

The basic idea is that if people are placed on jobs for which they are well suited and well trained, they will be personally satisfied and will perform effectively. What must be done, then, is to locate and attract to the organization people who are "right" for the jobs that are to be done—and then to train them to perform those jobs as competently as possible.

A great deal of effort has gone into the development of selection devices and training procedures in organizations. Job analysis methodologies, for example, provide rather precise means of identifying what skills are required for successful performance of almost any job (McCormick, 1976). Once job requirements are identified, numerous tests and placement models are available to ensure that all employees on a given job have at least the minimum capability to perform adequately (Dunnette, 1966; Guion, 1976). And when training is required to bring employee knowledge and skill up to the level needed for excellent performance, the capability to design and carry out that training is readily available (Bass and Vaughan, 1966; Goldstein, 1974).

Such procedures typically achieve their intended goals quite well and efficiently. And if the nature of the mismatch between the person and the job is that the person is not fully qualified for the position, then the use of existing selection and training procedures is appropriate and likely to be effective.

But if the problem is that people already are *over*qualified to do the work to which they will be assigned, as is often the case for jobs in the lower regions of organizations, then selection and training procedures may not help very much; indeed, they may actually worsen the fit between the people and the jobs they do (O'Toole, 1977).

What, for example, if the distribution of people and jobs in contemporary U.S. society approximated that shown in Fig. 2.1? The figure suggests that there are relatively more "simple" (routine, repetitive, easy-to-perform) jobs than there are "complex" (challenging, varied, uncertain) jobs. And there are relatively more "complex" (bright, skilled, upwardly mobile) people than there are "simple" (dull, uneducated, nonambitious) people. If jobs and people were distributed this way in the population, how could selection and training improve the overall fit between the people and the work they do in society?

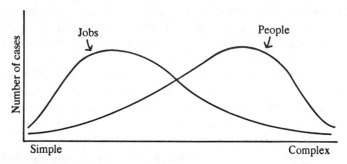

Fig. 2.1 Hypothetical distributions of people and jobs on a dimension of general complexity.

It appears that such devices would be appropriate only if they were used to select the *less* talented individuals for the simple jobs or to "de-train" more talented people so that they could survive psychologically and perform effectively on those jobs. However, such uses of selection and training are unlikely to gain wide acceptance. It would be difficult for managers to admit to themselves (let alone to their external constituencies and clients) that they are systematically selecting untalented or poorly qualified employees for the basic jobs in their organizations. Instead, public relations considerations (not to mention the personal attitudes of employing managers) tend to ensure that when selection, placement, and training techniques are used, they are used to upgrade (not downgrade) the quality of individuals sought and selected for work in the organization. Moreover, most managers hold the very reasonable view that the pool of human resources available for doing the work of the organization should be as rich and high-level as possible. This view prevails even when that resource pool is mostly unused in carrying out the work of the organization.

So we continue to see job candidates ordered in terms of their measured job-relevant knowledge and skill, and organizations selecting the "cream" of the applicants for employment, even if the lower quartile of those applying would be fully competent to do the work effectively. And we continue to see new employees given sophisticated training courses, even if the employees actually would be able to carry out the work with only a day or so of on-the-job training under the tutelage of an experienced employee. One airline, for example, routinely provides full-time training to its reservations agents for more than a week right after they are hired—even though agents who have worked on the job only a few weeks complain of the monotony and routineness of the work.

Even when the nature of the person-job mismatch is recognized as one of overqualification rather than ineptitude, the kinds of solutions proposed still often involve attempts to change the people to fit the jobs. One of the silliest is a $5 million plant donated by the General Electric Company to the Cleveland school system to support the training of students for assembly line work! And an Assistant Secretary of Labor suggested in a memo to the Department of Health, Education, and Welfare in 1972 that perhaps the problem of underemployment would be solved if the Office of Education would just stop educating so many people (reported by O'Toole, 1975).

Despite what seems an obvious overuse of selection and training procedures in attempting to fit people to undemanding jobs, these practices are likely to remain with us for two reasons. First, we know *how* to select, place, and train people. We tend to use heavily those techniques we are good at, sometimes regardless of their appropriateness for a given problem.

Secondly, it is easy to misperceive the *causes* of the problems we observe among people at work. When someone is behaving badly or performing poorly on the job, the human tendency is to attribute the reason for the difficulty to the person rather than to the situation (Jones and Nisbett, 1971). Following from that attribution, the cure that is prescribed typically is somehow to change the people—either by hiring "better" people, or by educating the people now on the job so they will know how to behave more competently.

If, however, the *real* root of the observed problems is that people are overqualified for the work they do (for instance, a talented person chaffing at an overcontrolled, routine job), then selection and training procedures are unlikely to help and may even lead to a worsening of the observed difficulties. Whereupon, the same perceptual biases might operate once again, and we would hear managers complaining, "I don't know about this younger generation—we took the very best people we could find, we spent lots of time training them, and they're still goofing off and screwing up on the job. What's wrong with them, anyhow?"

This refrain is frequently heard in these days of decently educated people with high personal aspirations for their life at work—

whether they are sitting at a desk in an air conditioned office or plugging away at assembly line work. And if the curves shown in Fig. 2.1 are even approximately accurate, we may expect the problem to worsen as the supply of well-educated, upwardly mobile workers continues to expand.

The arguments made here are *not* intended to suggest that selection, placement, and training are irrelevant to the effective utilization of human resources in organizations. On the contrary, when jobs are complex and challenging, it is critical to recruit competent people to work on them and to provide those people with the training they need to perform their jobs well. To be underqualified for a challenging, involving job is to be highly stressed and can lead to psychological or behavioral withdrawal from the job. The very real risks of ignoring questions of employee competence when jobs are expanded or "enriched" are explored later in this book.

So devices for identifying talented people and for increasing their task-relevant knowledge and skill have an important place in organizational management. The point of this section is that such devices often are overused in organizations and can result in negative consequences both for people and for their employing organizations when the real problem is that the people are *over-* rather than *under*qualified for the work they do.

CHANGING OTHER PEOPLE: SELECTING AND TRAINING SUPERVISORS

When attempts to select and train job incumbents for more effective on-the-job performance fail, managers often turn their attention to those who supervise the work and the workers. The idea is to select and train supervisors so that their behaviors elicit high productivity and high job satisfaction on the part of their subordinates. Responsibility for subordinate productivity and morale is placed on the shoulders of the boss, and the task is to find and develop leaders who are able to mold their subordinates into a committed, productive, and satisfied group of employees. Like the first approach reviewed, this one also has to do with changing people—but this time the people who manage the work rather than the people who actually do it.

The most efficient way to increase the quality of supervision, of course, would be to identify the characteristics of people who are superb leaders and then systematically to select those people for supervisory jobs. The problem is that decades of research have failed to identify attributes of people that reliably and powerfully predict effective supervisory performance. Long lists of "traits" held by good leaders have been generated—including self-confidence, intelligence (so long as it doesn't exceed by too much the intelligence of the people supervised), sociability, ambition, perseverance, willpower, absence of neuroses, and even height. But unfortunately the relationship between these traits and subordinate effectiveness is generally so low that their usefulness in selecting leaders is virtually nil.

In recent years, "assessment centers" have become an increasingly popular way of selecting individuals for managerial positions. These centers, typically involving one- or two-day situational tests in which candidates are observed and evaluated as they work on simulations of real managerial problems, have been shown to be better at predicting *future managerial success* (such as promotion) than are traditional paper-and-pencil tests (MacKinnon, 1975). However, assessment centers are not specifically oriented to selecting individuals who will be excellent supervisors of lower-level workers in organizations, and their validity for this purpose is uncertain.

In sum, attempts to identify and select excellent supervisors by measuring their enduring personal attributes are on the wane, largely because it has not been possible to identify those attributes that are key to successful supervisors. On the other hand, attempts to obtain top-quality supervision through leadership *training* are very much alive and well throughout the world. The idea is that if we cannot reliably identify those people who are sure to be top-notch supervisors, then perhaps we can take the people whom we do select (by whatever method) and train them to be effective supervisors of people and work.

So we have academic courses on theories of leadership and management, off-site human relations training, skills-oriented courses in which supervisors role-play effective behaviors, unstructured training sessions where participants share their experiences and learn from one another, and numerous other supervisory training techniques. Almost every moderately large organization sponsors managerial and supervisory training of one kind or another, based on one or another theory of leader effectiveness (Hinrichs, 1976).

There is no question that such training courses help expand the cognitive knowledge and self-understanding of the participants, and that they contribute to the participants' general education. Moreover, trainees usually find the courses stimulating and enjoyable: If a course or experience is well designed and competently executed, postcourse evaluations usually reveal that participants enjoyed the sessions, felt they learned a great deal, and would recommend the course to colleagues without hesitation.

What is at question is how much difference such training makes in the quality of the supervision that the subordinates of the trainee receive after the boss returns from the course and, ultimately, whether the overall effectiveness of the supervisor's work unit is improved as a result of the training received. For this more critical question there is less trustworthy evidence (measures of actual quality of supervision and unit effectiveness are much harder to obtain than are trainees' postcourse evaluations), but findings to date are not optimistic about the long-term effects of such training experiences (Campbell, Dunnette, Lawler, and Weick, 1970).

Why does supervisory training not have a greater impact on the productivity and work satisfaction of subordinates? There are at least three reasons.

1. *It is not altogether clear what the supervisors should be taught.* Should we train supervisors to keep their hands off subordinates as much as they can? Or to be very closely involved with them but only to help them develop their own approach to doing the work? Or to be closely involved and highly directive about what to do when? Or to be very democratic or participative in dealing with subordinates? All of these strategies work—sometimes. Other times they do not.

Then, perhaps, we should train supervisors to be *responsive* to their subordinates, to the imperatives of the task and technology, and to the organizational context in which the work is done—adapting their leadership styles and strategies to the situations in which they must carry out their leadership activities. This seems somehow more realistic, but what aspects of the people, the work, and the workplace are most critical, and what supervisory behaviors are best under which circumstances?

The hard fact of the matter is that we do not yet know for sure.

There has been lots of research on "consideration" and "initiation of structure" as leadership styles, for example.[1] However, it is not yet clear exactly how these important dimensions of leadership style affect the productivity of subordinates (although there does seem to be a reasonably stable finding that subordinates are more *satisfied* when supervisors behave considerately than when they do not). Research currently is delving into the contingencies that determine when "structuring" and "considerate" styles will be best for productivity and satisfaction. But at present we do not know enough about the circumstances under which one or another supervisory style is optimal, and it is starting to look as if the answer that eventually emerges is going to be fairly complex (Kerr, Schriesheim, Murphy, and Stogdill, 1974).

Indeed, there are so many complexities emerging from research on leadership style that we are beginning to doubt whether it will ever be realistic to satisfactorily "program" a supervisor about how to behave in different leadership situations. Instead, perhaps, the emphasis should be on identifying and selecting for supervisory positions those individuals who *intuitively* seem to know how they should behave in different circumstances. But this strategy, of course, brings us back to the original leader *selection* problem discussed earlier—and to our history of failure to solve that problem.

2. *It is difficult to get supervisors to transfer their learning from the training setting to the actual work setting.*   Most supervisory training courses take place away from the workplace to free the trainees from the interruptions and distractions that inevitably occur at work and to provide them with a setting specifically designed to enhance their learning. The problem is that even as the supervisor is changing as a result of the training, the workplace is not. And the outcome frequently is a supervisor who returns from training full of new knowledge, skill, and resolve—only to face the same unmanageable tasks,

---

1   Consideration reflects the degree to which leaders relate warmly to subordinates, show trust in them and listen to them, are willing to explain their actions, and so on. Initiation of structure is the degree to which leaders actively organize and structure the work and specify who is to do what under various task and organizational circumstances. The two dimensions of style are independent: it is possible to be high on one and low on the other, high on both or low on both.

structures, and people that had to be faced before. It turns out that the gap between the learning environment and the working environment often is so large that the supervisor is unable to build a bridge and apply the new lessons to the old situation (see Fleishman, 1955). Instead, the new ideas and skills tend gradually to fade away in the face of the old tasks and people and structures, and after a few months all that may remain of the training course is the glow that comes from having participated in a stimulating and enjoyable experience.

3. *The actual behavioral style of a supervisor may be largely out of his or her control in any case.*   Until rather recently most research and theory about supervisory style, and most training aimed at improving organizational functioning by changing leader behavior, was based on the assumption that the style of the leader *caused* changes in the work behavior and satisfaction of subordinates. It now appears, however, that the style of the leader may in many circumstances be as much a consequence of subordinate behavior as it is a cause of that behavior (e.g., Lowin and Craig, 1968; Farris and Lim, 1969). Specifically, if a supervisor is charged with managing a group of subordinates who are competent in carrying out the work and pleasantly cooperative with the supervisor, then the supervisor may "naturally" behave in ways that are considerate of the employees and be very participative with them in making work-related decisions. But if the subordinates are clearly incompetent in their jobs, and moreover behave with active hostility toward the supervisor, the "natural" course of action may be a much more structuring, directive, and autocratic style.

This is not to say that supervisory behavior makes no difference to the people being supervised. Obviously it does. But many supervisory training experiences appear to be based on assumptions that (1) supervisors are substantially in control of their behavior vis-a-vis subordinates and (2) supervisory behavior influences subordinate attitudes and work behavior much more than vice versa. There is a reason to be suspicious of both assumptions—and therefore to be skeptical about the degree to which substantial improvements in employee work behavior and satisfaction can be wrought simply by training supervisors to behave differently.

The cautions and skepticism expressed in this section are not intended as an unqualified damnation of selection and training activi-

ties that focus on supervisors. Without question, even ad hoc selection procedures can weed out individuals who would be grossly
incompetent as managers of people. And training procedures can
help supervisors learn *not* to engage in behaviors that are known to
be ineffective or destructive—such as excessively close supervision,
wholesale abdication of responsibility for the work or absence from
the workplace, gross favoritism, and so forth.

But when the work situation is basically satisfactory—or dis-
tressingly unsatisfactory—reliance on supervisory training as a strategy for organizational change and improvement may be little more
than whistling in the wind. Consider, for example, an organization in
which the jobs being done by rank-and-file employees are inherently
interesting and motivating, employees feel they are paid well and
fairly, and people are generally satisfied with their co-workers and
with working conditions. In this circumstance, supervision is relatively easy. And while supervisory training may be useful to prepare
managers for more responsible positions, it is unlikely to lead to
major improvements in the trainee's work unit—simply because few
improvements are needed.

If, on the other hand, subordinates are frustrated and bored with
highly fractionated, repetitive work, and if they also are furious about
unsatisfactory compensation and working conditions, then there may
be *no* way that the supervisor can behave vis-a-vis his or her subordinates to engender high morale and productivity among them. In this
case, the reasons for the observed problems lie more in the work and
in the organization than in the behavior of the supervisor, and
improvements in the managerial style of the supervisor are unlikely
to have much of a direct effect. The perceptive manager will, in such
circumstances, focus his or her energy upward (or outward) to improve those organizational systems that are creating the difficulties—
including how the work itself is designed—rather than attempt to
work directly with subordinates to create a happy and motivated
work force despite them (Oldham, 1976b).

CHANGING THE CONTEXT OF THE WORK

A third approach to improving individual-organization relationships
focuses on the context in which the work is done. The idea is to make
the organization a personally pleasant and socially satisfying place for

employees to be. And the hope is that if the work environment is sufficiently congenial, attractive, and convenient, then people will be both productive in their work and satisfied with their organizational experiences.

This approach has its roots in the "human relations" school of management, which developed from the seminal research conducted at the Hawthorne plant of Western Electric (Mayo, 1933; Roethlisberger and Dickson, 1939). These researchers found (contrary to their expectations) that alterations of working conditions such as rest pauses and illumination were *not* key in reducing employee boredom or increasing efficiency. Instead, it appeared that the work-group culture and the "informal organization" that existed among employees had an overriding influence on how employees experienced their work and how they reacted to it. The implication of the research, then, was that improvements in the social context of the work could increase the meaningfulness of even the most boring of jobs in an organization. Moreover, increases in both productivity and worker satisfaction would be expected when such improvements were made.

As a result of the Hawthorne studies, managers and social scientists gave increasing attention to improvements in the human relations climate of work organizations. Early innovations included counseling programs, courses to improve communication skills, increased teamwork and participation among rank-and-file workers, and more considerate, people-oriented supervision (Whyte, 1956). More recently, attempts to improve the work context have extended well beyond the early focus on interpersonal relationships and range from putting carpeting on the floor and music in the walls, to making work stations clean and quiet, and even to installing gymnasiums and swimming pools at the workplace, making some organizations appear to be more like country clubs than industrial plants. Currently very popular are innovations in work scheduling (such as flexitime and the four-day workweek) that are intended to make attendance at work more convenient and to reduce the difficulty of managing the boundary between work and the rest of one's life (Cohen and Gadon, 1978).

It is clear that most people like and appreciate satisfying social relationships at work, more convenient schedules, and on-the-job amenities. And for that reason, people may come to work more regularly and remain with the organization longer than they would if the workplace were unpleasant and work schedules inconvenient. So improving aspects of the work context can directly improve the quality of worklife for employees, which is of merit in its own right and which sometimes results in reduced absenteeism and turnover.

But what about work motivation and productivity? When the context is especially pleasant and satisfying will employees try especially hard to do a good job? Unfortunately, there are no data of which we are aware to support the view that improvements in the work context or the human relations climate of an organization will result in long-term gains in productivity or work efficiency. Indeed, those short-term gains that sometimes are noted when contextual improvements are made often are described using the name of the plant where the human relations movement began—that is, the "Hawthorne effect." Hawthorne effects cannot be counted on to persist over time.

Why not? Shouldn't people be willing to provide hard work on their jobs in return for the receipt of workplace amenities from management? Perhaps they *should* be, but it turns out the people do not adhere to a "norm of reciprocity" nearly as faithfully as some might wish them to. Instead, people come rather quickly to accept improved amenities as their legitimate lot in life and are likely to experience distress and anger if those amenities subsequently are taken away.

One of us recently had his office air conditioned. He was initially quite pleased about that. On hot summer days, it is now more likely than before that he will spend a full day at the office. But he does not find himself feeling constant gratitude to his university for the air conditioning, not even in the heat of August, nor does he feel that he owes the university any special loyalty or any extra on-the-job effort because university managers were nice enough to air condition his work space. If, however, the air conditioning unit were to be removed some July in a burst of energy-saving consciousness, then you can be sure that your author would notice the fact—and would be most unhappy with his employer.[2]

---

2   These reactions fit well with the arguments made by Frederick Herzberg (1976) that while aspects of the work context (which he calls "hygiene factors") are irrelevant to the level of *work motivation* exhibited by employees, they can lead to heightened employee dissatisfaction when they are mismanaged.

In sum, improving the context of the work may further reinforce employees' positive reactions to an already well-designed and well-managed organization, at least in the short term. But they are unlikely to be useful in compensating for work that is inherently meaningless, for a grossly inequitable compensation system, for capricious control procedures, or for discriminatory personnel practices. When basic features of the organization such as these are at issue, it surely is a better idea to deal with them directly than to try to gloss them over by introducing contextual amenities or improving the "human relations" climate of the workplace.

CHANGING REWARD CONTINGENCIES

By managing the contingencies between work behavior and organizational rewards, it often is possible to influence employee productivity directly and at the same time to create important spin-off effects on the quality of employees' work experiences. The idea is that when productive behavior is rewarded by the organization, people will work more effectively and thereby gain valued rewards that enhance their own satisfaction with the work and the organization.

Most commonly used in this regard are personal reinforcement by the supervisor (such as the pat on the back for a job well done) and pay (such as piece-rate incentive systems, end-of-year bonuses, and so on). For such rewards to be effective in eliciting and maintaining productivity, a number of conditions must be met. First, the reward must be *valued* by the individual. If you receive a trinket for your charm bracelet for doing especially good work, but do not even have a charm bracelet, the potency of that reward for eliciting good work in the future will be limited. If, however, you prize your bracelet and are always on the lookout for new and interesting charms to add, then the reward may work wonders.

Second, the reward must be administered on a *contingent* basis, that is, only when the desired behavior has actually occurred. If management runs around and hands out charms with wild abandon, perhaps in hopes of making everyone happy, then perhaps everyone will be happy (at least those who like charms), but the motivational impact of the reward will have been lost. Or if at odd intervals the supervisor appears with a charm and says, "Good for you," you may spend as much time wondering why those particular moments were chosen to pass out the rewards as you do working. And you may guess wrong.

But if the reward comes only when you sign up a new customer, then it gradually will become clear to you that signing up new customers is what is wanted and what is rewarded. Thus it is not sufficient that rewards be administered contingent upon the desired behavior; in addition, the employee must *understand* what it is that is wanted and rewarded. To meet this third condition, there must be a way to identify or measure the target behavior such that the reward giver and the potential reward receiver can agree when the behavior is present and when it is not.

In recent years, the fine old principle of administering organizational rewards contingent upon effective performance has been dressed up in the rather elaborate and sophisticated clothes of "behavior modification" as espoused by B. F. Skinner (see, for example, Luthans and Kreitner, 1975). The basic principles outlined above are adhered to in behavior modification programs, of course, but numerous refinements having to do with behavior measurement and reward schedules are added. One of the most important is the idea that after the desired behavior is being regularly exhibited, the reward giver should cease rewarding the behavior every time it occurs, and move to a variable schedule of reinforcement. Reinforcements appear on an occasional and (to the reward receiver) unpredictable schedule, and work becomes a bit like fishing: You keep casting because you know you get a strike every so often, but you don't know whether it will be the next cast, or the one after that, or five casts later. But so long as the fish occasionally cooperate, you keep casting; in technical terms, you show high "resistance to extinction."

The use of performance-contingent rewards would seem to have a great deal of potential for shaping employee behavior (and, indirectly, employee attitudes) at work. Indeed, some commentators have suggested that this approach should be standard operating procedure in work organizations. For example, Fein (1976a, p. 46) reports:

> In a study of over 400 plants across the United States, I found that when these plants instituted work measurement, their productivity rose an average of 14.6 percent. When plants instituted wage incentives where previously there was work measurement,

productivity rose an added 42.9 percent. The average increase from no-measurement to incentives was 63.6 percent.

Yet financial incentives and other organizational rewards do *not* always increase the level of motivated, productive behavior of the people to whom the rewards are given, even when those rewards are delivered contingent upon effective work behavior. Why not? Leaving aside the possibility that an incentive program might be poorly designed on technical grounds, three possibilities suggest themselves.

Getting Enough. At some point, employees may have obtained all of a particular reward they want. Praise and compliments from the supervisor, a frequently used reward in organizational behavior modification programs, would seem particularly prone to the satiation problem: If your boss were consistently to compliment you each time you complete a satisfactory piece of work, those compliments might eventually lose their reinforcing properties or even become irritating.

Those who vigorously advocate the use of incentive programs based on pay sometimes argue as if people are primarily (if not exclusively) oriented toward maximization of the economic benefit they receive from the hours they spend at work. However, if the last several decades of research on behavior in organizations has taught us anything, it is that people at work seek simultaneously *many* kinds of satisfactions, not just those with economic roots.

Any theory of managerial practice that assumes that a single motivational factor will suffice to understand employee behavior at work is assuredly incomplete—whether the factor espoused has to do with motivation for economic gain, for satisfying social relationships, or for personal growth and development. So those who seek to shape employee behavior at work must be careful to use rewards that are in fact valued by the target employees, and they must be watchful to make sure that the motivational properties of those rewards do not wear off significantly over time as employees become accustomed to them and, perhaps, even tired of them.

Becoming Dependent. Another problem with the use of behavior-contingent rewards has to do with the quality of the relationship that develops between the persons who are giving the rewards and those who receive them. If we were to attempt to control your behavior as powerfully as we could, we would first identify a reward about which you care very deeply (perhaps money, if you are so poor that your next meal is an uncertainty; or public praise and recognition if you are feeling well fed but terribly unappreciated). Then we would provide that reward to you, immediately and reliably, whenever you engage in the behavior that *we* desired. Soon, we predict, you would be doing exactly what we wanted you to do.

But you might also be resentful of our tactics and perhaps feeling pretty miserable about yourself for your slavish obedience. It is noteworthy that many of the early (and highly successful) applications of the principles of behavior modification have involved animals (such as pigeons), children, or institutionalized adults such as prisoners or mental patients. Individuals in each of these groups are *necessarily* dependent on powerful others for many of the things they most want and need, and their behavior usually can be shaped with relative ease.

But what works for the animals and the children may be met with serious resistance on the part of adults who have a strong wish to believe that they are personally in control of their lives and destinies. Many observers (e.g., Argyris, 1957; Whyte, 1977) have pointed out the dysfunctional consequences that can develop when normal, healthy adults find themselves in a relationship where they are wholly dependent on another person whom they must please in order to obtain the rewards they most value. In such circumstances, overt hostility, personal withdrawal, and even active deception and sabotage are not uncommon reactions.

Similarly, it has been shown that people become unpleasantly aroused when their experienced freedom to control their own behavior is curtailed (Brehm, 1972). Such arousal, or "reactance," often sets in motion attempts to restore a sense of control over one's destiny—sometimes by altering how one perceives or evaluates the situation, other times by taking specific behavioral action. In work settings, attempts to regain a sense of behavioral freedom might be expressed by deliberately engaging in prohibited behaviors, by colluding with others to "beat the system," or by directing aggressive feelings toward the reward giver, who is viewed as responsible for the threat to freedom.

Taken together, feelings of dependency and reactance can seriously compromise even technically sophisticated systems for linking rewards (and punishments) to desired employee behaviors. It is ironic that the more potent the contingent reward (and therefore the better the system should function from a technical perspective), the more likely it is that unanticipated and dysfunctional responses will be exhibited by those whose behavior is supposed to be shaped by the reward system.[3]

Experiencing Motivational Conflict. Finally, vigorous use of performance-contingent rewards may elicit conflicting motivational states on the part of employees and thereby induce internal stress and tension rather than the intended high level of performance motivation.

Consider the following question that might be asked of an employee about the perceived consequences of hard and effective work on the job:

> What happens when you try to work especially hard and productively on this job?

This question, which has its roots in the "expectancy theory" of work motivation (Vroom, 1964) can be an excellent device for gaining understanding of what the motivational pulls and restraints are to productive work on the job. The list generated by an individual whose job is lifting bricks from a pile onto a sled (to be carted away somewhere by someone else) might look something like this:

1. I get more tired, and I get grouchy.

2. My back starts to hurt earlier in the day, and if it's hot I'm likely to have a headache before noon.

3. The other guys kid me about being a rate-buster.

4. I start to wonder if I'm wearing out my body, and how many years I can keep this up.

---

3   Dependency-related problems with incentive programs sometimes can be reduced if the affected employees are involved in the design and management of those programs (Lawler, 1977). When employees participate in the design and installation of an incentive program, they probably will understand it better. In addition, they may feel that they "own" the program, and therefore that they (not the organization) are in control of it. Under such circumstances, the potency of the incentives to affect attitudes and behavior should remain high, but the risk of dependency-induced negative reactions should diminish considerably.

5. I think of myself more as a mule than as a person who has a brain in his head.

Not an inspiring list, and one that would lead us to a fairly confident prediction that the person would be *un*likely to try to work very hard on this job. The harder the person works, the more the *negative* outcomes.

Now imagine that a sophisticated piece-rate system is installed for the brick-loading job, in which a substantial monetary bonus is tied to the quantity of bricks moved by an individual in a day's work. Moreover, imagine that supervisors are trained to provide praise and recognition for individuals who handle a large number of bricks, and that individuals who consistently handle the most bricks over a several-month period are promised first opportunity to transfer to a less burdensome job.

With this change, we add some new items to the list of outcomes that the brick loader views as being contingent on hard and productive work:

6. I get more money.

7. The boss shows that he appreciates what I'm doing.

8. My chances of getting a better job improve.

Note that in adding the new, performance-contingent rewards, the first list of outcomes did not go away. Those outcomes are just as negative as they ever were and just as contingent on working hard as before.

So what will be the response of the brick loader to the new incentives? While we cannot predict with confidence how on-the-job behavior will change, we can be reasonably sure that the person will experience some internal stress and tension. The reason is that *no* behavior, neither loafing nor working extraordinarily hard, will lead to an optimal mix of work outcomes. Indeed, if we wished to drive someone insane, we might decide to do just what the brick loader's organization did: namely, arrange the work and the rewards so that strong *positive* and strong *negative* outcomes are *simultaneously contingent on the same behavior.* Under such circumstances, there is no way to win and no way to avoid the stress that derives from that fact.

Some of the problems of drug usage, alcoholism, and industrial sabotage that are observed in contemporary organizations may be rooted in precisely this state of affairs. That is, for some jobs, the work itself is arranged so that the harder one works the more negative the "intrinsic" outcomes received, but the organization is arranged so that hard work leads to positive "extrinsic" outcomes—or at least relief from negative extrinsic outcomes such as being "ridden" by one's supervisor.

On the other hand, if responses to the diagnostic question "What happens when you work especially hard?" reveal that productive work generally leads to positive outcomes (such as gaining a feeling of accomplishment, generating a useful product, providing an important service to others, or demonstrating competence on a tough job), then a solid basis for positive motivation already exists. Supplementing these built-in motivational incentives with performance-contingent extrinsic rewards can, in certain organizational circumstances, further reinforce employee motivation for hard and effective work.[4]

In sum, contingent rewards, when well selected and administered in appropriate organizational circumstances, can often enhance employee motivation and help people gain valued personal outcomes in return for their contributions to the attainment of organizational objectives. Yet the efficacy of contingent rewards, like that of the other approaches to change reviewed in this chapter, appears to depend substantially on how the work itself is designed. When jobs are poorly structured, then the use of performance-contingent rewards may result in a motivational "backlash." When, however, jobs are designed so that they provide built-in incentives for good performance, then performance-contingent rewards sometimes can help make an already decent motivational situation even better.

---

4   Motivational gains are not always realized when performance-contingent rewards are used on well-designed jobs, however. For one thing, providing extrinsic rewards for work on an interesting task can sometimes reduce the performer's *intrinsic* task motivation (Deci, 1975, Chapter 5). Moreover, certain organizational conditions (such as good measures of the desired performance outcomes and at least moderate trust between those who administer the rewards and those who receive them) may also be required if contingent rewards are to have their intended effects (see Chapter 6).

CONCLUSION

In this chapter we have reviewed a number of possible points of leverage for changing and improving the behavior and attitudes of people at work. We have suggested that these approaches, when used alone, may not be very powerful in bringing about real and lasting improvements in person-job relationships unless the *work itself* is also basically satisfactory to the individual. If a job is inherently dissatisfying, frustrating, or demotivating to the person who does it, then attempts to improve the overall person-job relationships using *only* the strategies reviewed in this chapter will be like swimming upstream against a very strong current.

The view of organizations suggested here can be illustrated through the device of a child's pegboard. The holes in the pegboard can be seen as jobs; the pegs, as the people who must fit those jobs. Traditionally what is done in staffing and managing organizations is to go to great lengths to get the pegs to fit the holes. Hundreds of pegs may be gathered (recruitment procedures) to find pegs that approximately fit the holes. Those that appear to be about the right size and shape are chosen (selection practices), assigned to the holes that seem the best match for them (placement), and then shaved and sanded to make the fit between the peg and the hole even better (training procedures). If the peg still won't go in the hole, then we may take the wooden hammer and beat on the peg a bit to force it in (supervisory practices and motivational programs).

At the risk of stretching further an already well-stretched analogy, the message of this chapter and this book is that perhaps we should be willing to change the holes as well as the pegs to achieve a good match—to try to achieve good person-organization relationships by adapting jobs to people as much as by adapting people to jobs. In the next chapter, we examine strategies for going about the design of jobs—ranging from traditional engineering approaches (which often result in the "fixed holes" into which people are placed) to state-of-the-art systems approaches that acknowledge the importance of adjusting *both* employees and jobs to achieve the best possible fit between people and their work.

FOR ADDITIONAL READING

Guion, R.M. Recruitment, selection, and job placement. In M.D. Dunnette (ed.), *Handbook of industrial and organizational psychology*. Chicago: Rand-McNally, 1976. This chapter provides a state-of-the-art review of techniques for personnel selection and placement. For a comprehensive review of existing theory and practice for training, see the chapter on "Personnel Training" by J. R. Hinrichs in the same volume.

Vroom, V.H. Leadership. In M.D. Dunnette (ed.), *Handbook of industrial and organizational psychology*. Chicago: Rand-McNally, 1976. A concise and lucid review of what is known about leader strategies for influencing subordinate attitudes and behaviors, and for improving decision making in organizations.

Perrow, C. *Complex organizations: A critical essay* (2nd ed.). Glenview, IL: Scott, Foresman, 1979. Chapter 3 of this book provides a nice summary of the "Hawthorne" studies that gave rise to the human relations movement and then moves on to a critique as readable as it is scathing of behavioral science approaches for changing and improving organizations.

Luthans, F., and D.D. White, Jr. Behavior modification: Application to manpower management. In J.R. Hackman, E.E. Lawler, and L.W. Porter (eds.), *Perspectives on behavior in organizations*. New York: McGraw-Hill, 1977. A sympathetic review of the usefulness and potency of behavior modification in organizations. For a cautionary note, see the article titled "Skinnerian Theory in Organizations" by W.F. Whyte, which follows the Luthans-White article in the same book.

3
APPROACHES TO CHANGE: THE WORK ITSELF

We turn now from strategies for change that focus on the people and the work context to those that involve alterations in the design of the work itself—that is, changing the actual structure of the jobs that people perform. There are many different approaches that can be taken in designing work and a variety of criteria that can be used in deciding what is a "good" or well-designed job. There is no single right way to design work.

Some of the approaches to be reviewed in this chapter focus on the minute motions and procedures that compose a job; others involve a more molar view of the whole task for which the job incumbent is responsible. Some approaches emphasize criteria of engineering efficiency in assessing how well designed jobs are; others focus more on the work motivation and satisfaction of the people who perform the jobs. And some approaches deal mainly with specific tasks performed by individual employees, while others address the larger tasks that are the responsibility of work groups or intact organizational units.

We have grouped the various approaches to work design, somewhat arbitrarily, into three categories: (1) traditional approaches, which derive from classical organization theory and the discipline of industrial engineering; (2) behavioral approaches, which emphasize the impact of jobs on the people who perform them; and (3) systems

44

approaches, which focus on networks of jobs that exist within larger organizational units.

At the end of the chapter, after these approaches have been reviewed and critiqued, we summarize our way of thinking about the design of work—the approach that will guide what we have to say throughout the remainder of this book.

TRADITIONAL APPROACHES

Imagine that you are the Manager of Audiovisual Services for a metropolitan area school system. Among the responsibilities of your department are ordering motion pictures and slide shows that will be used in classes, scheduling the use of audiovisual equipment (including motion picture and slide projectors, record players and tape recorders, overhead and opaque projectors, and portable television recorders and players), maintaining that equipment in working order, and helping teachers learn how to make good educational use of audiovisual equipment and materials in their classrooms.

Take a moment or two to consider how you would organize your department. What jobs would you create for effective use of your staff, and how would you link those jobs for effective unit performance? What supervisory or staff roles might be needed?

While construction of a detailed organizational chart obviously would require considerably more information than we have provided (including the number of classrooms served, the size of your staff, the rates of use of various kinds of equipment, the geographical dispersion of classrooms, and so on), we are willing to venture a prediction about the basic structure of the organization you generated.

First, you may have found it important to divide the work into categories that involve obviously different functions or skills. So you might have (1) a group of employees who maintain and operate the equipment; (2) a group who are responsible for clerical functions, including ordering materials and scheduling the use of equipment and personnel; and (3) one or more individuals responsible for "client relations"—educating teachers about your services, handling complaints, developing ideas for new services, and so on. Depending on your assumptions about the amount of work to be done, you might have created separate job categories for those people who operate and those who maintain the equipment (the skills are, after all, different) and for those who are responsible for scheduling and those who handle orders and payments for materials used.

You probably identified a need for two supervisors, one for equipment use and maintenance, and one for client services (which includes all scheduling, ordering, and teacher relations activities). In addition, you may have created a position for an instructor who would develop standardized procedures for using the audiovisual equipment and help staff members (and teachers, for client-operated equipment) learn how to operate the equipment to minimize foul-ups and accidental damage. And, perhaps, you would see the need for a receptionist to handle calls and visitors and channel them to the appropriate staff members.

If this is approximately the kind of design you generated, then you have created a number of clean, clearly defined jobs of limited scope and a management structure arranged to provide close and helpful supervision to the people who perform those jobs. And you have demonstrated just how pervasive "traditional" approaches to the design of work are when we think about ways of structuring organizations to get work done. For the design that we predict you generated in fact meets many of the criteria for a "good" work organization from the perspective of classical organization theory and the discipline of industrial engineering.

In the pages to follow, we briefly review the major tenets of classical organization theory and industrial engineering as they apply to the design of work. We will see some significant convergences in these two approaches as well as some unintended and dysfunctional consequences associated with their prescriptions about how work should be structured.

Classical Organization Theory

In the early decades of this century, organizational theorists attempted to develop a view of organizations, as well as a set of principles for managing them, that would enable organizations to function as *rationally* and as *efficiently* as possible. The idea was that operational efficiency was the ultimate criterion toward which organizations should strive, and that the use of rational administrative procedures would help managers approach this criterion.

Classical theorists developed and expounded a number of principles of managment that, they believed, would maximize rationality and efficiency in organizational functioning (see, for example, Gulick and Urwick, 1937; Mooney, 1947). These principles emphasize the importance of clear and unambiguous channels of authority to allow for centralized command and control of the organization; rules and regulations for coordinating organizational activities that minimize the chance for capricious managerial action; development of the ideal "span of control" for managers, to ensure that each manager has neither too few nor too many subordinates to supervise; and so on (Scott and Mitchell, 1976).

While such principles have clear implications for how organizations are designed and managed, one principle stands out as the fundamental pillar of the classical approach—and as the one that has the greatest implication for how work is designed in organizations. This, of course, is the principle of *division of labor*. In essence, this principle specifies that maximum work efficiency will be achieved if jobs are simplified and specialized to the greatest extent practicable. The notion is that organization members, employees and managers alike, will function most efficiently if they perform the same, specialized functions repeatedly rather than spreading their attention and their energies across several more complex or ambiguous tasks.

One of the oldest and clearest illustrations of how division of labor applies to the design of work was offered by Adam Smith in his description of the pin-making process:

> One man draws out the wire, another straights it, a third cuts it, a fourth points it, a fifth grinds it at the top for receiving the head: to make the head requires two or three distinct operations: to put it on is a peculiar business, to whiten the pins is another; it is even a trade by itself to put them into the paper; and the important business of making a pin is, in this manner, divided into about eighteen distinct operations, which in some manufactories, are all performed by distinct hands, though in others the same man will sometime perform two or three of them (Smith, 1850, p. 3).

While not so vivid an example as the pin maker, the design we outlined for jobs in the audiovisual department also follows the principle of division of labor. The work was to be partitioned according to various skill specialties—some people emphasizing equipment operation, some equipment maintenance, some clerical activities, some client relations, and so on. Employees would work in (and only in) their job specialties, and knowledgeable supervisors would help employees achieve high proficiency in their work. Obviously, this arrangement would be highly efficient.

But why? What is it about the division of labor that increases work efficiency? Several possibilities have been suggested (Fayol, 1948; Gulick and Urwick, 1937). For one, division of labor permits people to hone their special skills and abilities for doing a particular part of the work. When people are performing only one simple operation, they can become quite expert in completing it. Second, when tasks have been segmented and simplified employees can devote their full attention to very few objects, minimizing the degree to which extraneous objects divert their attention and reduce efficiency. Third, task simplification often reduces the need for a single employee to use different kinds of tools or equipment, and minimizes time spent *changing* tools in carrying out a piece of work. Finally, specialization enhances efficiency by removing the need for workers to move from one work station to another. All of the materials and equipment needed to complete the segmented task are available in one location, eliminating the need for time-wasting movement from place to place.

Specific procedural steps for designing work so that the principles of classical organization theory are achieved were not provided in detail by classical theorists. These more concrete matters were taken up by the industrial engineers, whose contributions to the theory and practice of work design we examine below.

Industrial Engineering

The discipline of industrial engineering shares with classical organization theory the overall objective of increasing the productive efficiency of organizations. And the basic principles of good industrial engineering practice are fully consistent with those of classical organization theory.

First, jobs are to be engineered so that any unnecessary work is eliminated, and so that the quickest and most efficient work methods are standardized for all employees who perform the same basic task. This will increase organizational efficiency because the efficiency of each subpart of the work is maximized. Second, all jobs in the organization, including supervisory jobs, are to be made as simple and routinized as possible. This increases the interchangeability of employees (because there is little training time involved in getting a person "up to speed" for a given task), and minimizes organizational dependence on the idiosyncracies and whims of specific organization members. Some commentators have actually referred to such practices as "idiot proofing" the work, that is, making the job so simple that any idiot can perform it competently (Meister and Sullivan, 1968).

The theorist most responsible for developing and evangelizing the principles of "scientific management" that underlie the industrial engineering approach to the design of work is Frederick W. Taylor (1911). Taylor's views can be summarized as follows.[1]

1. The work to be done should be studied scientifically to determine, in quantitative terms if possible, (a) how the work should be partitioned among various workers for maximum simplicity and efficiency and (b) how each segment of the work should be done most efficiently. Such analyses specify, for example, the exact details of equipment that should be used for dealing with various kinds of material and the exact spacing of rest breaks for maximum workday productivity.

2. Employees selected for the work should be as perfectly matched to the demands of the job as possible. Workers must, of course, be physically and mentally capable of the work, but care should be taken as well to ensure that they are not overqualified for the job.

3. Employees should be trained very carefully by managers to ensure that they perform the work exactly as specified by the prior scientific analysis of the work. In addition, many planners and supervisors are kept near workers to make certain that they are in fact performing the work as they are supposed to, and that there are no distractions or activities that workers must attend to other than the productive work itself. The work of the supervisors is subdivided into functional specialties just as is done for rank-and-file workers. In describing well-engineered shopwork, for example, Taylor specifies seven different supervisory roles: the inspector, the gang boss, the speed boss, the repair boss, the time clerk, the route clerk, and the disciplinarian.

---

1   This summary is adapted from Porter, Lawler, and Hackman (1975, p. 276).

4. Finally, to provide motivation for employees to follow the detailed procedures and work practices that are laid out for them and enforced by supervisors, a substantial monetary bonus should be established and paid upon successful completion of each day's work.

The procedures recommended by Taylor have been developed and perfected by industrial engineers over the last six decades. There now are highly sophisticated procedures for analyzing jobs (including systematic observation techniques using closed-circuit television) to determine the most efficient movements to be used in carrying out the work. Yet the goal of industrial engineering remains about the same—namely, improved efficiency through standardized operations and simplified work.

The influence of industrial engineering on how work is arranged and jobs designed is pervasive. In a study of work design practices in manufacturing firms in the 1950s, for example, researchers found that most jobs were designed consistent with the principles of scientific management (Davis, Canter, and Hoffman, 1955). Specifically, jobs were highly specialized and repetitive, training times were short because the skill requirements of the work were generally low, and the contributions of individual employees to accomplishing the overall work of the organization were quite restricted.

Findings such as these suggest that industrial engineering is flourishing in manufacturing organizations in the United States. Moreover, engineering principles increasingly are being used in structuring work in other types of organizations (such as hospitals and offices) and in other countries (Gardell and Dahlstrom, 1966). Thus, despite the fact that the approach was initially developed in the early 1900s, industrial engineering continues to shape the work (and working lives) of employees in an increasing diversity of work organizations.

Convergences Between Classical Theory and Industrial Engineering

Both classical organization theory and industrial engineering are dedicated, most of all, to rationality and efficiency in organizational operations. Both approaches specify that these objectives can be achieved through the simplification, standardization, and specialization of jobs in organizations. And both approaches are essentially universalistic; that is, they are based on the assumption that simplification and standardization create efficiency for all types of organizations, jobs, and employees.

There are, however, some differences in the two approaches. For one, industrial engineers tend to be more concerned than classical theorists with the development of specific techniques and procedures for simplifying work. For example, an industrial engineer might expend much effort and show great ingenuity in developing specific hand and arm movements that are optimally efficient for completing a given subtask; organization theorists, on the other hand, would simply propose that the labor be divided and the work simplified, and let it go at that.

Organization theorists give more attention than industrial engineers to how the work fits into the broader organizational context. They view the design of work for individual employees as only one part of a more general set of principles that, taken together, are intended to increase the overall efficiency of the work organization. Industrial engineers, on the other hand, tend to focus on employees as more or less isolated individuals who are to be helped to perform specific tasks as efficiently as possible.

Finally, industrial engineers traditionally have focused on production jobs in industry. Only relatively recently have engineering principles been extended to the design of work in people- and paper-processing organizations. Classical theorists, by contrast, have viewed their principles as relevant for all types of jobs and functions, whether in manufacturing or service organizations, and whether for rank-and-file employees or for managers.

The two approaches do appear to share a common blind spot—namely, the assumption that employees, if managed well, will work efficiently and effectively on simplified, routinized jobs. Managerial observations and research studies in organizations where work is designed according to traditional principles have shown that this is not always the case. Even studies conducted early in the century, when the level of education and affluence of rank-and-file employees was still relatively low, showed that many employees were quite vocal in their disaffection with routinized work (Vernon, 1924). Employees restricted their productivity on such jobs. Or they did not show up for work on time. Or they sabotaged their work or their equipment. In all, they simply did not behave like the "good and productive soldiers" they were supposed to be (Walker and Guest, 1952). These problems with traditional approaches to work design gave rise to a number of more behavioral approaches to the design of work, which are discussed next.

BEHAVIORAL APPROACHES

By mid-century it had become clear that there were numerous human difficulties with traditionally designed work, and some behavioral scientists concluded that the trend toward work simplification and routinization had gone too far. In response, they began developing alternative approaches to work design. Although various behavioral approaches have different theoretical underpinnings and different implications for action, they do share a common objective—namely, *to design work in a way that achieves high work productivity without incurring the human costs that are associated with traditional approaches.* Three relatively well-elaborated (and well-studied) behavioral approaches to the design of work are reviewed below.

Activation Theory

Imagine that you have a job that involves monitoring temperature and pressure gauges in a chemical plant. You sit at a console containing numerous gauges and take routine corrective action on those rare occasions when abnormal pressures or temperatures appear. Any serious difficulties are referred to the maintenance department, which is responsible for all equipment malfunctions.

How do you think you would react to this job? Since problems occur rarely and corrections are simple (turning a knob and, that failing, calling maintenance), you are likely to be pretty bored. Daydreaming would help pass the time and, although it is not allowed by company policy, you might bring a novel to work and do some reading when things seem especially routine. You might find frequent occasions to take papers to the front office, or to visit the restroom, or to do anything else you can think of to enliven things just a bit. You might even spend some time now and then speculating about what will happen when, inevitably, your job is automated: on the one hand, you will be happy to get off the job, but on the other you worry about whether there will be another position for you in the plant. With all of this daydreaming, reading, worrying, and errand running, you probably will fail to catch a number of deviations that do appear on your gauges, and you probably will get in trouble later for not paying attention. In all, it is not a very attractive work situation, but it is characteristic of many relatively mindless and repetitive tasks in organizations, especially monitoring tasks. (The problem in maintaining attention while monitoring building security using closed-circuit television, a job very similar to the one described above, is illustrated in Exhibit 3.1.)

What is it about the work that generates reactions such as those outlined above—reactions that may help people get through the day but at some cost to their work effectiveness? Part of the answer to this question is provided by activation theory. In essence, this theory proposes that the nature of the job influences an employee's psychological and physiological activation (or excitation) at work. When a job is repetitive, it provides little stimulation to the job incumbent, and activation level declines. A number of studies show that people react to chronic states of underactivation at work by engaging in arousal-enhancing behaviors, some of which (like those illustrated in the above example) clearly impair work effectiveness (Scott, 1966). These findings suggest that activation theory can be helpful in understanding jobs that are highly repetitive, and in planning for task

Exhibit 3.1
Work Design Problems in Museum Security

The problem with the closed-circuit television system is that while it may perfectly well show someone sneaking up the back stairs or unlimbering an acetylene torch, the system is really only as alert as the guard in the back room monitoring the television screens where the cameras report what they see. And guards, although their payroll constitutes a substantial portion of museum budgets, simply aren't as attentive as one might guess. In fact, a Federal agency in Boise, Idaho, completed an 18-month-long test last spring which came up with a conclusion sure to raise blood pressure in the ranks of the Veteran Police Association. Several thousand covert intrusions were conducted within view of closed-circuit television cameras monitored by professional guards, and only 5 percent were detected.

From W.H. Honan. "The Perils of Guarding King Tut's Treasures." *The New York Times Sunday Magazine.* December 17. 1978. p. 110. ©1978 by The New York Times Company. Reprinted by permission.

designs that minimize the dysfunctional consequences of underactivating work.[2]

However, if activation theory is to be used in designing work in organizations, more information is needed about the specific properties of tasks that affect activation levels and about the amounts of these properties that are associated with desirable levels of jobholder activation. On step in this direction has been taken by Schwab and Cummings (1976), who identified three dimensions that affect how activating a task will be: (1) the *magnitude* of the stimulation provided by the task, (2) the *variation* of the stimulation, and (3) the *number of sensory modalities* (visual, auditory, olfactory, gustatory, and tactile) that are affected by the task. Although research has yet to be conducted on these dimensions, they could in theory provide clear guidelines to those interested in designing stimulating jobs. For example, the number and variability of sound decibels could be re-engineered for a given task to create a higher (or lower) activation level.

The actual redesign of work using this approach probably should wait until additional data are collected on the effects of the three dimensions. Moreover, three thorny conceptual problems must also be overcome before the theory can receive widespread application. The first has to do with differences among individuals in how activated they are by their jobs and in the amount of activation they prefer. Clearly, people have different optimal levels of activation, that is, levels at which they are most alert, neither bored nor over-stimulated. Moreover, there is increasing evidence that personality affects how an individual will act when over- or understimulated (cf. Sales, 1970). Such differences among people are obviously important in applying activation theory to job redesign. But at present the theory provides little explicit guidance about how these differences should be dealt with in designing jobs and tasks.

A second problem in applying activation theory to work design derives from the fact that people tend to adapt rather quickly to changes in the level of stimulation they experience. A person's level of activation decreases markedly as a function of familiarity with a

---

2   While we are emphasizing here work that is underactivating, it should be noted that there also are dysfunctional consequences associated with tasks that induce excessively high levels of activation. For an excellent discussion of stressfully overstimulating work, see McGrath (1976).

given stimulus situation. But after a period of rest, re-presenting the same stimulus situation will again raise the level of activation (Scott, 1966). More complete understanding of the waxing and waning of activation in various circumstances could have significant implications for such job design practices a job rotation. Those who advocate job rotation claim that worker motivation can be kept reasonably high by rotating individuals through several different jobs, even though each of the jobs would become monotonous and boring if an individual were to remain on it for a long period of time. If future research can identify ways to maintain activation at nearly optimal levels through planned stimulus change, then the theory can increase substantially the usefulness of job rotation as a motivational technique. If, however, it turns out that there are general and inevitable decreases in activation over time regardless of how different tasks and rest periods are cycled, then the long-term usefulness of job rotation would seem to be limited.

Finally, it appears that the "ideal" level of activation for task effectiveness (as distinct from employee motivation or satisfaction) varies for different kinds of work. High activation increases effectiveness for certain types of tasks, but decreases effectiveness for others. Why? The answer derives from the fact that a person who is highly activated is more likely to exhibit *dominant* responses in a task situation, that is, responses that are well learned and ready to be emitted (Zajonc, 1965). For this reason, high activation fosters effective performance on tasks for which the dominant response is also the correct response (tasks that Zajonc calls "performance" tasks). But high activation *impairs* effectiveness on tasks for which the dominant response is likely to be wrong (tasks he calls "learning" tasks). Thus, if I know just what to do and how to do it (perhaps because I have done it many times) then more activation is better. If, however, I am struggling with the task and groping for the right way to respond (such as trying to speak a foreign language in which I am not quite fluent), then the higher my activation the worse my effectiveness. Further study is needed to learn how the "performance" and "learning" aspects of jobs can best be identified and described, and to understand how these task properties interact with the talent and experience of employees in affecting their work performance under varying levels of arousal.

In sum, while activation theory is very helpful in understanding how people react to very routine jobs (and to very complex ones), a number of conceptual and measurement problems make it difficult to apply the theory rigorously in actual work redesign situations. For this reason, the theory may be useful mainly as a heuristic for identifying jobs that grossly understimulate (or overstimulate) people and for determining the kinds of changes that should be made to reduce the negative effects of such jobs. In its present form, the theory offers little specific guidance about how jobs should be structured to elicit positive, self-reinforcing work motivation.[3] A quite different conceptual approach to the design of work, and one that does identify specific conditions that promote positive work motivation is examined next.

Motivation-Hygiene Theory

By far the most influential behavioral approach to work redesign to date has been Frederick Herzberg's two-factor theory of satisfaction and motivation (Herzberg, 1966; 1976). In essence, this theory proposes that the primary determinants of employee satisfaction are

---

3   Some interesting leads for pursuing this question are provided by the work of Hunt (1965). According to Hunt, people are motivated to seek an *optimal level of incongruity* between the stimulation they experience and some comparison standard (that to which they are accustomed). Thus, if a person experiences too little incongruity in performing work (as might be the case for someone who has overlearned a relatively simple task) he or she will be motivated to seek out and deal with increasingly incongruous situations. When, on the other hand, a person experiences too much incongruity (as might be the case for our pressure and temperature monitor, if suddenly all the gauges failed and simultaneously turned bright purple) the individual would be motivated to reduce the incongruity. The person's motivation would be to achieve an optimal level of incongruity, that is, a point at which there were still engaging discrpancies from normal expectations—*not* a point at which everything was predictable and routine.

Following this model, tasks should foster positive work motivation if they provide performers with moderate (that is, near-optimal) amounts of *incongruity* as the work progresses. Individual differences in how people respond to different tasks, a matter not handled well by basic activation theory, would be dealt with in terms of the amount of incongruity that different people experience as optimal. While the incongruity model strikes us as having intriguing possibilities for developing designs for work that engage the positive motivation of employees, such applications have not yet been attempted.

factors intrinsic to the work that is done—recognition, achievement, responsibility, advancement, and personal growth in competence. These factors are called *motivators* because employees are motivated to obtain more of them, for example, through good job performance. Dissatisfaction, on the other hand, is seen as being caused by *hygiene factors* that are extrinsic to the work. Examples include company policies, supervisory practices, pay plans, and working conditions. The Herzberg theory specifies that a job will enhance work motivation only to the degree that motivators are designed into the work. When this is done, a job is said to be "enriched." On the other hand, changes that deal solely with hygiene factors are not expected to generate motivational gains.

Much to the credit of Herzberg's theory, it has prompted a great deal of research and inspired a number of successful change projects involving job redesign (e.g., Paul, Robertson, and Herzberg, 1969). Especially noteworthy is the series of job enrichment studies done at AT&T (Ford, 1969). These studies appear to demonstrate, for a diversity of jobs, that job enrichment can lead to beneficial outcomes both for the individuals involved and for the employing organization. Moreover, a set of step-by-step procedures for implementing job enrichment was generated as part of the AT&T program, and these procedures continue to guide many job redesign activities throughout the country.

The Herzberg theory (specifically, the distinction between motivators and hygiene factors) provides a clear and straightforward way of thinking about employee motivation and of predicting the likely impact of various planned changes on motivation. The phrases "Yes, but that's really only a hygiene factor" and "But would it change the work itself?" have undoubtedly been used to good effect thousands of times as managers have considered various strategies for attempting to improve employee work motivation and satisfaction.

More often than not, applying the Herzberg theory has helped keep job design activities focused on issues that are central rather than peripheral to employee motivation and satisfaction. Consider, for example, such recently popular interventions as the four-day workweek and flexible scheduling of working hours. As noted in Chapter 2, these changes legitimately can be viewed as devices for improving the quality of the work experiences of employees in organizations. Yet motivation-hygiene theory would suggest that such alterations of work schedules are *not* likely to lead to long-term improvements in worker satisfaction, motivation, or productivity. Why? Because the nature of the work itself is not changed by innovations in scheduling. If the work is more frustrating than fulfilling, then about all that reasonably could be expected from flexible scheduling of work hours and the four-day workweek would be a decrease in some dissatisfactions that derive from conflicts between personal plans and work schedules. Indeed, problems arising from dissatisfying aspects of the work might actually be exacerbated rather than relieved under a four-day arrangement, because more hours would be spent on the job on any given workday.

In sum, what the Herzberg theory does, and does well, is point attention directly to the considerable significance of the *work itself* as a factor in the ultimate motivation and satisfaction of employees. And because the message of the theory is simple, persuasive, and directly relevant to the design and evaluation of actual organizational changes, the theory continues to be widely known and generally used by managers of organizations in this country.

Despite its considerable merit, there are several difficulties with motivation-hygiene theory that compromise its usefulness. For one thing, a number of researchers have been unable to provide empirical support for the major tenets of the two-factor theory. (See, for example, House and Wigdor, 1967. For analyses of the evidence that are favorable to the theory, see Herzberg, 1966.) In particular, it appears that the original dichotomization of aspects of the workplace into motivators and hygiene factors may have been partly due to methodological artifact. Moreover, some aspects of the workplace can serve at times as motivators and at other times as hygiene factors. Non-specific praise from a supervisor or an end-of-year raise in pay, for example, would not be classified as motivators by the theory. Yet to the extent that praise or pay raises are provided by the organization (and experienced by the employee) as recognition for achievement, such items would help motivate the employee, because recognition is included in the theory as a motivator. Thus, the motivating factors are not concretely defined in and of themselves; instead, the status of various factors depends in large part on the dynamics of the particular organizational situation.

This difficulty compromises the degree to which the presence or absence of the motivating factors can be *measured* for existing jobs. At the least, the measurement problem makes empirical testing of the theory in organizations very difficult. It also raises practical difficulties in using the theory to plan and implement actual job changes, because there is no way to diagnose systematically the status of jobs prior to change, or to measure the effects of job enrichment activities on the jobs after changes have been carried out.

Finally, the theory does not provide for differences in how responsive people are likely to be to enriched jobs. In the AT&T studies based on the theory, for example, it was assumed that the motivating factors potentially could increase the work motivation of all employees, although the implementation procedures devised for these studies specified that enriching tasks should be added to a job only when an employee showed readiness for new responsibilities. But the theory does not specify how determinations of readiness should be made. Because it is clear that some individuals are more likely to respond positively to an enriched, complex job than are others (Hulin, 1971), it would be useful if the theory were elaborated to specify in concrete terms how individual differences should be dealt with, both conceptually and in the design and implementation of actual change.

Job Characteristics Theory

A third behavioral approach to the design of work focuses on the objective characteristics of employee jobs. The basic idea is to build into jobs those attributes that create conditions for high work motivation, satisfaction, and performance. In addition, the approach acknowledges that people will respond differently to the same job. Therefore, the theory requires that the characteristics of jobholders as well as of the jobs themselves be considered when work is designed.

Job characteristics theory has its roots in a major study by Arthur Turner and Paul Lawrence (1965) that examined the relationship between certain objective attributes of tasks and employees' reactions to their work. Among the task attributes studied were the amount of variety in the work, the level of employee autonomy in performing the work, the amount of interaction required in carrying out task activities (and the number of opportunities for optional interaction), the level of knowledge and skill required, and the amount of responsibility entrusted to the jobholder.

Turner and Lawrence predicted that the higher a job's standing on these attributes, the more satisfied (and regular in attendance) jobholders would be. To test their ideas, the researchers combined the several task attributes into a single index (the separate attributes were positively associated with one another anyway) and examined the relationship between the scores of 47 industrial jobs on the index and the satisfaction and attendance of employees who worked on those jobs. It turned out that the expected positive relationships were found only for workers in factories located in small towns. For employees in urban work settings, satisfaction was negatively related to scores of jobs on the index, and absenteeism was unrelated to the index. Turner and Lawrence concluded that employees with different subcultural backgrounds reacted differently to "good" jobs (those high on task attributes such as variety and autonomy), and this view was supported in later research (e.g., Blood and Hulin, 1967).

Further evidence that measurable job characteristics are directly associated with employee attitudes and behaviors at work was provided in a study of telephone company jobs by Hackman and Lawler (1971). These researchers focused on four job characteristics: variety, task identity (doing a whole piece of work), autonomy, and job-based feedback. They predicted that if these characteristics were present in a job, then jobholders would experience a positive, self-generated affective "kick" when they performed well and that this internal reinforcement would serve as an incentive for continued good performance.

In addition, Hackman and Lawler suggested that the previously found differences in how members of subcultural groups responded to their jobs might most simply be explained in terms of employees' personal needs for growth and development at work. Specifically, they predicted that the stronger an individual's need for growth, the more likely he or she would be to respond positively to a job high on the four core dimensions. Results of the Hackman-Lawler research generally support their predictions.

The present authors (Hackman and Oldham, 1975; 1976) have further extended and revised job characteristics theory, with emphasis on ways the theory can be made most useful in carrying out work redesign activities.[4] The revised model is discussed in detail in the next section of the book. As will be seen, one of its major features is its amenability for use in prechange diagnoses of work systems and in postchange evaluations of the effects of job changes.

---

4   Simultaneously, Blood (1978) has developed a promising related theory, which examines self-rewarding behaviors of employees under various job and organizational circumstances.

Because the key job characteristics in the model are specified at a low level of abstraction, they provide a relatively concrete set of criteria for use in deciding what kinds of change in jobs are (and are not) likely to result in motivational improvements. One could, for example, evaluate alternative designs for the school systems audio-visual department (described earlier in this chapter) in terms of the expected standing of departmental jobs on characteristics such as variety, autonomy, feedback, and so on. And because job characteristics are readily measured, the theory makes possible greater "fine tuning" of planned changes, and greater accountability for their effects, than heretofore has been possible.

Like motivation-hygiene theory, job characteristics theory deals only with aspects of the job that can be altered to create *positive* motivational incentives for jobholders. The theory does not deal directly with the dysfunctional aspects of repetitive work (as does activation theory), although presumably a job designed according to the theory would not turn out to be excessively routine or repetitive.

In addition, job characteristics theory focuses on jobs that are done independently by individuals working more or less alone. Existing versions of the theory offer little guidance about how work should be designed for interacting teams of employees, nor do they address social, technical, and situational factors that affect how work systems function. At core, job characteristics theory, like motivation-hygiene theory, is a theory of individual motivation.

An alternative conceptual approach, one that does deal specifically with the properties of work systems and that emphasizes the use of groups in performing work, is discussed below.

SYSTEMS APPROACHES

Work is not, of course, performed in a vacuum. Work is done in *organizations,* and for that reason it is imperative that we understand how organizations, as social systems, influence the way work is designed and managed.

While there are numerous useful system-oriented approaches to the analysis of work organizations (see, for example, Katz and Kahn, 1978), one theory stands out as having the most relevance to the design and redesign of jobs and work systems. This is sociotechnical systems theory, as developed and espoused by scholars such as Albert

Cherns, Eric Trist, and Louis Davis (Cherns, 1976; Davis, 1975; Trist, Higgin, Murray, and Pollock, 1963). We focus on that theory here.

The Sociotechnical Approach

A key feature of the sociotechnical approach to work design is an emphasis on creating work systems in which the social and the technical aspects of those systems are integrated and as supportive of one another as possible. This involves attempting to "jointly optimize" the social and the technical systems that operate in work organizations, rather than optimizing the functioning of the technical system at the expense of the social system (as sometimes is done in traditional approaches to work design), or vice versa.

Another important feature of the sociotechnical approach is its recognition of the fact that all organizations are imbedded in, and affected by, an outside environment. To understand how an organization functions and to make constructive changes in that organization, one must pay close attention to the environmental forces that operate on it. Especially important are cultural values that specify how organizations "should" function, and generally accepted roles that individuals, groups, and organizations are supposed to play in society. Thus, there is constant interchange between what goes on in any given work organization and what goes on in its environment—a fact that is dangerous to ignore when work systems are designed or changed (Davis and Trist, 1974).

Sociotechnical systems theory has evolved gradually over the past two decades. It has been informed by findings from numerous change projects in work systems, originally primarily in overseas organizations but increasingly in the United States as well. Many of these projects have provided vivid illustration of the interactions between the social and technical aspects of work and have also proven successful as action projects (e.g., Rice, 1958; Trist *et al.,* 1963; Trist, Susman, and Brown, 1977).

As revealed through reports of such experiments, sociotechnical systems theory appears to be at the same time very general and very specific. It is general in the sense that the principles of the theory are framed and discussed at a rather molar or general level of analysis, and few explicit conceptual links are forged between the tenets of the theory and the particular actions taken or outcomes observed in various applications. It is specific in the sense that the characteristics of the organizations where the experiments are conducted (and the specifics of what happens during the course of the projects) are usually described in rich and complete detail.

The generality of the theory is one of the elegant features of the sociotechnical approach, since it allows the theory to be adapted with ease to almost any organizational situation and used to understand and explain almost anything that happens there. Thus, the theory remains open to continual improvement and revision on the basis of increased experience with it in actual change situations. Moreover, the theory seems quite unlikely to fall into the trap of a "new Taylorism," that is, mechanistically overspecifying the details of tasks and relationships that are expected to contribute to an improved quality of life in organizations (Davis, 1975).

Sociotechnical theory offers some clear advantages over both traditional and behavioral approaches to work design. Traditional approaches often ignore the personal needs of the people who carry out the work (especially social needs that can be fulfilled by group memberships) and are so oriented toward the efficiency of the technical system that critical aspects of the social system may be ignored. Psychological approaches tend to give insufficient attention to the operation of the technical system when work is designed and almost always underestimate the importance of group relations and the organizational environment in affecting what happens in the workplace. By contrast, changes that are undertaken from a sociotechnical perspective involve *simultaneous* modification of technical and social systems to create designs for work that can lead both to greater task productivity and to increased fulfillment for organization members.

Features of Sociotechnical Changes

There are two characteristic features of most sociotechnical change projects: multiply focused interventions and the creation of work groups.

Sociotechnical changes are virtually never carried out in piecemeal fashion. While jobs, rewards, physical equipment, spatial arrangements, work schedules, supervisory relationships (and more) may be altered in a sociotechnical intervention, none of these is taken as the primary focus of change activities. Instead, organization members (often including rank-and-file employees and representatives of organized labor as well as managers) examine *all* aspects of organizational operations that might affect how well the work is done or the quality of organization members' experiences. Changes that emerge from these explorations invariably involve numerous aspects of both the social and the technical systems of the organization and, it is hoped, result in holistic changes in how the organization functions.

Despite the view of sociotechnical theorists that there is no single "right" lever for initiating organizational change, it turns out that sociotechnical interventions almost always involve the formation of groups of employees who share responsibility for carrying out a significant piece of work. Indeed, one of the major contributions of the sociotechnical approach to the theory and practice of work design is the idea of the *autonomous work group* (Cummings, 1978; Gulowsen, 1972).

Typically, such groups are relatively small (less than 20 members), and members share among themselves much of the decision making about how the work of the group should be planned and executed. The task of the group is designed so that it is a whole and meaningful piece of work on which members can perform a variety of different roles. Members are encouraged to develop close ties with one another and a joint commitment to the task. Consistent with the spirit of the sociotechnical approach, other aspects of the workplace (such as compensation arrangements and management roles) also are changed when autonomous work groups are formed, so that the group, its task, and the surrounding organization are as congruent with one another as possible.

Autonomous work groups have become an increasingly popular organizational innovation in recent years and now are frequently seen even in change projects that are not explicitly guided by sociotechnical theory. One such case is the well-known General Foods pet-food plant in Topeka, Kansas (Walton, 1972). One of the innovative features of the new plant at Topeka was the organization of the work force into teams. Each team was given nearly autonomous responsibility for a significant organizational task. In addition to carrying out the work required to complete their task, team members collectively performed many activities that traditionally are reserved for management. These included coping with manufacturing problems, distributing individual tasks among team members, and participating in making organization-wide decisions. Members were encouraged to share their task-relevant knowledge and skill with one another, both to increase internal flexibility in getting the work done and to prepare members for even more challenging assignments. Outside observations indicated that the use of autonomous work teams was an important ingredient of the early success of the Topeka experiment (Walton, 1975a).

Limitations of the Approach

Perhaps the greatest difficulty in attempting to design and implement changes in work systems using the sociotechnical approach is a pervasive lack of specificity in the theory. It is difficult to determine, for example, what exactly is meant by terms such as "joint optimization," "autonomy," and even "social systems" (Van der Zwaan, 1975). It is unclear how (and under what circumstances) the work, the social surround, and the outside environment affect one another. There are no theory-specified principles or procedures for carrying out sociotechnical changes in work systems. Nor are there clear and theory-based criteria for use in determining just what is (and what is not) a "well-designed" job or work group. Some progress in clarifying these matters has been made in recent years (see, for example, Cherns, 1976; Cummings, 1978; Davis and Trist, 1974). Yet the various prescriptions and criteria that have been set forth differ from one another in numerous specifics, and they appear to be based more on experiences in given research or action projects than on derivations from the basic tenets of the theory itself.

In addition, the sociotechnical approach does not adequately deal with differences among organization members in how they respond to work that is designed from the sociotechnical perspective. For example, in a recent study of work groups formed in a coalmining organization it was assumed that all members would respond similarly to the experience of working in autonomous groups (Trist et al., 1977). However, as we have noted previously, there is now abundant evidence that there are great individual differences in how people react to various work arrangements. Sociotechnical theory would be strengthened (and made more useful in practice) if it were elaborated to better account for such differences among people and to provide guidance about how these differences should be dealt with in the design and conduct of change projects.

In sum, the sociotechnical perspective on work organizations is of considerable value as a way of thinking about work and its redesign, and as a framework for planning changes in work systems. Yet sociotechnical systems theory in its present form is difficult to test empirically, and the theory provides little explicit and concrete guidance about what organizational changes should be made under what circumstances.

CONCLUSION

The traditional approaches to work design, discussed first in this chapter, assume that most people can work productively and efficiently on routinized, standardized jobs. The behavioral approaches, on the other hand, suggest that work effectiveness will be enhanced if employees have jobs that are *not* simple and repetitive—that are, instead, complex, meaningful, and challenging. And the sociotechnical systems approach accepts the major premises of the behavioral approaches, but goes beyond them in asserting the importance of group relationships and organization-environment transactions in establishing effective work systems.

Our approach to the design and redesign of work, the approach that will guide the models and prescriptions for change presented throughout the remainder of this book, is something of a hybrid of the behavioral and systems approaches. Its major features can be summarized as follows:

• It focuses squarely on the actual work that people perform in organizations. We assume that the problems stemming from poor person-job relationships can, in many instances, be remedied most powerfully and permanently by restructuring the jobs that are performed. We draw heavily on one of the behavioral approaches to work design, job characteristics theory, in specifying the attributes of jobs that create conditions for positive work motivation. And we find that work motivation often can be enhanced by increasing the levels of responsibility, meaningfulness, and feedback that are built into jobs.

• It deals separately with the design of work for individuals and the design of work for groups. We will show that the choice between individual and group designs is one of the most important choices to be made in structuring a work system, and that the conditions required for optimal individual work effectiveness are different from those needed for high team effectiveness. For individuals, the emphasis is on the person-job relationship; for groups, one must consider person-job, person-group, and group-job relationships, as well as how these components fit together. It turns out that designing work for groups is *not* merely constructing a "team version" of a good individual job design.

• It deals explicitly both with individual differences in how people react to jobs and with aspects of the systemic context that affect the feasibility, potency, and persistence of work redesign efforts. Our approach is neither an "individual differences" theory nor a "systems" theory in that we maintain throughout our focus on person-job (or person-group-job) relationships. Nevertheless, we acknowledge the potency of both individual and systemic properties in affecting what happens when people perform work in organizations. And we deal systematically with these properties in our models for individual and group work design.

• It emphasizes the importance of collecting diagnostic data about a work system before it changed. There are, we believe, few (if any) universals regarding the design of work. What is appropriate in one set of organizational circumstances will wholly miss the mark in another. And what changes intuitively "seem right" to managers or workers when they first think about work restructuring often turn out to be wrong or irrelevant. For these reasons, theory-guided diagnoses of work systems are critically important to effective work redesign, and our change models explicitly incorporate a diagnostic component.

• Finally, our approach highlights the links between basic theory about behavior in organizations and practical technologies for the design and redesign of jobs. If a theoretical proposition has no implications for action, then we are likely to suffice by noting it as a matter of passing scholarly interest. And if a seemingly plausible change technique has no conceptual basis, then (assuming we cannot generate one) we may not mention it at all. We share with Lewin the view that there is nothing so practical as a good theory, and we have tried very hard to keep the conceptual and the practical aspects of our approach tied together.

Throughout, we have attempted to develop some strategies for work design that offer realistic alternatives to traditional approaches, alternatives that neither compromise the integrity of people to achieve work efficiency nor compromise organizational productivity to make people happy. If, by book's end, you and we have managed to avoid both the Scylla of pure efficiency and the Charybdis of pure happiness, then you should be able to return to the audiovisual department with which we began this chapter, generate three or four innovative but realistic designs for work there, and draw up a fairly complete list of additional information that you would need to decide which of those designs would be most appropriate for that work system.

FOR ADDITIONAL READING

Scott, W.G., and T.R. Mitchell. *Organization theory* (3rd ed.). Homewood, IL: Irwin, 1976. Chapters 1 and 2 provide a good introduction to classical organization theory and show the implications of the theory for how work is designed.

Scott, W.E. Activation theory and task design. *Organizational Behavior and Human Performance,* 1966, *1,* 3-30. An excellent (albeit technical) review of research and theory on activation theory, which gives special attention to the implications of the theory for the design of work in organizations.

Herzberg, F. *The managerial choice.* Homewood, IL: Dow Jones-Irwin, 1976. The most recent and comprehensive statement of Herzberg's views. Includes a statement of motivation-hygiene theory, examples of applications of the theory, and a very readable question-and-answer defense of this approach to the design of work.

Turner, A.N., and P.R. Lawrence, *Industrial jobs and the worker.* Boston: Harvard Graduate School of Business Administration, 1965. The pioneering study of the relationship between measurable task attributes and employee responses to their work.

Cherns, A. The principles of sociotechnical design. *Human Relations,* 1976, *29,* 793-792. One of the most concrete statements available of the sociotechnical systems theory approach to work design, presented as nine "principles" for the design of work systems.

PART TWO
DESIGNING WORK FOR INDIVIDUALS

4
MOTIVATION THROUGH THE DESIGN OF WORK

How can work be structured so that it is performed effectively and, at the same time, jobholders find the work personally rewarding and satisfying? In this chapter, one approach to answering that question is developed. We begin by examining the basic conditions that promote high performance motivation and satisfaction at work, and then work backwards to determine how those conditions can be created.[1]

When people are well matched with their jobs, it rarely is necessary to force, coerce, bribe, or trick them into working hard and trying to perform the job well. Instead, they try to do well because it is rewarding and satisfying to do so. Recall the diagnostic question posed in Chapter 2: "What happens when you try to work especially hard and productively on your job?" When there is a good fit between the person and the job, responses to that question will be mostly positive: "I get a nice sense of accomplishment," or "I feel good about myself and what I'm producing."

The term we use to describe this state of affairs is "internal motivation." When someone has high internal work motivation, feelings are closely tied to how well he or she performs on the job.

---

1   The theoretical position presented in this chapter is developed in more detail by Hackman and Oldham (1976).

Good performance is an occasion for self-reward, which serves as an incentive for continuing to do well. And because poor performance prompts unhappy feelings, the person may elect to try harder in the future so as to avoid those unpleasant outcomes and regain the internal rewards that good performance can bring. The result is a self-perpetuating cycle of positive work motivation powered by self-generated (rather than external) rewards for good work.[2]

A number of other personal and work outcomes (such as improved work effectiveness and increased job satisfaction) tend also to appear when conditions for internal work motivation are created. For ease of presentation, we will deal solely with internal motivation in the pages to follow, and fold in these additional outcomes toward the end of the chapter.

CREATING CONDITIONS FOR INTERNAL MOTIVATION

When will internal motivation occur on the job? As shown in Fig. 4.1, our theory suggests that there are three key conditions. First, the person must have *knowledge of the results* of his or her work. If things are arranged so that the person who does the work never finds out whether it is being performed well or poorly, then that person has no basis for feeling good about having done well or unhappy about doing poorly.

Secondly, the person must *experience responsibility* for the results of the work, believing that he or she is personally accountable for the work outcomes. If one views the quality of work done as depending more on external factors (such as a procedure manual, the boss, or people in another work section) than on one's own initiatives or efforts, then there is no reason to feel personally proud when one does well or sad when one doesn't.

---

2   Concepts that are related to internal motivation as we use the term here include Deci's (1975) more general notion of "intrinsic motivation" and Csikszentmihali's (1975) more focused idea of the "flow experience." Perhaps closest in meaning to internal motivation is Blood's concept of "self-rewarding." Self-administered rewards, according to Blood, are both immediate and contingent on behavior; in colloquial terms, extreme positive self-rewarding can be characterized as pride, and extreme negative self-rewarding as shame (Blood, 1978, p. 94).

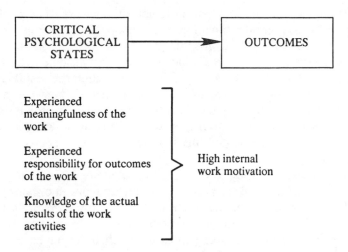

Fig. 4.1 The three psychological states that affect internal work motivation.

And finally, the person must *experience the work as meaningful,* as something that "counts" in one's own system of values. If the work being done is seen as trivial (as might be the case for a job putting paper clips in boxes, for example), then internal work motivation is unlikely to develop—even when the person has sole responsibility for the work and receives ample information about how well he or she is performing.

It appears necessary for *all three* of these factors, labeled "critical psychological states" in Fig. 4.1, to be present for strong internal work motivation to develop and persist. One of your authors, like many college teachers, finds that his day is made or broken by how well the morning lecture goes. The task is meaningful to him (he finds lecturing challenging and believes it to be important); he feels that the quality of the lecture is *his* responsibility (he's never quite learned how to attribute responsibility for a bad class to the students); and his knowledge of results is direct and unambiguous (undergraduates are expert in using subtle cues—and some not so subtle, such as newspaper reading—to signal how much they feel they are learning from the day's class). So all three of the psychological states are present in the lecturing task, and internal motivation to do well is very high indeed.

If any one of the three psychological states were to be removed, your author's internal motivation would drop. If, for example, he did not experience the task as meaningful—perhaps because he did not believe in the lecture as a teaching device, or because he was so good at it (or so poor) that it was not a challenge—then the results would not matter so much. The same would be true if he were merely reading lecture notes prepared by someone else (his personal responsibility for the outcome would be minimal), or if he were insulated from knowledge about how his lecture was being received by the students.

It is ironic that the three psychological states often characterize games played for pleasure better than they do work in organizations. Consider, for example, the game of golf. Knowledge of results is direct and immediate: the player hits the ball and sees at once where it goes. Moreover, tallies of scores for each hole played are kept, providing cumulative and comparative data about performance effectiveness. Experienced personal responsibility for the outcomes also is clear and high, despite the tendency of golfers sometimes to claim that the slice was due to someone whispering behind the tee, or perhaps to a little puff of wind that came up 100 yards down the fairway just after the ball had been hit. Experienced meaningfulness also is high, despite the fact that the task itself is mostly devoid of cosmic significance.

Why is experienced meaningfulness high for the game of golf? The reason is that golf provides continuous opportunities for players to express and test their personal skills and abilities—specifically their judgment and motor coordination. As will be seen in the next section of this chapter, people tend to experience as meaningful almost *any* task that provides chances to use and test personal skills and abilities, regardless of whether the task is inherently significant (such as performing surgery) or trivial (such as hitting white balls around green pastures). Moreover, the meaningfulness that grows from the challenge to players' skills is often reinforced by golfing partners, who provide social validation of the importance of the activity and may even attach monetary outcomes to the day's play.

So, in golf, the three psychological states are present, and internal motivation among regular golfers is usually quite high. Indeed, golfers exhibit an intensity of behavior that is rarely seen in the workplace: getting up before dawn to be first on the tee, feeling jubilation or despair all day depending on how well the morning round was played, sometimes even destroying the tools and equipment of the game—not out of boredom or frustration with the work (as is sometimes seen in industrial settings) but rather from anger at oneself for not playing better.

Now consider another kind of task, such as assembling aircraft brakes, which clearly is of great human significance. For this task, good versus poor performance can literally mean the difference between life and death for someone aboard an aircraft that must stop before the runway does. An aircraft brake assembler is likely to experience the work as highly meaningful, which provides a good basis for creating conditions of high internal work motivation. The irony is that in many such significant jobs, precisely *because* the task is so important, management designs and supervises the work to ensure error-free performance and destroys employee motivation for high quality work in the process.

For example, managers in one organization were very concerned that an assembly task (not assembling brakes, but similar in many respects) be performed at the highest possible level of quality, with virtually no errors. A detailed manual was prepared specifying how the assembly should be carried out, with step-by-step instructions about the order of assembly, the use of different tools, and so on. Supervisors were instructed to monitor closely the performance of the assemblers, to ensure that they performed the task exactly "by the book," and to demonstrate the correct use of tools and procedures when they deviated from standard procedure in any way. Moreover, an independent inspection section was created and located in a distant wing of the plant. Also in that wing was a small repair section where any assemblies that failed to pass inspection were to be repaired. Each supervisor received an end-of-week report giving the number of faulty assemblies produced by his group and documenting the nature of the problems discovered by the inspectors. Supervisors were expected to take any corrective action needed to eliminate recurring problems.

The work system described above, which is typical for jobs deemed especially critical by management, seems at first glance appropriate and rational. How did the assemblers respond to the system? The experienced meaningfulness of the work was high: almost to a person the employees agreed that the work itself was significant and important. But they experienced very little *personal* responsibility for the outcomes of the work and felt well insulated from knowledge of the results of their work activities.

The reasons for these perceptions and feelings are not hard to fathom. Because the job required the assemblers to follow the procedure manual to the letter, and because supervisors enforced that requirement, the assemblers viewed themselves as relatively small cogs in a carefully engineered machine. Many employees assumed that if an error were made, or if the assembly materials or tools were out of specification, an inspector would catch it—that was, after all, their job. Moreover, no assembler learned about the results of his or her work: all testing was done by the inspectors, and the information received by the supervisor at the end of each week was about the group (not the individual). This led many assemblers to conclude that reported problems probably were the fault of *other* members of the work group, not themselves.

In sum, two of the three psychological states were low for most of the assemblers (that is, experienced responsibility and knowledge of results), resulting in a low level of internal work motivation to perform well, despite the inherent significance of the task. And work quality was such a problem that management expressed dismay at the shoddy work being done by the "shoddy people" in the assembly section. Given how the work was designed, with little real chance for assemblers to feel responsibility for what they produced or to learn about the quality of their production, it was almost inevitable that there would be motivational problems among them. But as is often the case, management viewed the problem solely in terms of the apparent impact of the people on the work and failed to consider the effects of the work on the people.

In fact, most people exhibit "motivational problems" at work when their tasks are designed so that they have little meaning, when they experience little responsibility for the work outcomes, or when they are protected from data about how well they are performing. If, on the other hand, a task is arranged so that the people who perform it richly experience the three psychological states, then even individuals who view themselves as chronically lazy may find themselves putting out a little extra effort to do the work well. It appears, then, that *motivation at work may actually have more to do with how tasks are designed and managed than with the personal dispositions of the people who do them.* But what are the task characteristics that create conditions for internal work motivation? We turn to this question next.

THE PROPERTIES OF MOTIVATING JOBS

The three psychological states discussed above are, by definition, internal to persons and therefore not directly manipulable in designing or managing work. What is needed are reasonably objective, measurable, changeable properties of the work itself that foster these psychological states, and through them, enhance internal work motivation. Research suggests that the five job characteristics shown in Fig. 4.2 may be useful in this regard (Hackman and Lawler, 1971; Hackman and Oldham, 1976; Turner and Lawrence, 1965). Three of these five job characteristics are shown in the figure as contributing to the experienced meaningfulness of the work, one contributes to experienced responsibility, and one contributes to knowledge of results.

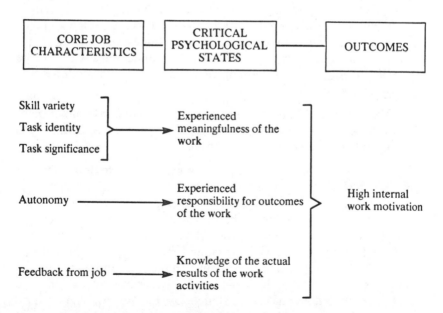

Fig. 4.2 Job characteristics that foster the three psychological states.

Toward Experienced Meaningfulness

There are a number of different ways that work can take on personal meaning for the person who performs it. Three characteristics of jobs that seem especially powerful in influencing the experienced meaningfulness of work are (1) *skill variety,* (2) *task identity,* and (3) *task significance.*

> **Skill variety:** The degree to which a job requires a variety of different activities in carrying out the work, involving the use of a number of different skills and talents of the person.

As noted earlier, when a task requires workers to engage in activities that challenge or stretch their skills or abilities, they almost invariably experience that task as meaningful, and the more skills involved, the more meaningful the work is likely to be. The link between skill variety and experienced meaningfulness is probably "wired in" for human organisms. Numerous researchers have shown that people, from newborn infants to mature adults, seek out occasions to explore and manipulate their environments and to gain a sense of efficacy by testing and using their skills (Kagan, 1972; White, 1959). The substantive content of the materials being dealt with is not critical in establishing experienced meaningfulness; even work that is not very significant or important in an absolute sense can still be meaningful to a person if doing that work taps and stretches the performer's skills and talents.

> **Task identity:** The degree to which a job requires completion of a "whole" and identifiable piece of work, that is, doing a job from beginning to end with a visible outcome.

People care about their work more when they are doing a whole job. When workers have an intact task, such as providing a complete unit of service or putting together an entire product, they tend to see that task as more meaningful than is the case when they are responsible for only a small part of the job. A social worker in a public welfare department who is responsible for dealing with *all* the needs and problems of his or her clients will find the work more meaningful than a colleague who deals only with issues relating to income maintenance or homemaker assistance. By the same token, it is more meaningful to assemble a complete toaster than to solder electrical connections on toaster after toaster—even if the skill levels required for the two jobs are about the same.

Task significance: The degree to which the job has a substantial impact on the lives of other people, whether those people are in the immediate organization or in the world at large.

Experienced meaningfulness of the work usually is enhanced when workers understand that the work being done will have a substantial impact on the physical or psychological well-being of other people. Employees who tighten nuts on aircraft engines are likely to experience their work as more meaningful than workers who tighten nuts on decorative mirrors, simply because lives are at stake in the first task and are not in the second. When we know that what we do at work will affect someone else's happiness, health, or safety, we care about that work more than if the work is largely irrelevant to the lives and well-being of other people.

Each of the three job characteristics described above contributes to the overall experienced meaningfulness of the work. If a given job is high on all three of the characteristics, an employee is very likely to experience the work as meaningful: putting together a complex heart pacemaker is an example of such a task. Yet because three different task characteristics contribute to experienced meaningfulness, a person can experience the work as meaningful even if one or two of these task characteristics are quite low. Even our assembler of decorative mirrors, whose task is surely below average in significance, could find meaning in the work if it were sufficiently high in skill variety and/or task identity.

Toward Increased Responsibility

The characteristic of jobs that fosters increased feelings of personal responsibility for the work outcomes is *autonomy*.

Autonomy: The degree to which the job provides substantial freedom, independence, and discretion to the individual in scheduling the work and in determining the procedures to be used in carrying it out.

When the job provides substantial autonomy to the persons performing it, work outcomes will be viewed by those individuals as depending substantially on their *own* efforts, initiatives, and decisions, rather than on, say, the adequacy of instructions from the boss or on a manual of job procedures. As autonomy increases, individuals tend to feel more personal responsibility for successes and failures that occur on the job and are more willing to accept personal accountability for the outcomes of their work.[3]

Toward Knowledge of Results

Knowledge of the results of one's work is affected directly by the amount of *feedback* one receives from doing the work.

Job feedback: The degree to which carrying out the work activities required by the job provides the individual with direct and clear information about the effectiveness of his or her performance.

Note that the focus here is on feedback obtained *directly from the job*, as when a television repairman turns on the set and finds that it works (or doesn't work) after being repaired, when a sales representative closes the deal and receives a check from the customer, or when a physician treats a patient and sees the patient get well. In each case, the knowledge of results derives from the work activities themselves, rather from some other person (such as a co-worker or a supervisor) who collects data or makes a judgment about how well the work is being done. While this second type of feedback (which will be termed "feedback from agents") can also contribute to the overall knowledge an employee has of the results of his or her work, the focus here is on feedback mechanisms that are designed into the work itself.

The Overall Motivating Potential of a Job

Because a given job can be very high on one or more of the five characteristics described above and simultaneously quite low on

---

3   There has been a good deal of research in social and clinical psychology documenting the negative consequences for people of constrained autonomy to make decisions about their life and work (see Wortman and Brehm, 1975 for a review.) Moreover, there are some intriguing findings that suggest that increased control can have beneficial effects on learning (Perlmuter and Monty, 1977), on responses to stressful situations such as crowding (Baron and Rodin, 1978), and on happiness and health (Rodin and Langer, 1977). There are, however, few studies in which control has been increased by direct alteration of task structure, or which provide direct tests of the link proposed here between objective increases in autonomy and enhanced feelings of personal *responsibility* for work outcomes (Sogin and Pallak, 1976; Wortman, 1976).

others, it always is useful to consider the standing of a job on each of the job characteristics. Nevertheless, it also can be informative to combine the five characteristics into a single index that reflects the *overall* potential of a job to foster internal work motivation on the part of job incumbents.

Following the model diagrammed in Fig. 4.2, a job high in motivating potential must be high on at least one (and hopefully more) of the three characteristics that prompt experienced meaningfulness, *and* high on both autonomy and feedback as well, thereby creating conditions that foster all three of the critical psychological states. When numerical scores are available, they are combined as follows:

$$\text{Motivating potential score (MPS)} = \left[\frac{\text{Skill variety} + \text{Task identity} + \text{Task significance}}{3}\right] \times \text{Autonomy} \times \text{Job feedback}$$

As can be seen from the formula, a very low score on *either* autonomy or feedback will reduce the overall MPS of the job very substantially. This is as it should be, because the model requires that both experienced responsibility and knowledge of results be present if internal work motivation is to be high, and autonomy and feedback, respectively, are the job characteristics that prompt those two psychological states.

On the other hand, a low score on one of the three job characteristics that contribute to experienced meaningfulness cannot, by itself, seriously compromise the overall motivating potential of a job. The other characteristics that prompt experienced meaningfulness can, to some extent, compensate for low scores on one or even two of these three characteristics.

Techniques for measuring the five core job characteristics are discussed in detail in the next chapter. A diagnostic instrument is described there that yields scores for each job characteristic, ranging from a low of 1 to a high of 7. Following the above formula, this means that the lowest possible MPS for a job is 1 and the highest possible is 343 (7 cubed). In practice, the lowest MPS we have ever observed was 7 (an *overflow* typing pool, in which a number of employees sat by their typewriters for hours on end waiting for occasions when one of the regular typing pools was overloaded, at which time they would be given some pages to type until the work-load in the regular pools once again became normal). The highest we have observed was over 300, for an autonomous organization development consultant working in a moderate-sized corporation. An average MPS score for jobs in U.S. organizations is about 128.

It should be emphasized that the objective "motivating potential" of a job does not *cause* employees who work on that job to be internally motivated, to perform well, or to experience job satisfaction. Instead, a job that is high in motivating potential merely creates conditions such that *if* the jobholder performs well he or she is likely to experience a reinforcing state of affairs as a consequence. Job characteristics, then, serve only to set the stage for internal motivation. The *behavior* of people who work on a job determines the action that unfolds on the stage. And, as will be seen below, some people are much better positioned to take advantage of the opportunities offered by "enriched" jobs than are others.

THE ROLE OF DIFFERENCES AMONG PEOPLE

Some employees "take off" on jobs that are high in motivating potential; others are more likely to "turn off." There are many attributes of people that affect how they respond to their work, and we cannot review all of them here. We have, however, selected for discussion three characteristics of people that seem especially important in understanding who will (and who will not) respond positively to high MPS jobs. These three factors, which we believe should be taken into account in planning for possible changes in jobs, are identified as "moderators" in Fig. 4.3 and are examined separately below.

Knowledge and Skill

Recall once again the essential property of internal work motivation: positive feelings follow from good performance, and negative feelings follow from poor performance. If a job is low in motivating potential, then internal motivation will be low, and one's feelings will not be affected much by how well one does. But if a job is *high* in MPS, then good performance will be highly reinforcing, and poor performance will lead to very unhappy feelings. The consequence of this state of

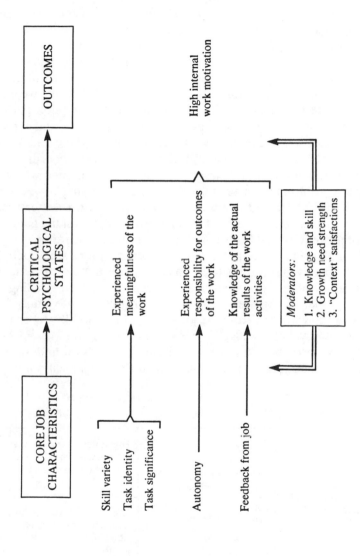

Fig. 4.3 Moderators of the relationship between the job characteristics and internal motivation.

affairs for the work motivation and satisfaction of job incumbents is shown in Fig. 4.4.

For jobs high in motivating potential, then, people who have sufficient knowledge and skill to perform well will experience substantially positive feelings as a result of their work activities. But people who are *not* competent enough to perform well will experience a good deal of unhappiness and frustration at work, precisely because the job "counts" for them and they do poorly at it.

To return to our example of golf, a high MPS task, we find talented golfers frustrated at times with occasional poor performance, but always motivated, returning for more practice, and netting a good deal of self-satisfaction with themselves and the game. However, those of us who are not blessed with good hand-eye coordination may show equally high motivation early in our experience with the game, but eventually we tend to give it up. Spending a weekend morning trying hard and being miserable at failing, time after time, eventually leads all but the most masochistic to abandon the game in favor of an activity that brings more pleasure than frustration.

A similar phenomenon can occur in organizations when people are given highly motivating tasks that they are unable to perform successfully: rather than continually accept the pain of failing at something that is experienced as important, such individuals frequently opt to withdraw from the job—either behaviorally, by changing jobs, or psychologically, by convincing themselves that in fact they do *not* care about the work. Either outcome is an undesirable state of affairs both for the individual and for the organization.

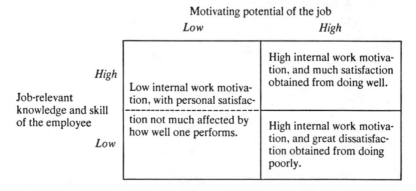

Fig. 4.4 The outcomes of work on high and low MPS jobs as a function of employee knowledge and skill.

Growth Need Strength

Jobs high in motivating potential create opportunities for considerable self-direction, learning, and personal accomplishment at work. Not all individuals appreciate such opportunities, even among employees who would be able to perform the work very competently. What determines who will respond positively to a complex, challenging job, and who will not?

As noted in Chapter 3, some researchers (e.g., Turner and Lawrence, 1965; Blood and Hulin, 1967) have suggested that the critical factor may be subcultural: people from rural settings may more strongly endorse middle-class work norms than people from urban settings, and therefore respond more positively to jobs high in motivating potential. An alternative view, and the one we endorse, is that the *psychological needs* of people are critical in determining how vigorously an individual will respond to a job high in motivating potential (Hackman and Lawler, 1971; Hackman and Oldham, 1976).

Some people have strong needs for personal accomplishment, for learning, and for developing themselves beyond where they are now. These people are said to have strong "growth needs" and are predicted to develop high internal motivation when working on a complex, challenging job. Others have less strong needs for growth and will be less eager to exploit the opportunities for personal accomplishment provided by a job high in motivating potential.

Growth need strength may affect how people react to their jobs at two different points in the model shown in Fig. 4.3: first at the link between the objective job characteristics and the psychological states, and again between the psychological states and internal motivation. The first link specifies that people with high growth need strength will *experience* the psychological states more strongly when their objective job is high in MPS than will their low growth need strength counterparts. And the second link means that individuals with high growth need strength will *respond more positively* to the psychological states, when they are present, than will low growth need individuals.

For both of these reasons, individuals with strong needs for growth should respond eagerly and positively to the opportunities provided by enriched work. Individuals with low needs for growth, on the other hand, may not recognize the existence of such opportunities, or may not value them, or may even find them threatening and balk at being "pushed" or stretched too far by their work.

Satisfaction with the Work Context

Up to this point our discussion has focused on the motivating properties of the work itself and on characteristics of people (specifically their job-relevant knowledge and skill, and their growth need strength) that affect how people respond to jobs that are high or low in motivating potential. However, it is also the case that how satisfied people are with aspects of the work *context* may affect their willingness or ability to take advantage of the opportunities for personal accomplishment provided by enriched work.

Consider, for example, an employee who is very upset about her work context. She feels exploitively underpaid for the work she does; she is worried that she is about to be fired, partly because her supervisor seems to go out of the way to make life at work miserable for her; and she doesn't get on at all well with her co-workers, to the point that she believes her co-workers are ridiculing her behind her back.

Now imagine that this woman is asked if she would like to have her (currently rather routine) job made more complex and challenging. Even if she is presently more than qualified to do the work that would be required on the enriched job, would she respond with enthusiasm to the opportunity being offered? It is not very likely. She is *so* dissatisfied with the contextual aspects of life at work that most of her energy is absorbed merely in coping with those issues from day to day. Only if these problems were resolved (or if the employee found a way to adapt psychologically to them) would she become able to experience, appreciate, and respond with high internal motivation to enriched work.

We expect, therefore, that individuals who are relatively satisfied with pay, job security, co-workers, and supervisors will respond more positively to enriched and challenging jobs than individuals who are dissatisfied with these aspects of the work context. And if individuals who are satisfied with the work context also have relatively strong growth need strength, then a *very* high level of internal work motivation would be expected.

What of employees who are both dissatisfied with the work context and low on personal need for growth? For these individuals, work motivation may be only minimally affected by the motivational characteristics of the jobs they do: they are likely to be distracted from whatever richness exists in the work itself (because of their dissatisfaction with contextual factors) and at the same time oriented toward satisfactions *other* than those that can come from effective performance on enriched jobs (because of their low need for personal growth at work).

Research tests of these ideas provide some support for the proposition that the impact of a job on a person is moderated both by the person's needs and by his or her context satisfaction (Oldham, 1976a; Oldham, Hackman, and Pearce, 1976). The findings of the Oldham, Hackman, and Pearce study are summarized in Fig. 4.5. Overall, we found that the higher the motivating potential of a job, the stronger the work motivation and on-the-job performance of the employee. This was not unexpected: task characteristics usually turn out to predict outcomes such as satisfaction and performance in this kind of research.

Yet it also was found in this study that the *strongest* relationships between MPS and the outcomes were obtained for those employees who were highly desirous of growth satisfaction and simultaneously satisfied with the work context (that is, those employees in the upper right-hand cell of Fig. 4.5. And when both growth need strength and context satisfaction were at low levels (the lower left-hand cell), some *negative* relationships were obtained between MPS and the outcomes—a quite unusual finding. Apparently those individuals who were both low in growth need strength *and* dissatisfied with the work

	Growth need strength	
	Low	*High*
High	*Moderate positive relationship*	*Strong positive relationship:* The higher the MPS of the job, the higher the motivation and performance of the job incumbent.
Low	*No relationship (or small negative relationship):* Motivation and performance are unrelated (or slightly negatively related) to the MPS of the job.	*Moderate positive relationship*

Satisfaction with the work context

Fig. 4.5 Relationship between the motivating potential of a job and the motivation and performance of job incumbents.

context found a complex and challenging job so far out of line with their needs that they were unable to perform well on it. When, on the other hand, these individuals worked on a simple and routine job (one low in MPS), they reacted positively to it, probably for two related reasons. First, the job may have fit better with their personal needs (which were for other than growth satisfactions); secondly, because the job ws not very challenging, these individuals probably could carry out the work satisfactorily and still have energy left over to use in attempting to deal with the dissatisfying work context.

Summary

In the preceding pages, we have reviewed three factors which qualify the general proposition that increases in the motivating potential of a job foster greater internal work motivation on the part of the people who perform it. These factors are a person's job-relevant knowledge and skill; growth need strength; and level of satisfaction with aspects of the work context, particularly satisfaction with job security, compensation, co-workers, and supervision.

While each of these factors may, in its own right, affect the responses of a person to a job, they become especially significant when they occur in combination. The "worst possible" circumstance for a job that is high in motivating potential, for example, would be when the job incumbent is only marginally competent to perform the work *and* has low needs for personal growth at work *and* is highly dissatisfied with one or more aspects of the work context. The job clearly would be too much for that individual, and negative personal and work outcomes would be predicted. It would be better, for the person as well as for the organization, for the individual to perform relatively more simple and routine work.

On the other hand, if an individual is fully competent to carry out the work required by a complex, challenging task *and* has strong needs for personal growth *and* is well satisfied with the work context, then we would expect both high personal satisfaction and high work motivation and performance. The work, in this case, would fit well both with the talents and the needs of the individual, and the outcomes should be beneficial both to the individual and to the organization.

OUTCOMES OF ENRICHED WORK

Thus far, we have focused on internal work motivation as one key outcome of enriched work. We now broaden our view and examine a number of other personal and organizational outcomes that often are associated with motivating jobs, outcomes that may be affected when the motivational structure of work is changed. The expanded set of outcomes is shown in Fig. 4.6, which provides a complete overview of the job characteristics model of work motivation that has been developed in the preceding pages.

Personal Outcomes

The personal outcomes asociated with the motivating potential of jobs are, in addition to internal motivation, *growth satisfaction* and *general satisfaction*. When a job is high in MPS, jobholders have enriched opportunities for personal learning and growth at work, and they tend to report that they find those opportunities personally satisfying. Employees on enriched jobs also express relatively high general satisfaction, as measured by questions such as "Generally speaking, how satisfied are you with your job?" and "How frequently do you think of quitting this job?" (reverse scored).

Not included among the outcomes in Fig. 4.6 is satisfaction with various aspects of the work context. What is changed when work is redesigned is the relationship between the person and the work itself. While improvements in that relationship should affect the overall satisfaction of individuals with their jobs, there is no reason to expect that it should also lead to specific improvements in satisfaction with job security, pay, supervision, or co-worker relationships. Indeed, as will be seen later in this book, job enrichment sometimes leads to decreases in satisfaction with pay and supervision, particularly when compensation arrangements and supervision are not altered to mesh with the new responsibilities and increased autonomy of the persons whose jobs are redesigned.

Work Effectiveness

The model in Fig. 4.6 specifies that employee work effectiveness is expected to be high when jobs are high in motivating potential. As we

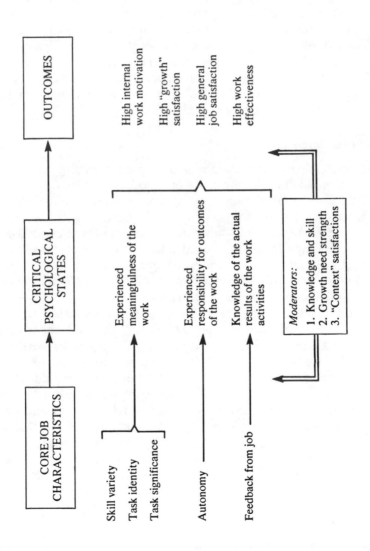

Fig. 4.6 The complete job characteristics model.

choose to use the term, work effectiveness includes both the quality and the quantity of the goods or services produced. These two components of overall effectiveness relate to the motivational structure of jobs somewhat differently.

The reasoning regarding work *quality* is straightforward: When a job is high in motivating potential, people who work on that job tend to experience positive affect when they perform *well*. And performing well, for most people, means producing high-quality work of which one can be proud. Thus, on enriched jobs, we find error-free products being manufactured, or especially considerate and helpful service being given to clients, or an extra-careful piece of library research being done.

On the other hand, merely producing a great *quantity* of work—such as making many calls, turning out lots of products, or handling hordes of customers—may not be viewed as a very good reason for patting one's self on the back. Such self-rewards are especially unlikely when, as is sometimes the case, it has been necessary to cut some corners in quality to rack up great quantities of work.

But if the motivational payoff of enriched work has more to do with producing excellent products or services than with producing lots of them, then why are improvements in work quantity obtained in many work redesign projects (Katzell, Bienstock, and Faerstein, 1977)? There are, we believe, three reasons. First, work redesign may remove the "demotivating" effects of a traditionally designed job. As noted in chapter 3, if work is extremely routine and repetitive employees often engage in behaviors that minimize the amount of work they actually have to do. This may involve diversion of attention from the work (daydreaming or sleeping), finding ways to leave the job (taking unnecessary breaks or feigning the need for help from the supervisor), or even engaging in directly counterproductive behaviors (causing machine malfunctions or deliberately restricting output). So even if employees do not become motivated to produce especially great quantities of output when their work is enriched, productivity increases may still be obtained, simply because dysfunctional behaviors such as those noted above are no longer exhibited.

Second, hidden inefficiencies in the use of time and support staff may be eliminated when traditional jobs are redesigned. While in traditional designs each subpart of the work to be done is engineered for maximum efficiency, it often is necessary to add extra coordinating, supervising, and quality control staff for the work system as a whole to function smoothly. Moreover, when work must be passed from person to person repeatedly to complete an entire task, employees necessarily spend nonproductive time receiving the work, getting started on it, and passing it on to the co-worker who is to perform the next operation. In some (not all) work systems, these inefficiencies of time and staff can be reduced substantially when the numerous small parts of the total task are recombined into a meaningful whole.

Finally, it often is possible to refine and simplify the overall work system when jobs within that system are redesigned. Whenever jobs are changed substantially, it usually is necessary to rethink the way related jobs are structured and how work flows from person to person and from job to job. Often such scrutiny of the workflow (which previously may have been taken as "given") unearths some simple systemic inefficiencies—such as redundant work activities, work being done that does not contribute to the final product or service (reports written for files that are never used, for instance), or time-wasting work rules and procedures. Once these inefficiencies are brought to light they are likely to be corrected, resulting in higher system productivity.

In sum, improvements in work effectiveness generally are to be expected when the motivational makeup of jobs is improved through work redesign. The quality of performance should improve as a direct function of the increased motivating potential of the work. The quantity of work produced also may increase, but this is a more complicated and less predictable matter. In our view, the likelihood of quantity improvements depends on the state of the work system *prior* to work redesign, specifically whether (1) employees were exhibiting low productivity because they were "turned off" by exceedingly routine or repetitive work, (2) there were hidden inefficiencies in the use of time or support staff in getting the work done, or (3) there were redundancies or time-wasting procedures built into the work system itself. If one or more of these problems preexisted in the work unit, then increases in the quantity of work performed are likely to appear after the work is redesigned. If these problems were not present, then we would not expect work redesign to yield increases in production quantity.[4] Indeed, decreases in quantity may even be noted as people work especially hard to produce high *quality* work.[5]

Attendance at Work

Why is reduced absenteeism not in the outcome list in Fig. 4.6? One would expect that when jobs are motivationally improved, employees would find the workplace more attractive and would want to come to work more regularly. The fact that general satisfaction (which is typically associated with absenteeism) usually improves when jobs are enriched would further strengthen the expectation that attendance should improve when the design of work is improved. Yet research results on the question are far from conclusive: Some studies report improvements in attendance when jobs are enriched, some report no change, and some have even reported worse absence problems than before (e.g., Hackman, Pearce, and Wolfe, 1978).

Our view is that whether attendance improves or deteriorates as a consequence of work redesign depends heavily on the *competence* of the employees whose jobs are changed. We argued earlier in this chapter that while jobs high in motivating potential lead to increased occasions for self-reinforcement among people who are competent in the work, they also provide more frequent occasions for self-generated *negative* affect for those who are not. If this is true, then changes in jobs that increase internal motivation might simultaneously prompt decreased absenteeism for more competent employees and increased

---

4   This suggests that findings from laboratory studies of the effects of work redesign on productivity should be interpreted with caution. It is doubtful, in such studies, that control conditions will contain the kinds of systemic inefficiencies that often build up over time in real organizations, or that control subjects in the laboratory will exhibit the kinds of antiproductive behaviors that sometimes appear when employees have extended experience on poorly designed jobs. Thus, a laboratory finding that work redesign has no impact on productivity may not generalize to problem-ridden real organizations.

5   In such circumstances, devices such as goal setting and contingent financial rewards may be helpful in maintaining a balance between the quantity and quality of work produced (cf. Umstot, Bell, and Mitchell, 1976).

absenteeism for their less competent co-workers. Any overall indicator of absenteeism for the work group as a whole would be misleading because of the different effects of the change on the absence rate of the two subgroups.

This notion awaits systematic research testing. If it should be borne out, it would have some interesting implications for the management of employee attendance—and, perhaps, even for issues of work-force retention. Specifically, it appears that designing enriched jobs might be one way to foster the retention of the best workers and to ensure their regular attendance, while at the same time creating conditions such that their less competent colleagues would find it advantageous to stay away from work. For some managers, this would be a pleasant reversal of present difficulties in getting competent workers to stay with the organization and in getting incompetents to stay away.

Summary

When the motivational properties of work are improved, one can usually count on increases in internal work motivation, general satisfaction, and growth satisfaction. Employee satisfaction with aspects of the work context, such as job security, pay, supervision, and co-workers are not likely to increase and may even show a decline.

Work effectiveness should improve when jobs are enriched, especially the quality of the work done. Production quantity may also increase, but this is likely only when there were relatively severe motivational problems or built-in inefficiencies in the work system prior to redesign. Although additional research is required before confident predictions can be made regarding the effects of work redesign on absenteeism and voluntary turnover, it may be that enriched work leads to greater behavioral commitment to the work and the organization for more talented employees and to less commitment among employees who are less capable.

Work redesign assuredly is *not* a panacea for all organizational problems. It is a viable and useful change strategy for some personal and work outcomes but not for others. And, as will be seen in subsequent chapters of this book, even to obtain those outcomes listed in Fig. 4.6 requires careful and competent planning to ensure that the changes made are appropriate for the kind of work being done, for the people who do the work, and for the broader organizational context.

THE JOB CHARACTERISTICS MODEL: TRUTH OR FICTION?

Just how correct and complete is the model of work motivation presented in this chapter? The literature relevant to the many propositions in the model cannot be reviewed here, and it is probably too early for a definitive assessment of the validity of the model in any case. Based on evidence available, it is fair to say that the model probably is more right than wrong, but that it is surely inaccurate and incomplete in numerous specifics.[6]

We believe that it is very important for people to be guided by some theory or model when they plan and implement organizational changes. Yet it is also important for those who would base their change activities on a given theoretical model to be aware of known problems, ambiguities, and omissions in that model, especially those that might affect how the changes are carried out. Here, then, are a number of concerns about the job characteristics model that we believe should be kept in mind by readers who might use our approach in redesigning work.

1. Evidence for the proposed moderating effects is scattered. The moderating effects of knowledge and skill have not been systematically tested, and only a few studies have addressed context satisfaction as a moderator of job characteristic-outcome relationships. A relatively large number of studies have examined the moderating effect of growth need strength, with mixed results. Some studies

---

6   While there are numerous studies of devices for *measuring* job characteristics (see Barr, Brief, and Aldag, 1978 for a review), relatively few studies have been made of the *conceptual* propositions of job characteristics theory. Recent tests of the theory that came to our attention as this book was going to press are: Arnold and House, in press: Champoux, in press; Orpen, 1979; and Wall, Clegg, and Jackson, 1978. The Arnold and House study is of special interest because of its innovations in the use of regression techniques to test the theory; the Orpen study is of special interest because it is the only *experimental* test (that is, involving random assignment of employees to enriched and unriched conditions in a real organization) of which we are aware. While there is not yet a review of studies testing the job characteristics model in the research literature, a more general review that questions the entire metatheory on which the model is based is provided by Salancik and Pfeffer (1977).

have, and others have not, found the predicted moderating effect. Moreover, several other individual difference variables (such as need for achievement, alienation from middle-class work norms, and intrinsic versus extrinsic work values) have been proposed as alternatives to growth need strength in determining how people react to their work. That there are important differences among people in their motivational readiness for work on enriched jobs seems not at issue, but how best to construe and measure those differences remains very much an open question.

2. While existing evidence generally suggests that the job characteristics affect the outcomes *through* the psychological states as specified by the model, a number of anomolies have been found. Some of the job characteristics (particularly autonomy) appear in some investigations to affect psychological states other than those specified in the model. And some of the psychological states are, on occasion, influenced by other than model-specified job characteristics. In sum, the links between the job characteristics and the psychological states are not as neat and clean as suggested in Fig. 4.6.

3. While the model treats the several job characteristics as if they were independent (that is, mostly uncorrelated with one another), this is not always true. Instead, jobs that are high on one job characteristic often are high on others as well. Skill variety and autonomy are especially closely associated in many organizations. Intercorrelations among the job characteristics can diffuse their effects on the psychological states, as noted above. Moreover, the appropriateness of the multiplicative formula for MPS (given earlier in this chapter) is compromised to the extent that these intercorrelations are high. In many situations, therefore, an estimate of the motivating potential of jobs obtained by simply summing the scores of the job characteristics will be just as good (or better) than one that uses the more complex MPS formula (cf. Brief, Wallace, and Aldag, 1976).

4. The concept of feedback used in the model is flawed. It sometimes is difficult to determine just what is (and what is not) "job-based" feedback, and we frequently find supervisors, job incumbents, and outside observers disagreeing about how much feedback a given job actually provides. Moreover, the model does not address feedback from nonjob sources (such as supervisors, co-workers, or one's self) that also affect knowledge of the results of the work, let alone the complex interactions that no doubt exist among these sources of information about performance. This is important because the ef-

fects of job-based feedback may be altered by data about performance that is received from nonjob sources.[7]

5. How the objective properties of jobs relate to people's perceptions of those properties is not completely clear. It is known that people "redefine" their tasks to be consistent with their personal needs, attitudes, and values, and in response to cues or direct influence from other people about the meaning of the work (Hackman, 1969; Weiss and Shaw, 1979). Yet the job characteristics model in its present form does not differentiate between objective and perceived properties of tasks, and it is not known whether the motivational benefits of "enriched" work derive primarily from objective task characteristics (even if those characteristics are not perceived by the performer) or from employee perceptions of task characteristics (even if those perceptions are influenced by nonjob factors).

In sum, while there is support in the research literature for the basic job characteristics model, it would be inappropriate to conclude that the model provides a correct and complete picture of the motivational effects of job characteristics. Instead, this model, like the alternative models proposed by Herzberg (1968) and by sociotechnical systems theorists (Davis and Trist, 1974), is perhaps best viewed as a guide for further research and as an aid in planning for changes in work systems. An especially important part of that planning process, and one for which a conceptual model of some kind is almost essential, is the prechange diagnosis of a work system. It is to the diagnostic task that we turn in the next chapter, where a diagnostic strategy based on the job characteristics approach is developed and discussed.

FOR ADDITIONAL READING

Hackman, J.R., and G.R. Oldham. Motivation through the design of work: Test of a theory. *Organizational Behavior and Human Performance,* 1976, *16,* 250-279. This is the original statement of our version of job characteristics theory, which includes an empirical assessment of the strengths and weaknesses of the model.

---

7   For a more differentiated view of the concept of feedback and its consequences in work systems, see Herold and Greller (1977) or Ilgen, Fisher, and Taylor (1977).

Wanous, J.P. Individual differences and reactions to job characteristics. *Journal of Applied Psychology*, 1974, *59*, 612-622. This study compares the usefulness of (1) growth need strength, (2) endorsement of the Protestant Work Ethic, and (3) urban versus rural background in determining how people react to "enriched" work. It is found that growth needs are the best moderator of reactions to work and that urban-rural background is the worst. Implications for the practice of work design are drawn. (It should be noted, however, that other studies have not been as supportive of the moderating effects of growth need strength as is this one.)

Umstot, D.D., C.H. Bell, and T.R. Mitchell. Effects of job enrichment and task goals on satisfaction and productivity: Implications for job design. *Journal of Applied Psychology*, 1976, *61*, 379-394. The authors created an organization to study and found that enriched jobs improved employee attitudes (but not productivity), while goal setting improved productivity (but not attitudes). Interesting implications for the *joint* use of work design and goal setting in managing work are suggested.

Locke, E.A., D. Sirota, and A.D. Wolfson. An experimental case study of the successes and failures of job enrichment in a government agency. *Journal of Applied Psychology*, 1976, *61*, 701-711. A well-documented field investigation showing the opposite of the Umstot, Bell, and Mitchell results: namely, that job enrichment improved productivity but had no effect on attitudes. Note the interesting discussion about why these results may have been obtained.

Pierce, J.L. and R.B. Dunham. Task design: A literature review. *Academy of Management Review*, 1976, *1*, 83-87. A relatively thorough and thoughtful assessment of the state of the evidence regarding the effects of job design. Although there have been many studies of work design published since this review was completed, the authors' implications and recommendations are still worth careful attention.

5
DIAGNOSING WORK SYSTEMS

Imagine that you are a manager considering the redesign of certain jobs within a unit of your organization. How do you decide whether work redesign is feasible for that unit? How do you distinguish between those aspects of the jobs that need improving and those that are fine as they are? How do you tell how ready the people who will be involved are for change, and how well the changes will fit with their needs and their skills? How do you assess the readiness of the organization itself for changes that involve work restructuring?

This chapter explores what is involved in obtaining answers to these questions and reviews some tools and techniques that may be useful in that undertaking. We begin by pointing out the risks of relying on intuition for prechange diagnoses of work systems and the advantages of gathering systematic data about people and their jobs using multiple methodologies. We then describe in detail one diagnostic instrument (the Job Diagnostic Survey) and show how JDS data can help answer some of the questions posed above. The chapter concludes with a discussion of six diagnostic issues that we believe to be key in assessing the *need* for work redesign and the *feasibility* of carrying it out in various organizational circumstances.

THE CASE FOR SYSTEMATIC DIAGNOSIS

Some kind of diagnosis is always carried out when work is redesigned. Often the diagnosis is done implicitly, as when a manager
decides that job enrichment "seems right" for a given job and then
proceeds to install some changes intended to improve that job. Other
times diagnosis is an explicit and important part of the prechange
planning process, involving the collection of extensive data from both
employees and managers.

The Risks of Intuition

When managers rely exclusively on their own perceptions of what is
going on in a work unit, the result can be a flawed diagnosis of the
situation that leads to inappropriate changes. In many cases, problems are too quickly defined in terms of their symptoms, and then
solutions are implemented that deal with those symptoms rather than
with the underlying problem. In one manufacturing organization, for
example, managers were concerned about work quality. Inspectors
were finding excessive numbers of defects in the products, and
customers were returning malfunctioning products at an alarmingly
high rate. Clearly something had to be done. Managers from production, customer service, and quality-control departments met to
figure out how to deal with the problem. Little time was spent trying
to understand the problem or its causes. Instead, managers quickly
agreed that workers were using shortcuts and poor assembly procedures, and that inspectors (who examined a 20 percent sample of
completed products) were letting too many poor-quality products out
the door.

The solution that the group came up with dealt with both of
these perceived difficulties. Employees were reminded by their supervisors of the importance of doing high-quality work, and supervisors
were instructed to monitor employee performance more closely until
quality improved. In addition, inspection standards were tightened
and additional inspectors were brought in to allow a 50 percent
sample of products to be inspected. The solutions seemed to work.
Quality increased, the problem disappeared, and after a few months
supervisors relaxed and the percentage of products inspected was
dropped to its former level. Unfortunately, work quality also declined
after the return to "business as usual"—this time to a level below that
which prompted the management meeting in the first place.

What had happened? One possibility is that the problem was not solved because it initially had been misdiagnosed. If managers had examined how the work was designed, they would have found that there was little built-in incentive for quality. Each employee did a small piece of the overall task; only the final assembler saw the whole product. Employees had no autonomy in how they carried out their work, and they received feedback only on those occasions when a supervisor informed the entire crew that "quality is down." The quality problem, apparently, was at least partly rooted in poorly designed jobs—a possibility overlooked by the managers when they met to discuss it.

Moreover, the solutions generated by the managers on the basis of their diagnosis (tightening supervisory control over work behaviors and inspecting more products) may have increased the disaffection of employees with their work. The initial misdiagnosis, then, prompted a "fix" that was only temporarily effective and that made things worse rather than better in the long haul. A more careful and thorough diagnosis of the work system might have led to different conclusions about what was at the root of the quality problem and to more appropriate strategies for dealing with it.

A second risk of relying on *ad hoc* or intuitive diagnoses of problems in work systems has to do with the human tendency, noted in Chapter 2, to misperceive the causes of the behavior of other people. Specifically, we often give excessive weight to the characteristics of the *person* in understanding someone's behavior and insufficient weight to the characteristics of the *situation* in which that person is behaving (Jones and Nisbett, 1971).

When performance is poor, we tend to blame those who did the work: they are lazy, irresponsible, incompetent, or all three. When performance is excellent, we are likely to sing the praises of the bright, motivated workers who can be counted on to do good work. There are, of course, real differences in the motivation, attitude, and talent of people at work, and we should not pretend that such differences do not exist. But intuitive diagnoses tend to overestimate the *person* part of person-situation interactions and therefore lead to misapprehensions of the causal forces that are actually operating in a given work situation.

The Importance of Multiple Methods

Because of the high risk of error when *ad hoc* procedures are used to diagnose work systems prior to planned change, it usually is advantageous to carry out some kind of systematic diagnostic study before deciding whether to redesign work. The idea is to collect and compile data about the work and people's reactions to it that are as comprehensive and trustworthy as possible.

It is, however, difficult to obtain data that really can be trusted. There are special problems with *every* methodology that can be used to assess jobs and people's reactions to them. Likewise, any observer of a work situation—employee, manager, or disinterested outsider—is prone to some special kinds of distortion in what he or she sees and understands.

Only by using multiple methodologies, involving data from multiple observers, can diagnosticians protect themselves from systematic distortions in the conclusions they reach. Thus, if reports of the properties of jobs are obtained using a questionnaire, those reports might be supplemented with information obtained by interviews or by structured observations. If data from employees who will be affected by a job change are collected (usually a good idea), then those data can be supplemented by information obtained from managers or from observers who are not personally invested in the work unit.

Ideally, diagnostic data should be collected using *both* multiple methods (questionnaires, interviews, observations) and multiple observers (job incumbents, supervisors, staff members, outside consultants). If the findings obtained from these multiple methods and observers are generally consistent, then one can be reasonably sure that the results reflect the phenomena being studied rather than some idiosyncracies of the methods or of the observers. If the findings are not in agreement, then further diagnostic probing is indicated to identify and understand the reasons for the differences. Such activities might include additional interviews and observations that focus on the points of disagreement or discussions of possible reasons for the disagreements.

Only when all interested parties agree that the diagnostic data provide a reasonably accurate assessment of the work situation should actual plans for change be laid. To shortcut this process risks developing changes based on an incomplete or incorrect understanding of the people and the work, which is one of the quickest and surest routes to a work redesign failure.

THE JOB DIAGNOSTIC SURVEY

The Job Diagnostic Survey (JDS) is a data collection instrument that can be useful as *part* of a multiple-method diagnosis. The major intended uses of the JDS are (1) to diagnose existing jobs prior to work redesign, as one input in planning whether and how redesign should proceed, and (2) to evaluate the effects of work redesign—for example, to determine how much jobs have changed, to assess the effects of the changes on employee motivation and satisfaction, and to test for any spin-off effects of the job changes on employee growth need strength or satisfaction with the work context.[1]

The JDS was constructed by the authors to tap each major class of variables in the theory of work motivation presented in the previous chapter (Hackman and Oldham, 1974; 1975). The specific concepts measured are summarized in Table 5.1. Definitions of theory-specified concepts, and the relationships among them, were presented and discussed in Chapter 4.

Two concepts in the theory are not assessed by the JDS: the level of employee knowledge and skill, and employee work effectiveness. These factors are idiosyncratic to particular work settings, and therefore defy meaningful measurement across organizations. Also, two job characteristics that are not in the motivational theory are measured by the JDS: *feedback from agents* and *dealing with others.* Feedback from agents is often useful in supplementing JDS information on feedback from the job itself. Dealing with others reflects the extent to which the job requires work with other people, which can alert planners to the possibility that meaningful change may require attention to an interconnected *set* of jobs rather than to the single job that may have prompted the diagnosis. These two supplementary concepts are defined as follows:

---

1   Alternative instruments for assessing characteristics of jobs have been provided by Jenkins, Nadler, Lawler, and Cammann (1975) and by Sims, Szilagyi, and Keller (1976). The Jenkins *et al.* instrument involves structured observations of jobs; the Sims *et al.* instrument is a paper-and-pencil device that (like the job characteristics portion of the JDS) elicits respondents' perceptions of the attributes of their jobs.

Feedback from agents: The degree to which the employee receives clear information about his or her performance from supervisors or from co-workers.

Dealing with others: The degree to which the job requires employees to work closely with other people in carrying out the work activities (including dealings with other organization members and with external organizational "clients").

Perhaps the best way to get a "feel" for each of the JDS measures is to examine the specific items that compose them. This can be done by turning to Appendices A and C, where the instrument and its scoring key are reproduced.[2] After scoring, all JDS concepts are expressed on 7-point scales, where 1 is low and 7 is high. The overall motivating potential score (MPS) of a job, which was described in the previous chapter, ranges from 1 to 343. As is seen in Appendix C, all JDS concepts (except for growth satisfaction and the context satisfactions) are measured using two different response formats in two different sections of the instrument. This, it is hoped, decreases somewhat the degree to which JDS results are method specific.

Norms for the JDS

The Job Diagnostic Survey has been used extensively in research and change projects over the last few years, and data from many of these projects have been compiled recently by Oldham, Hackman, and Stepina (1979). Average JDS scores across 876 different jobs in 56 organizations are shown in Table 5.1, and Appendix E provides JDS means and standard deviations for a number of job families (clerical, sales, benchwork, managerial, and so on). Additional normative data are provided in the Oldham-Hackman-Stepina report, including breakdowns of the averages by respondent characteristics (age, sex,

---

2   The Job Diagnostic Survey is not copyrighted. The "manual" for the instrument (which includes information on the psychometric properties of the JDS scales) is available from the National Technical Information Service (ordering information is included under Hackman and Oldham, 1974 in the reference list at the end of this book). Printed copies of the JDS are available in quantity from the Roy W. Walters and Associates consulting firm, which also provides a computerized scoring service for the instrument. The address of the Walters organization is included in Appendix C.

education), by type of job (job level, compensation arrangements, Dictionary of Occupational Titles job category), and by type of organization in which the job is located (organization size, geographic location, primary organizational function).

Table 5.1
Job Diagnostic Survey National Norms

Job characteristics

Skill variety	4.7
Task identity	4.7
Task significance	5.5
Autonomy	4.9
Feedback from job	4.9
Feedback from agents*	4.1
Dealing with others*	5.6

Critical psychological states

Experienced meaningfulness of the work	5.2
Experienced responsibility for work outcomes	5.5
Knowledge of results	5.0

Affective outcomes

General satisfaction	4.7
Growth satisfaction	4.8
Internal work motivation	5.6

Context satisfactions

Job security	4.9
Pay	4.3
Co-workers	5.4
Supervision	4.9

Individual growth need strength	5.0

Motivating Potential Score (MPS)	128.

Note: From Oldham, Hackman, and Stepina (1979). These norms are based on the responses of 6930 employees who work on 876 different jobs in 56 organizations. The norms were computed by averaging the scores of employees who work on each of the 876 jobs and then computing overall means across those jobs.

*Supplementary measures; see text.

The norms shown in Table 5.1 provide a relatively stable set of standards for use in interpreting JDS diagnostic results. For illustration, we have provided in Fig. 5.1 the diagnostic results for about 100 organization development consultants who have attended workshops on job design over the past three years. Each participant completed the JDS for his or her job, and the results were averaged later to generate the profile shown in the figure.

The average motivating potential score (MPS) for the consultants is 183, substantially above the national average of 128. Consultants viewed their jobs as particularly high on skill variety and autonomy; on the other hand, the consultants were only slightly higher than the norms on task identity and feedback from the job. Interviews with a sample of the consultants confirmed that they felt their jobs were, on the whole, challenging and motivating, but to the extent that there were problems, those problems had to do with inadequate feedback about the results of their work and infrequent opportunities to complete a whole piece of work with a clear and visible beginning and end (task identity).

The validity of the consultants' job perceptions is further supported by the average scores for the three psychological states. Both experienced meaningfulness and experienced responsibility are quite high, as they should be given the high standing of the jobs on skill variety and task significance (which contribute to meaningfulness) and on autonomy (which contributes to responsibility). Knowledge of results is lower, which is understandable given the relatively low scores on the two job dimensions that describe the amount of feedback received by the consultants.

In general, the affective responses of the consultants to their work are positive. Internal work motivation and growth satisfaction are especially high. This is to be expected, given that the job is high in MPS *and* that the consultants have, on the average, strong needs for growth. General job satisfaction, while somewhat lower than internal motivation and growth satisfaction, is still substantially higher than the national average for this variable. This may be due not only to the work itself, but also to the consultants' satisfaction with co-workers, job security and pay—all of which are noticeably above the national averages.

Finally, we note that the consultants are quite high on the supplementary job dimension "dealing with others." This fits with the

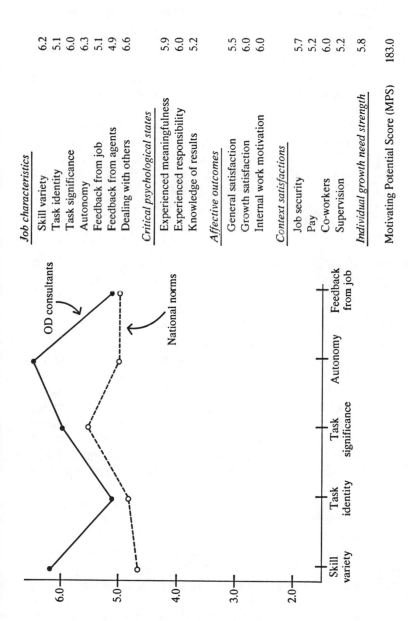

Job characteristics	
Skill variety	6.2
Task identity	5.1
Task significance	6.0
Autonomy	6.3
Feedback from job	5.1
Feedback from agents	4.9
Dealing with others	6.6
Critical psychological states	
Experienced meaningfulness	5.9
Experienced responsibility	6.0
Knowledge of results	5.2
Affective outcomes	
General satisfaction	5.5
Growth satisfaction	6.0
Internal work motivation	6.0
Context satisfactions	
Job security	5.7
Pay	5.2
Co-workers	6.0
Supervision	5.2
Individual growth need strength	5.8
Motivating Potential Score (MPS)	183.0

Fig. 5.1 JDS diagnostic profile for 100 organization development consultants.

consultants' verbal descriptions of their day-to-day activities as involving extensive interaction with colleagues and clients. Apparently these interactions are felt to be satisfactory by the consultants, as shown by their average score on the measure of satisfaction with coworkers.

All in all, we would conclude from the findings reported in Fig. 5.1 that the basic job of OD consultants is well designed and that most of the job incumbents are prospering in it. Planned redesign of the consultants' work would *not* be indicated for this large (and, it should be kept in mind, heterogeneous) group. Nevertheless, attempts by the consultants and their managers to increase the clarity of consultants' tasks and to improve the feedback they receive (both from the job itself and from the people with whom they work) might help to make a good job somewhat better.

Limitations of the JDS

When shown the diagnostic results summarized in Fig. 5.1, most organization development consultants conclude that the findings provide a reasonably accurate assessment of the strengths and weaknesses of their jobs. Yet just how much can results such as these be trusted? How reliable and valid are the JDS measures?

A number of researchers have addressed these questions and have identified several limitations of the instrument and offered cautions regarding its use (see Appendix D for citations of the relevant research studies). These limitations have primarily to do with the lack of independence among measures of the job characteristics, the relative ease with which respondents who are so inclined can "fake" their scores by deliberately distorting their answers to JDS items, restricted reliabilities of some scales, and an absence of firm evidence about the validity of some of the JDS measures, especially growth need strength.

These issues are addressed in detail in Appendix D, which provides a set of guidelines for administering the JDS and cautions to keep in mind when interpreting JDS results. Prospective users of the instrument are strongly encouraged to study that appendix to counter any tendency to rely too heavily on data from the JDS or to spend too little effort considering special problems and opportunities in using the instrument.

The risk of overreliance on available paper-and-pencil instruments, we believe, far exceeds the risk that users will be excessively conservative and cautious in interpreting and applying findings from such instruments. Our hope is that the caveats and limitations highlighted in Appendix D will tilt the balance slightly toward caution when the JDS is used, and encourage careful and appropriate applications of what we believe to be a good, but flawed and incomplete, diagnostic tool.

ASSESSING THE NEED FOR WORK REDESIGN

Before plans are laid for restructuring the jobs of organization members, two key issues should be addressed:

1. Whether there is a demonstrable *need* for the redesign of work, or whether some other approach to change (or none at all) is more appropriate.

2. Whether it is *feasible* to redesign individual jobs, given the present structure of those jobs, the characteristics of the people who do them, and the state of the organizational milieu in which they are done.

We examine these two issues in this section and the next. Throughout we suggest ways that diagnostic data (from the JDS and from other devices) can be helpful in determining need and feasibility. And, as we proceed, we identify a number of specific questions that can be used to guide step-by-step diagnoses of work systems. We begin with four questions that are critical in assessing the *need* for work redesign.

Question 1: Is There a Problem or an Exploitable Opportunity?

Sometimes work is redesigned for silly reasons. In one organization, for example, a line vice-president went off to an executive development program where he attended a seminar on the benefits of job enrichment. The idea so captured his imagination that, upon his return, he strongly suggested that all of his subordinate managers consider "trying out job enrichment" in their units. Most of the subordinate managers felt, understandably, that they should give it a try, even though many of them had only a passing familiarity with the idea.

Some of these managers selected jobs that turned out to be nicely appropriate for job enrichment. Others selected jobs that were peripheral to their main activities, thereby minimizing the risk of severe disruption if something went wrong. Still others selected work units that had so much wrong with them—ranging from poor employee-supervisor relations to unpleasant working conditions—that job enrichment could not possibly have made a noticeable difference. Needless to say, there were more work redesign failures than successes in the vice-president's division, and job enrichment soon was laid to rest as yet another seemingly good idea that "just doesn't work in the real world."

If work redesign is implemented, as in the above example, only because someone says it should be, failure is just around the corner. Before seriously considering redesigning jobs as a change strategy, then, one should attempt to identify as specifically as possible just what the problem is that is being addressed or, alternatively, just what kinds of improvements might be achieved. In many cases, it will turn out that a specific problem or opportunity cannot be identified, in which case the idea of "doing job enrichment" can be set aside early in the game, before excessive time and energy are wasted tooling up for something that cannot help.

Question 2: Does the Problem or Opportunity Centrally Involve Employee Motivation, Satisfaction, or Work Effectiveness?

We suggested in Chapter 4 that the positive outcomes of work redesign have primarily to do with (1) the work motivation and satisfaction of employees and (2) their performance effectiveness, especially the *quality* of the work they produce. Sometimes work redesign is implemented when employees are basically satisfied with their jobs and the quality of their work is fully acceptable. Work redesign is unlikely to help very much in such circumstances. Other times, there are real problems in work effectiveness, but these problems have little to do with the motivation of the people who do the work. It might be, for example, that the roots of the observed difficulties are in an error-prone computer, or in faulty tools and equipment, or in bad raw materials. Work redesign, obviously, will not help in these circumstances either.

Judgments about the quality of performance must be made by managers who are familiar with the technology and with the product or service being provided. A diagnostic instrument such as the Job Diagnostic Survey cannot help in that assessment. JDS data can be useful, however, in determining whether or not motivation and satis-faction are at issue. In particular, one would examine JDS scores on *internal work motivation, general satisfaction,* and *growth satisfac-tion.* If the responses of employees indicate that motivation and satisfaction are near or below the national averages for these scales, then one would proceed to the next diagnostic step. If they are significantly above the national averages, then the problem probably has little to do with the "fit" between the people and their work, and work redesign may not be appropriate.[3]

Question 3: Might the Design of the Work be Responsible for Observed Problems?

There are many possible reasons for poor performance, motivation, or satisfaction. Work redesign is an appropriate change strategy only if there is reason to believe that observed problems may have their roots in the motivational properties of the work itself.

Interviews with employees about how they see their jobs can be quite helpful in making this assessment, as can the motivating po-tential score (MPS) provided by the JDS. One would compare the MPS score for the focal unit either with the national norms or with scores for other units in the organization. If MPS is low, then it is reasonable to conclude that the work itself may be contributing to the performance, motivation, or satisfaction problems previously documented; if MPS is high, then it would be advisable to look to other aspects of the work situation (such as supervision, compen-sation, or co-worker relations) as possible causes of the observed difficulties

Question 4: What Aspects of the Job Most Need Improvement?

If a diagnosis has proceeded this far, we know that the way the work is designed may be constraining the motivation, satisfaction, or work effectiveness of employees on a given job. But we do not yet know what the specific strengths and weaknesses of that job are or what the focus of any changes in the job should be. As will be seen below, even

---

3   As noted in Appendix E, the standard deviations of JDS scores can be used to determine how much of a difference between the scores of two jobs (or between one job and the national norms) is a "significant" difference (see also Oldham, Hackman, and Stepina, 1979).

jobs that are nearly identical in MPS can require quite different changes if they are to be motivationally improved.

We recently surveyed a number of rank-and-file jobs in the headquarters organization of a large manufacturing firm. The MPS scores of these jobs ranged widely, but two jobs came out exceptionally low.[4] One was a data coding job in the headquarters payroll department. Jobholders are responsible for coding changes in compensation arrangements (including pay level) on computer-readable forms for all headquarters personnel. Departmental administrative assistants submit compensation changes to the coders. Using special numbers and symbols, the coders transfer the data onto computer forms and give completed forms to their supervisor, who checks them and passes them on to the data processing manager. The MPS for the coding job was 56, compared to a national average of 128 (see Table 5.1).

The other job was that of laboratory technician. These individuals test various materials developed by engineers in the research and development department. They receive batches of materials and a list of tests to be performed from the engineers. After completing the specified tests and recording the results on standardized forms, they submit those forms (together with any special comments or observations they have about the materials or the test results) to the laboratory supervisor. The supervisor takes the forms to the client engineers and deals with any questions the engineers may have about the results. The MPS for this job was 48.

Both jobs, clearly, are low in motivating potential, and employees in both work groups report low work satisfaction and show obvious signs of poor performance motivation. Yet the specific problems with the two jobs, despite their nearly identical MPS scores, are quite different, as can be seen in the diagnostic profiles reproduced in Fig. 5.2.

For the data coders the design problems have to do with skill variety and autonomy. The job is quite high in task significance (what the coders do directly affects other people's paychecks) and in feedback (the computer is programmed in such a way that most incorrectly coded forms do not run and are returned to the coder who

---

4   Details of the jobs have been slightly simplified and altered in the presentation to follow.

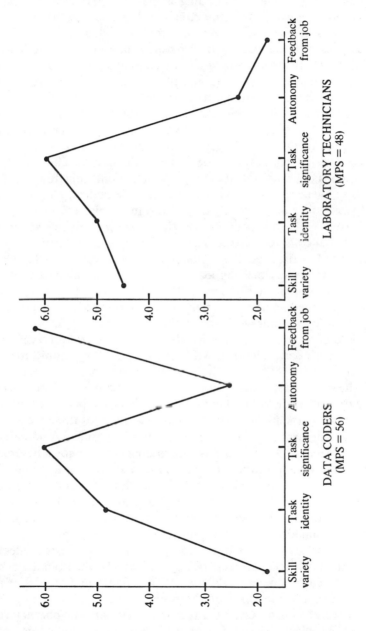

Fig. 5.2 JDS diagnostic profiles for two problem jobs in a corporate headquarters.

prepared them). The data coding manager reported that *precisely because the job was so significant* nothing was left to chance: all procedures and problems were covered in a detailed manual, and employees were instructed that anything that could not be handled using the manual was to be given to the manager for coding. Thus, high significance—a motivational plus—was more than neutralized by the constraints on autonomy it prompted.

For the laboratory technicians, the problems are autonomy and feedback. The technicians do a variety of laboratory procedures from start to finish, and they understand the importance of their results for the firm's product development activities. Thus, the three job dimensions that contribute to experienced meaningfulness of the work are generally satisfactory. But, like the coders, all procedures and techniques are prescribed, and the technicians are not authorized to alter those procedures on their own initiative (a supervisor must be called in for any special problem or deviation from standard procedure). Moreover, the technicians receive very little feedback: they do what they are supposed to, fill out the laboratory report forms, and submit these forms to the supervisor. They do not learn what happened to the materials they have tested or whether the engineers found their work acceptable.

The change implications for these two jobs are quite different, despite the nearly identical MPS scores. For the technicians, one would immediately address the problems in autonomy and feedback. For the data coders, one would focus first on autonomy and secondarily on skill variety. (Skill variety is less pressing because both task identity and task significance are relatively high for the coders.)

Because profiles of job characteristics are critical in identifying those aspects of a job that most need change, it is not advisable to rely *solely* on employee-provided data in constructing them. The views of supervisors (and, when possible, those of disinterested outsiders) also should be collected and considered in identifying the specific motivational strengths and weaknesses of a job. Such data can be obtained by using the Job Rating Form, a companion instrument to the JDS that is designed specifically for use in collecting assessments of job characteristics by individuals who do not work on the job (Hackman and Oldham, 1974). The Job Rating Form is reproduced in Appendix B of this book.

Usually it turns out that the *shape* of the job characteristic profiles provided by supervisors and by job incumbents are quite similar, with supervisors having a somewhat more optimistic view of the motivating characteristics of a job than do the job incumbents. This state of affairs, for a hypothetical job, is shown in part (a) of Fig. 5.3. Sometimes, however, the shape of the profile does differ for employees and supervisors, as shown in part (b) of the figure.

When the shapes of the profiles for employees and supervisors are similar, then planning for change can proceed with little reason for concern. When, however, employees and supervisors disagree about what are the relatively best and worst aspects of the job, as in part (b) of the the figure, then additional data are required before planning for change proceeds. (In such cases, we often seek the views of nonsupervisory staff members in the organization, using the Job Rating Form, and compare their profiles with those developed from employee and supervisor data. Frequently the views of the outside observers fit well with either those of the employees or those of the supervisors.) Employees and supervisors are encouraged to discuss those aspects of the job about which they disagree, referring to any data from outside observers that have been collected. A shared view of what about the job does (and does not) need changing usually emerges from these discussions.

In sum, it is not enough to know that a job is low in motivating potential. We also must identify what it is about the job that most needs to be improved and confirm this assessment by making sure that those who perform the job and those who supervise it are in rough agreement about its best and worst features.

After the four questions reviewed above have been addressed, it should be clear whether work redesign is a sensible change strategy for the organization under study and, if so, just what aspects of the existing jobs should be the prime targets for change. If the diagnostic signs are favorable at this point, then it is time to explore the *feasibility* of actually getting needed changes made in the target jobs.

DETERMINING THE FEASIBILITY OF WORK REDESIGN[5]

Even if we knew precisely what it was about a given job that most required improvement, it would be foolhardy to start making those

---

5   In this section of the book we are focusing on the design of work for individuals — that is, what is typically done in "job enrichment" projects. In Chapter 7, as we discuss the design of work for groups, we will suggest ways of determining the feasibility of creating self-managing (or "auto-nomous") work groups in various kinds of organizational settings.

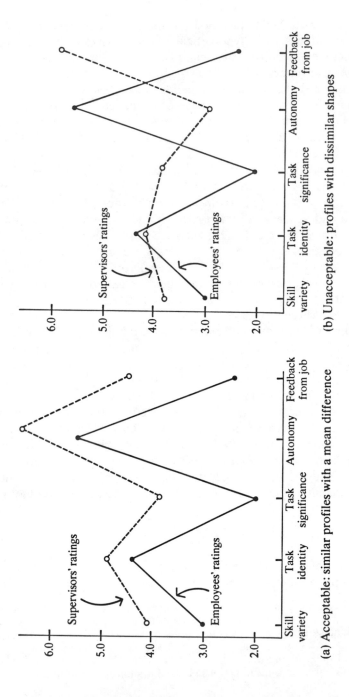

Fig. 5.3 Comparisons of employee and supervisor job characteristic profiles for a hypothetical job.

changes without some indication of the *readiness of the people* for change and the *hospitability of the organization* to getting the changes installed. We take up these two questions of feasibility below.

Question 5: How Ready are the Employees for Change?

If those aspects of a job that constrain its motivating potential are in fact changed, how are jobholders likely to react? Will they respond eagerly to increased complexity and challenge, or is it more probable that they will react only tentatively, or even negatively, to enriched work?

The answers to such questions can affect not only the decision about whether to proceed with work redesign, but also choices about how substantial the changes should be and how they should be implemented. If, for example, there are signs that people are severely underutilized and underchallenged in their present work, then it may be appropriate to install major changes in the work with dispatch. But if the people do not appear desirous of, or ready for, enriched work, the decision might be to start with smaller changes and to introduce them gradually and cautiously.

The theory set forth in Chapter 4 specifies three characteristics of people that are predicted to affect responses to enriched work.

1. *Employees' Task-relevent Knowledge and Skills.* Enriched work requires different talents than does traditionally designed work; moreover, the psychological costs of performing poorly on an enriched job are greater than for a less involving job. Because the particular knowledge and skill required depends substantially on the nature of the work being done, there is no general test that can be given to predict whether employees are competent enough to handle more challenging work. Yet it is important, whenever possible, to bring *some* kind of systematic data to bear on this question, as managers are very likely to underestimate the competence of employees based on their observations of them as they perform relatively simple and routine tasks. Without data to counter that conservative tendency, there is real risk that a decision will be made not to change the job (or change it only in token ways) because of a fear that "those people just couldn't handle much more than they're doing now; heaven knows we have too many errors and dumb mistakes to deal with now!" That the errors and dumb mistakes may be occurring because of the way the job currently is designed is unlikely to be

seriously entertained by managers who have their hands full trying to get the work done right.

2. *Employees' Needs for Growth.* The growth need strength scale of the JDS can be helpful in estimating whether people are likely to prosper on enriched jobs (although JDS scores should always be supplemented with other data, such as interviews with a sample of employees, before drawing conclusions about the psychological readiness of the people for enriched work).

Even a relatively low growth need strength score does not ensure that a person will balk at enriched work. Since people's needs are shaped throughout life by their experiences, very much including their work experiences, it may be that a low expressed need for growth is best interpreted as a statement about how a person has *adapted* to a worklife that provides few opportunities for personal responsibility and growth. Thus, it might be advisable to proceed, albeit cautiously and slowly, with enrichment of the work even for people who have relatively low measured growth need strength. For many such individuals, we suspect, the "spark" of growth motivation will be rekindled as they become comfortable—and find they can be successful—in handling complex, challenging tasks on their own.

3. *Employees' Context Satisfactions.* The JDS context satisfaction measures are useful indicators of the degree to which job incumbents may be preoccupied with problems of pay, job security, co-worker relationships, and supervision, and therefore psychologically unable to exploit the opportunities for growth and personal development that an enriched job can provide.

It should be noted that the JDS measures of context satisfaction are relatively brief scales that capture only the outcroppings of possible problems in the work context. More complete assessments of the functioning of organizational units can be obtained using other diagnostic instruments, such as the Survey of Organizations (Taylor and Bowers, 1972), the Organizational Assessment Instrument (Van de Ven and Ferry, in press), or the Michigan Assessment Package (Seashore, Lawler, Mirvis, and Cammann, in press).

In Fig. 5.4 we violate our own prohibition about constructing diagnostic profiles for single individuals (see Appendix D) and present for illustrative purposes the profile of a peripheral machine operator in the data processing department of a government agency. This individual, whom we will call Kenneth Brewer, physically prepares tapes and cards to be processed by a large computer. The job is

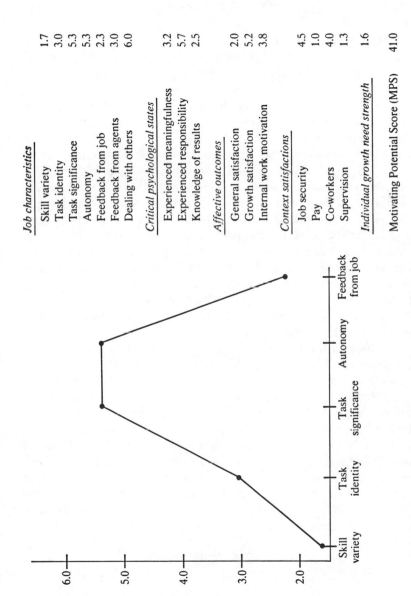

Job characteristics	
Skill variety	1.7
Task identity	3.0
Task significance	5.3
Autonomy	5.3
Feedback from job	2.3
Feedback from agents	3.0
Dealing with others	6.0
Critical psychological states	
Experienced meaningfulness	3.2
Experienced responsibility	5.7
Knowledge of results	2.5
Affective outcomes	
General satisfaction	2.0
Growth satisfaction	5.2
Internal work motivation	3.8
Context satisfactions	
Job security	4.5
Pay	1.0
Co-workers	4.0
Supervision	1.3
Individual growth need strength	1.6
Motivating Potential Score (MPS)	41.0

Fig. 5.4 JDS diagnostic profile for a peripheral machine operator.

simple and largely routine. Should it be enriched? Take a moment to study the diagnostic profile in Fig. 5.4 and generate your answer to this question.

What do you conclude? Kenneth's general satisfaction and internal motivation are low (2.0 and 3.8 respectively on the 7-point JDS scale), suggesting that there indeed is a problem. The MPS of 41 raises the possibility that the problem might be rooted in the work itself. Skill variety, task identity, and feedback appear to be particularly troublesome aspects of the work. So is work redesign indicated to improve the situation?

Probably not. While we have no data about Kenneth's competence, his level of dissatisfaction with aspects of the work context gives us pause. Satisfaction with co-workers and with job security are acceptable, but he is extremely unhappy with his compensation and with the supervision he receives. These factors alone could be responsible for the relatively low general satisfaction score.

Moreover, Kenneth's growth need strength is a very low 1.6, and his growth *satisfaction* is above average (5.2). Apparently he does not seek much challenge and complexity at work and is relatively happy with the amount he has in his job as it presently is designed.

The implication, then, is that attention to questions of pay and supervision are clearly warranted to understand (and possibly improve) whatever it is that has resulted in Kenneth's dissatisfactions in these areas. Full-scale job enrichment, however, appears inappropriate for Kenneth and might well be resisted by him. The one job change that may be appropriate is to increase the feedback that he receives. At present, Kenneth reports getting little feedback either from the job itself or from the people with whom he works. (See also the relatively low score for the psychological state "knowledge of results.") He probably has only a foggy idea of what he does well and what he does poorly. This should be corrected, since information about the adequacy of one's performance often directly improves performance independent of any motivational considerations associated with enriched work.

Question 6: How Hospitable Are Organizational Systems to Needed Changes?

Sometimes it turns out that those aspects of the work that most need to be improved are not readily changeable. When work redesign is carried out under such circumstances, the result may be the implementation of changes that are not nearly substantial enough to yield measurable differences in employee attitudes and behavior. We call this phenomenon the "small change" effect, and its pervasiveness in work redesign projects (e.g., Frank and Hackman, 1975) highlights the need to assess the hospitability of existing organizational systems to improvements in the motivational properties of jobs.

The small change effect often starts to develop as managers come to realize that major changes in the design of work would require that other organizational systems be substantially altered as well. When possible enriching changes in jobs are discussed, for example, we frequently have heard comments such as, "Yes, but we couldn't really do that, because . . . ," followed by a description of how the contemplated changes would not fit with some existing organizational system or practice.

Usually the concerns are valid: large changes in one organizational system (in this case, the work itself) invariably require alterations in related systems. These alterations are anxiety arousing for the people involved, or expensive to make, or contrary to organization-wide policies, or, frequently, all of the above. So numerous small compromises are made from the "ideal" work design to minimize the disruptiveness and cost of the changes. The net effect, in many cases, is a project that meddles with the work rather than redesigns it. The changes are safe, feasible, inexpensive—and ineffectual.

What differentiates between those organizational circumstances in which substantial changes in the design of work can be made and those where only small changes in jobs are feasible? The answer, we suggest, has primarily to do with the properties of three organizational systems: (1) the technological system, (2) the personnel system, and (3) the control system. Because these systems can severely constrain the magnitude of changes in the work itself, they bear close scrutiny in the diagnostic phase of a change project.[6]

The Technological System.   The technology of an organization can constrain the feasibility of work redesign by limiting the number of

6   The material that follows is adapted from a more detailed discussion of work redesign in the organizational context that is published elsewhere (Oldham and Hackman, 1980).

ways that jobs within the technology can be designed. In certain kinds of technologies, for example, it simply is not possible to build meaningful amounts of autonomy, variety, or feedback into the jobs (Slocum and Sims, 1978).

A well-worn but illuminating example of such a technology is the automobile assembly line. Employees working on the line have little control over work pace—this is controlled by the line itself. Moreover, both the size of the work unit for which employees are responsible and the variety of skills needed to complete the work of the unit are severely limited for technological reasons. What remains in many assembly line technologies are fractionalized, segmented jobs—jobs that must remain that way as long as the technology is the way it is.

Perhaps a key in understanding how technology limits the characteristics of jobs is the concept of employee *discretion* (Rousseau, 1978). When little employee discretion is required or allowed by the technology, work procedures are necessarily standardized and structured to a considerable extent. Under such conditions, employees' jobs are usually segmented and routinized, and contain little variety, autonomy, identity, and significance for the people who perform them. In essence, the technology usurps many of the most desirable features of the work.

Any effort to redesign work in a technology that permits little employee discretion is probably doomed to failure from the outset because of the mechanics of the system itself. The only redesign activities that are likely to be feasible are those that involve relatively small changes in the work itself (like giving employees some choice of tools). However, as we suggested earlier, this usually amounts to meddling with the work rather than enriching it, and the effects are likely to be neither substantial nor long lasting.

These views suggest that if work is to be meaningfully redesigned in an organization either (1) the technology must be of the type that provides at least moderate employee discretion or (2) the technology itself must be changed to be compatible with the characteristics of enriched work.

The latter route was taken, apparently successfully, when the management of Volvo planned its new automobile assembly plant at Kalmar (Gyllenhammar, 1977). It was decided early in the planning process to create enriched, challenging jobs at the new plant. The idea, however, was to design these jobs within a traditional conveyor line technology. As planning progressed, Gyllenhammar and his associates realized that the traditional technology and the innovative jobs were inherently incompatible. It became clear that if nontraditional, enriched jobs were to be created, a nontraditional technology also would be required. This realization led to cancellation of plans for the conveyor line and, instead, the development and installation of a technology permitting large amounts of employee discretion (through movable automobile carriers).

The cost of altering technologies can be very high and in many cases will be prohibitive. Volvo's nontraditional technology, for example, entailed an initial investment that was 10 percent higher than would have been the case if the traditional technology had been installed. However, unless such an investment is made, the possibility of creating substantial and meaningful jobs is sharply reduced. Indeed, in many cases it will be advisable *not* to try to enrich work for traditional technological systems, but instead to find ways to manage people as effectively and humanely as possible within those systems.

The Personnel System. In the interest of having a clear, fair, and concrete basis for employee recruitment, selection, placement, and training, elaborate personnel systems are often developed in organizations. These systems often result in a set of fixed job descriptions that specify not only who is to do what work, but also exactly how they are to go about it, complete with lists of tools and procedures that are to be used (Fine and Wiley, 1974).

While explicit and detailed job descriptions can be helpful in the smooth operation of many personnel functions, they can also constrain the feasibility of work redesign. In particular, it may be virtually impossible to meaningfully alter the design of jobs in personnel systems where adherence to precise specifications of permissible actions, tools, and work procedures is enforced.

Sometimes, of course, it is possible to change constraining aspects of the personnel system simultaneously with changes in jobs, or even to make arrangements for the focal jobs to be placed outside the domain of the personnel system. However, these alternatives are sure to be resisted by individuals who have vested interests in maintaining the system as it exists. Personnel managers who created the system and who may be charged with refining and enforcing it are unlikely to be enthusiastic about alterations that seem to compromise its integrity or its elegance. Neither are training managers likely to support changed job requirements and responsibilities that make obsolete their carefully constructed courses for employees who work on specific existing jobs.

Moreover, fixed job descriptions and personnel practices are sometimes the product of years of union-management negotiations, enforced by a legal and binding contract. When a great deal of work has gone into the development of mutually acceptable personnel practices, both managers and union officials may be extremely hesitant to reconsider existing practices, especially if it seems likely that compensation rates for various jobs might have to be revised as well.

In one instance, the administration of a university was convinced that work redesign was desirable for numerous secretarial jobs throughout the university. However, the personnel system of the university included a set of rigid secretarial job descriptions that had been accepted by both personnel officers and the employees' union. The implementation of the work redesign program would have involved substantial revisions in the secretarial job descriptions and salary schedules. This, of course, would have required new union-management negotiations concerning the job descriptions as well as additional discussions about salary for any revised job descriptions. After considering the possibility of these additional negotiations, the administration scrapped the entire work redesign project.

It appears, therefore, that the personnel system should be examined prior to work redesign to determine if there is enough room in the way jobs are being defined for meaningful changes to be made. If there is not sufficient slack in existing job descriptions and personnel practices, and if it is not possible to circumvent the personnel system or to introduce additional flexibility in that system, then the project risks falling victim to the "small change" effect. Better, in our view, would be to do as university managers did in the above example and decide not to attempt work redesign under conditions that make meaningful change unlikely or unacceptably costly.

The Control System.   The organization's control system can also constrain the feasibility of work redesign. By control system we mean any "mechanical" system that is designed to control and influence employee behavior in an impersonal, impartial, and automatic fashion (Reeves and Woodward, 1970). Control systems include budgets and cost accounting systems, production and quality control reports, attendance measuring devices, and so on.

Control systems help organizations minimize redundancies and inefficiencies in carrying out work, allow for careful monitoring of important aspects of organizational performance (productivity, financial expenditures, or staffing levels), and provide a concrete basis for taking corrective action when system-provided data do not conform to standards.

However, control systems also tend to limit the complexity and challenge of jobs (Clegg and Fitter, 1978). Because it is important to pinpoint accountability, control systems often specify in considerable detail exactly who is to do what specific tasks, thereby restricting the autonomy in employees' jobs. Also, control systems often rigidify and standardize the work, so that performance indices can be developed and applied to all employees and work activities within the system.

An example of the effects of control systems on work design is provided in a study of the purchasing department in a large organization (Lawler and Rhode, 1976). A financial control system was designed both to provide information about work outcomes to higher management and to prevent fraud and theft. In this situation, the control system required that employees who handled payments to vendors not talk with those vendors, and specified that each employee handle only a few of the activities necessary to pay the vendors. Thus, the jobs were necessarily routine and highly repetitive in order to meet the criteria for a "good" control system. The result in this particular case was low employee satisfaction and work performance.

Any subsequent attempt to redesign work in the purchasing department described above (or in other departments with rigid control systems) would probably result in only small changes in the work itself. For one thing, many control systems simply would not work if the complexity of the work done by individual jobholders were increased or if people were given greater autonomy in managing their own work processes and procedures.

Moreover, it is often difficult to increase job-based feedback (a common change made when work is redesigned) and still have the control system function as intended. The reason is that data collected as part of the control system are typically supplied to staff personnel and line managers for use in managing unit performance. To redesign the work so that feedback comes naturally to the persons who are doing the work (for example, by having the jobholders do their own testing and inspection or by placing them in direct contact with the "clients" of the work) would throw many control systems into disarray. Such problems will be particularly severe if the *form* of the naturally occurring feedback is not readily quantifiable or if it varies from job to job within the organizational unit. Nonquantitative and nongeneral data are anathemas to most well-designed control systems.

To avoid the "small change" trap when work is redesigned in organizations where rigid control systems are already in place, it often is desirable to alter the control systems themselves as part of the work redesign activity. Unfortunately, significant redesign of control systems (and in particular "loosening" of them) is unlikely in many instances. Indeed, tampering with a control system may sometimes even be illegal. Certain government agencies, for example, require organizations to engage in specific, strict quality control activities. Or a contract may be awarded to an organization (or withheld from it) because of the organization's quality control procedures. The costs to an organization of loosening its procedures in such circumstances would usually (and justifiably) be considered unacceptably expensive.

In addition, there may be large internal costs associated with altering or scrapping a control system. Establishing a good control system often involves a large initial investment, perhaps including the purchase of computer hardware and the development of sophisticated programs to assess unit productivity and management performance. Altering such a system could involve the costly development of new control system technology in addition to the person-hours required to set up the technology. Finally, as was noted earlier, there are always personnel in organizations *whose own jobs* depend on the maintenance of existing organizational systems. Therefore, attempts to change the control system (particularly if the idea is to "loosen" technically sophisticated controls) are very likely to encounter resistance from those who have a personal and professional interest in the preservation and refinement of existing control procedures in essentially their present form.

Summary.   It appears that rigidities built into the technological, personnel, and control systems of an organization can seriously compromise the magnitude of changes that can be made in how work is designed, and therefore reduce the feasibility of work redesign as a change strategy. For this reason, the hospitability of these three systems to contemplated changes should be carefully assessed prior to initiating the change process. Diagnostic devices that are specifically designed to assist in making this assessment, unfortunately, are not presently available. So despite the importance of the issue, it will be necessary to use ad hoc procedures for bringing data to bear on it.

It is ironic that the organizational systems addressed in this section not only constrain the feasibility of work redesign, but also are part of the reason why the jobs may *need* to be changed. That is, each of the three systems reviewed tends to influence how jobs are structured, and we have seen that the type of job design that is consistent with a traditional technological, personnel, or control system often tends to involve work that is routinized and simplified rather than complex and challenging.

So work redesign may be especially difficult to carry out successfully under precisely the circumstances when it is most needed to improve work motivation and the personal satisfaction of employees. As we have noted throughout this section, the alternatives in such circumstances are three. The first is to decide not to redesign the work and to look to other devices for improving the functioning of the organizational unit. The second is to proceed with work redesign despite the constraints posed by the technological, personnel, or control systems. This alternative risks on the one hand succumbing to the "small change" pitfall (if the systemic constraints are not overcome) and on the other to throwing the existing systems into disarray (if substantial changes somehow do get made but are inconsistent with the functioning of the established systems). And the third alternative is to redesign the organizational systems themselves, either prior to or simultaneously with redesign of the work, so that they can accomodate and support employees' work on the enriched jobs. This alternative obviously is not an easy, risk-free, or inexpensive undertaking. But in many cases it may be the only way to proceed if the risk of small change and the risk of organizational disarray are to be simultaneously avoided when work is redesigned.

CONCLUSION

In the last half of this chapter, we have walked through six questions that can be asked usefully as part of a prechange diagnosis of a work system. These questions are summarized in Table 5.2.

Table 5.2
Summary of Six Questions to Ask in Diagnosing Work Systems
Prior to Work Redesign

Assessing the need for work design

1. Is there a problem or an exploitable opportunity?
2. Does the problem or opportunity centrally involve employee motivation, satisfaction, or work effectiveness?
3. Might the design of work be responsible for the observed problems?
4. What aspects of the job most need improvement?

Determining the feasibility of work redesign

5. How ready are the employees for change?
6. How hospitable are organizational systems to needed changes?

A decision not to proceed with work redesign can be made on the basis of a negative answer to any one of these six questions. If the diagnostic results are taken seriously, many work redesign projects will not get off the ground, even though planners initially think that changing jobs would be a good idea. Such conservatism is appropriate, in our view, because of the numerous failures we have seen that came about because the setting was not appropriate for the job-focused intervention that was carried out.

Yet one must also be careful not to overinterpret diagnostic results or to rely too heavily on answers to the questions posed in Table 5.2. As noted earlier, all diagnostic instruments and procedures are in some way flawed and incomplete, and it is probably as impossible to generate a "perfect" diagnostic assessment of a work system as it is to paint a portrait that captures all the nuances of the subject's appearance and personality.

If, for example, a job "passes" all six of the diagnostic tests discussed here, there may still be some very good organizational reasons for not proceeding to change jobs—such as managerial reluctance, an impending reorganization, a planned technological innovation that will radically alter the work that is done, high interdependence between the focal job and other jobs that cannot be changed, and so on.

On the other hand, occasionally jobs can be beneficially changed even when diagnostic results are negative. If, for example, top managers have a clear and informed commitment to enriching jobs throughout the organization, and if these individuals are prepared to support changes that are consistent with their vision through thick and thin, then it may make sense to proceed with work redesign even in units where the diagnostic results suggest that meaningful changes in jobs will be difficult to design and install.

The conclusion, then, is that the choice to redesign work, or not to do so, is a complex managerial decision. A well-done diagnosis can help inform that decision, and we believe that diagnostic results should enter significantly into managerial choices about whether and how to proceed with changes in jobs. But diagnostic data are only a part of the story. The data must be fitted together carefully with other information about the people and the organization, and they must be tested against dominant values about how the organization is to be managed. Even if diagnostic data are highly favorable, work redesign is probably a bad idea if those who ultimately must support and diffuse the changes *believe* it to be a bad idea.

FOR ADDITIONAL READING

Hackman, J.R., and G.R. Oldham. Development of the Job Diagnostic Survey. *Journal of Applied Psychology,* 1975, *60,* 159-170. Describes the development of the JDS, summarizes its uses, and provides data about its psychometric properties.

Dunham, R.B., R.J. Aldag, and A.P. Brief. Dimensionality of task design as measured by the Job Diagnostic Survey. *Academy of Management Journal,* 1977, *20,* 209-223. Summarizes data from 20 samples of workers (totaling almost 6000 people) who took the job characteristics portion of the JDS, and concludes that the number of separate job dimensions measured by the instrument varies from sample to sample.

Seashore, S.E., E.E. Lawler III, P.H. Mirvis, and C. Cammann. *Observing and measuring organizational change: A guide to field practice.* New York: Wiley-Interscience, in press. A guide to the Michigan instruments for measuring various aspects of organizational functioning. Separate measurement devices and methods are presented as separate "modules," allowing the user to piece together validated instruments to make up a customized measurement package.

Rousseau, D.M. Characteristics of departments, positions, and individuals: Contexts for attitudes and behavior. *Administrative Science Quarterly,* 1978, *23,* 521-540. Explores the ways organizational factors (such as technology) affect the characteristics of jobs and, through them, the responses of people to their work.

6
CREATING AND SUPPORTING ENRICHED WORK

Suppose you have recently completed the diagnosis of a work system along the lines suggested in the previous chapter. You first identified some specific problems in the motivation, satisfaction, and work effectiveness of employees who work on the job you studied. Data from the Job Diagnostic Survey and from interviews indicated that the job is low in built-in motivating potential, and you have identified the specific job characteristics that most require change. The people who work on the job are relatively well satisfied with the work context, they are talented enough to handle more challenging work, and they score high on measures of growth need strength. Moreover, your diagnosis revealed that key organizational systems (including the technology, control, and personnel systems) will present no major obstacles to making substantial changes in how the job is structured. In sum, the answers you generated to the diagnostic questions posed in Table 5.2 suggest that work redesign is in order, and you are ready to move.

But what specifically should you do? To be sure, you know what aspects of the job need attention, but what specific *action steps* should you take to improve the standing of the job on these characteristics? And how should these changes, once made, be *managed and supported* so that their effects persist over time?

This chapter provides some guidance for dealing with these questions. In the first half of the chapter, we review several principles for redesigning work and show how each of these principles is linked to one or more of the core job characteristics. Then we turn to questions about the management of people on enriched jobs—specifically, what can be done to improve the fit between how the work is structured and how the organization is managed after jobs are redesigned.

We begin with a look at one specific job that appears to be a good candidate for change and use that job to illustrate five principles of job redesign.

THE TREADFREE KEYPUNCHERS: A CASE[1]

All keypunching for the Treadfree Manufacturing Corporation is performed in one organizational unit, headed by a Manager of Keypunching Services. This manager is responsible for two supervisors, two clerks, and about twenty keypunch and verifying machine operators. Most of the operators are young, on their first or second full-time job, and have high school diplomas.

As seen in Fig. 6.1, most work to be keypunched comes from five departments: accounting (30 percent), engineering (10 percent), sales (20 percent), personnel (20 percent), and production staff (10 percent). Another 10 percent of the work comes from miscellaneous departments throughout Treadfree.

Representatives of client departments bring work to be done to a receiving clerk, who has a desk at a corridor window in the keypunch room. The clerk accepts the work, completes a work order form that indicates job specifications (such as special cards or codes) and the date the cards are needed. The data and work order form are then given to Supervisor I, who checks the materials to make sure that they are clear and legible, and that the due date is realistic given other work in progress. If there is any problem with the work as submitted, Supervisor I returns it to the receiving clerk, who calls the client and resolves the difficulties. Problems having to do with due dates are negotiated directly between Supervisor I and the client.

Supervisor I keeps a queue of jobs to be done on the shelves by her desk, and when a keypuncher becomes free, gives the next job to

---

1   While based on an actual organizational situation, numerous aspects of this case have been altered for presentation here.

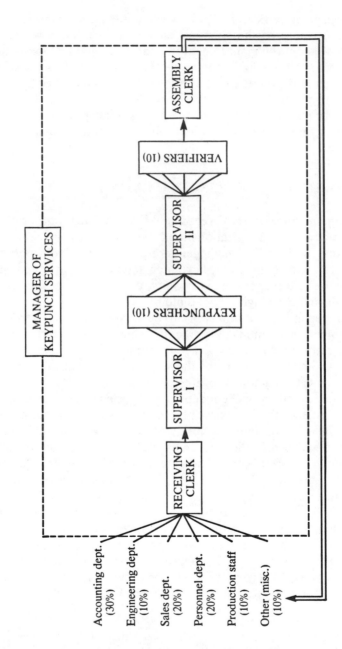

Fig. 6.1 Workflow for keypunchers.

be done to that individual. For especially large or especially urgent jobs, the supervisor may break the work into several parts and give the parts to several operators. Occasionally it is necessary to have a keypuncher set aside work in progress to do part of a rush job.

When a job (or portion of a job, if the work was broken up when assigned) is completed, it is given by the keypuncher to Supervisor II. This supervisor makes a quick check for accuracy of codes, formats, and card types, and notes the due date for the work to be completed. He then places the work in a queue on his shelves and gives the next highest priority job to the next available verifier. Because of a history of errors in keypunched work, all jobs are verified, which essentially involves repunching the data, except that the verifying machine merely confirms that the right punches already have been made on completed cards. Verifiers correct any mispunches they find.

After a job (or portion of a job) has been verified, it goes to the assembly clerk. The assembly clerk compiles the completed cards and, when all portions of the job are finished, prints the cards on a line printer. The assembly clerk then calls the client to say that the job may be picked up at the assembly clerk's corridor window.

Supervisor I is responsible for the receiving clerk, the ten keypunchers, and any problems having to do with scheduling or due dates. When work is especially heavy, she may obtain permission from the manager to bring on some part-time help. Supervisor II is responsible for the assembly clerk, the ten verifiers, and any problems having to do with quality and accuracy. If clients discover problems in the work after picking it up, they contact Supervisor II, who will have someone who is free (or can be made so) among the verifying staff do the corrections. Since it takes somewhat longer to initially punch the cards than it does to verify them, having the verifiers do any corrections or repunching tends to "balance" the workloads of the keypunchers and verifiers. Nevertheless, on occasion it is necessary for Supervisors I and II to move someone from keypunching to verifying or vice versa to deal with a "lump" in the workflow.

An evaluation of the job using the JDS reveals the diagnostic profile shown in Fig. 6.2. The job characteristic scores have been confirmed using multiple observers (in this case supervisors and outside researchers) and multiple methods (interviews in addition to the JDS).

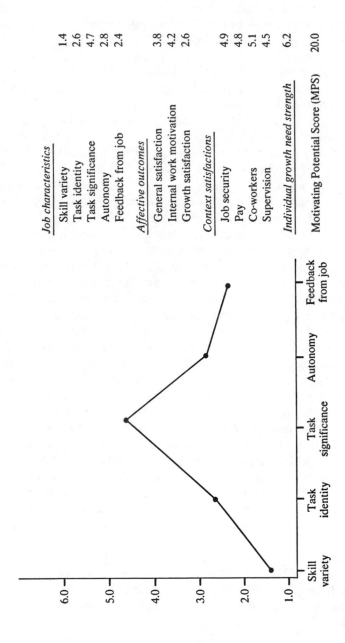

Job characteristics	
Skill variety	1.4
Task identity	2.6
Task significance	4.7
Autonomy	2.8
Feedback from job	2.4
Affective outcomes	
General satisfaction	3.8
Internal work motivation	4.2
Growth satisfaction	2.6
Context satisfactions	
Job security	4.9
Pay	4.8
Co-workers	5.1
Supervision	4.5
Individual growth need strength	6.2
Motivating Potential Score (MPS)	20.0

Fig. 6.2 Diagnostic profile for keypunchers.

Given the results of the diagnosis, how would you change this job? What specific steps would you take to improve the standing of the job on the core job characteristics?

SOME IMPLEMENTING PRINCIPLES[2]

In this section we present several principles for implementing work redesign that can be useful in dealing with the questions posed above. These principles are (1) combining tasks, (2) forming natural work units, (3) establishing client relationships, (4) vertically loading the job, and (5) opening feedback channels. As shown in Fig. 6.3, each of the principles is especially powerful in affecting the standing of a job on one or more of the core job characteristics.

Combining Tasks

Both the skill variety and the task identity of a job can be increased by putting together existing, fractionalized tasks to form new and larger modules of work. When tasks are combined, all tasks required

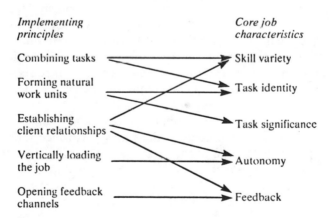

Fig. 6.3 Links between the implementing principles and the core job characteristics.

---

2   This section is based on materials from Hackman, Oldham, Janson, and Purdy (1975) and Walters and Associates (1975).

to complete a given piece of work are performed by one person, rather than by a series of individuals who do separate, small parts of the job.

The tasks involved in providing nursing care to hospitalized patients, for example, might be combined so that each nurse would have responsibility for many aspects of the care and treatment of a given set of patients. This would contrast with a design for nursing work in which each nurse is responsible for only one or two tasks for a larger number of patients. Similarly, the job of a toaster assembler might be designed so that each employee completes a whole toaster from beginning to end, rather than perform one small operation (such as attaching the line cord) and passing the toaster on to another employee who does another small operation.

When a number of tasks are combined to form a single large module of work, skill variety almost invariably increases. Moreover, task identity often improves as well because the employee is able to identify with the complete product or service. It is far easier to identify with a shiny toaster, tested and ready for shipment, than with an electrical cord firmly attached to an empty toaster chasis.

In thinking about how to combine tasks, it often is helpful to draw a workflow diagram similar to the one shown in Fig. 6.1. How does the work get to each employee, and where does it go next? How do the separate tasks that are performed relate to one another? How feasible would it be to combine those tasks into a single, larger job? Examining the workflow can help generate answers to these questions and can prompt ideas for combining tasks to create enriched jobs.

In the toaster case, for example, the workflow diagram might identify six or seven separate operations now performed serially that could be put together and carried out readily by individual "toaster makers." For the keypunchers in the case described at the beginning of this chapter, the tasks of punching, verifying, printing, and delivering completed cards might be combined into a single job.

Forming Natural Work Units

When work is formed into "natural" units, the items of work handled by employees are arranged into logical or inherently meaningful groups. At present, the work of the keypunchers in our case is randomly assigned to whomever happens to be free, regardless of the nature or source of the work. Natural work units could be formed by giving each keypuncher continuing responsibility for specific departments or accounts. Under this arrangement, employees would have more task identity ("I do the keypunch work for the Treadfree production department"). In addition, the keypunchers would probably develop a growing sense of how their work affects people in the department they serve—an increase in task significance.

Among the possible bases for forming natural work units suggested by Walters and Associates (1975) are the following:

- *Geographical.* Salespersons might be given a particular section of the city, state, or country as their "turf."

- *Type of business.* Insurance claims adjusters might be assigned to business groups, such as utilities, manufacturers, and so on.

- *Organizational.* Typists might be given work that originates in a particular department of the larger organization.

- *Alphabetical or numerical.* File clerks could be made responsible for materials in specified alphabetical groups (like A-D), or library shelf readers might check books in a certain range of the library's numerical cataloging system.

- *Customer groups.* Employees of a public utility might be assigned to serve particular institutional or business accounts.

Other categories for forming groups of work items can be readily invented for various types of jobs. All that is required is that there be some logical or meaningful basis for grouping the items of work, a basis that makes good intuitive sense to those who will carry out the work.

Establishing Client Relationships

As noted above, natural work units can often be formed around specific groups of "clients" of the work. In such cases, it may be possible to put the employee in direct contact with those clients and give him or her continuing responsibility for managing relationships with them.

Client relationships could be established for the keypunch operator job we have been discussing by giving the keypunchers personal responsibility for managing their relationships with specific client departments. The keypunchers (rather than the supervisors) would negotiate due dates and priorities with clients, discuss with them any problems in the legibility of work submitted, receive complaints, perform any corrections needed after the job had been completed, and so on.

Creating client relationships is a three-step process. First, the client must be identified—not always an easy task. Second, the most direct contact possible between the worker and the client is established. Third, criteria are set up by which the client can judge the quality of the product or service received. And, whenever possible, the client should have a means of relaying his or her judgments directly back to the worker.

The contact between worker and client should be as great as possible and as frequent as necessary to reduce the chance that messages will be distorted or delayed. Face-to-face contact is highly desirable, at least occasionally. When that is impossible or impractical, telephone and mail can suffice. In any case, it is important that the performance criteria used by the client be mutually understood and agreed upon.

By enabling employees to establish direct relationships with the clients of their work, improvements are often realized simultaneously on the three core dimensions. Feedback increases because of additional opportunities for individuals to obtain direct and immediate praise or criticism of their work outputs from the persons who receive the work. Skill variety increases because of the need to exercise interpersonal skills in maintaining the client relationship as well as technical skills in completing the task itself. And autonomy increases because individuals have personal responsibility for deciding how to manage their relationships with the clients.

Vertically Loading the Job

When a job is vertically loaded, autonomy increases. Workers are given increased control over the work by "pushing down" responsibility and authority that formerly were reserved for higher levels of management. In effect, the gap between the doing and the controlling parts of the work is narrowed.

There are several ways to vertically load a job. Jobholders can be given discretion in setting schedules, determining work methods, and deciding when and how to check on the quality of the work produced. Employees can make their own decisions about when to start and stop work, when to take breaks, and how to assign priorities. They can be encouraged to seek solutions to problems on their own, consulting with other organization members as necessary, rather than calling immediately for the supervisor when problems arise. In all, the idea is to advance employees from a position of highly restricted authority to one of reviewed authority and, eventually, to near-total authority for their work.

Consider, for example, the job of a teacher. In some schools, teachers are required to submit lesson plans to their principal for approval one week prior to the use of the plans. Textbooks are selected by the principal and must be used in all classrooms. Class periods are scheduled for 50 minutes, after which breaks must be taken regardless of the status of the lesson at that time. If such a job were to be vertically loaded, external controls would be reduced and teachers granted new authority. Lesson plans would no longer need to be submitted for approval. Teachers would have discretion in selecting texts (perhaps from a district-approved set), and could establish class times that uniquely fit the needs of the students and the requirements of the material.

This implementing principle also can be applied to the keypunch operator case. Operators could be given authority to set their schedules, to establish priorities for their daily work, and to correct on their own obvious errors in materials clients submit for keypunching. Moreover, operators with demonstrated competence might be given authority to decide when (and when not) to verify their work. The net effect of such changes should be an increase in keypunchers' feelings of personal responsibility for their work and, ultimately, an improvement in their internal work motivation.

Opening Feedback Channels

In virtually all jobs there are ways to open channels of feedback to help employees learn how they are performing and whether their performance is improving or deteriorating over time. While information about performance effectiveness can be obtained in many ways, including appraisals from the supervisor, it generally is better for workers to learn about their performance directly from doing the job itself.

Job-provided feedback usually is more immediate and private than supervisor-supplied feedback, and it increases the worker's feelings of personal control over his or her work in the bargain.

Moreover, it avoids many of the potentially disruptive interpersonal problems that can develop when the only way a worker has to find out how he or she is doing is through direct messages or subtle cues from the boss.

Exactly what should be done to open channels for job-provided feedback will vary from job to job and organization to organization. Yet in many cases the changes involve simply removing existing blocks that isolate the worker from naturally occurring data about performance rather than generating entirely new feedback mechanisms. For example:

• Establishing direct relationships with clients. As suggested above, this often provides the worker with naturally occurring data about how well the product or service provided meets the needs of those who receive it.

• Placing quality control close to the workers (perhaps even in their hands). Quality control efforts in many organizations eliminate a natural source of feedback. The quality check on a product or service is done by persons other than those responsible for the work, and feedback to workers is belated and diluted if it is provided at all. This fosters a tendency to think of quality as "someone else's concern." Doing their own quality checks can dramatically increase the quantity and quality of data people have about their performance.

• Providing summaries of performance records directly to workers (as well as to their supervisors), thereby ensuring that they have at hand the data they need to improve their performance. Tradition and established procedure in many organizations dictate that records about performance be kept by a supervisor and transmitted up (not down) the organizational hierarchy. Sometimes supervisors even check the work and correct any errors themselves. The people who made the errors never know they occurred and are denied the very information that could enhance both their internal work motivation and the technical adequacy of their performance.

• Using computers and other automated devices to provide individuals with information now inaccessible to them. Many clerical operations, for example, are now performed on computer consoles. These consoles can often be programmed to provide the clerk with immediate feedback in the form of a CRT display or a printout indicating that an error has been made. Some systems have even been programmed to provide the operator with a positive feedback message when a period of error-free performance has been sustained.

How might the principle of opening feedback channels be applied to the keypunch operator job? One idea would be to allow the clients to return incorrect cards directly to the operators (rather than to the supervisor), and then permit the operators to correct their own errors. Each operator might also be required to keep a file of copies of his or her errors, which could be reviewed to determine trends in types and frequencies of errors. Finally, operators could be provided with a weekly (or monthly) printout of their errors and productivity.

In summary, opening feedback channels typically involves removing barriers or blocks that isolate employees from existing information about their work performance. In doing this, the intent is to provide employees with *direct, immediate,* and *regular* feedback about their performance effectiveness. If the removal of barriers is not sufficient to provide direct feedback, new feedback mechanisms may have to be established. This may be as simple as instructing employees to maintain their own charts of their performance, or as complex as the development of sophisticated surveys to reveal how clients perceive the quality of the work they are receiving (Nadler, 1977; Walters and Associates, 1975).

Conclusion: Implementing Principles

In this section we have reviewed several action-oriented principles for redesigning jobs to improve their standing on the core job characteristics. Throughout we have suggested ways that each implementing principle might be applied to the job of the keypunch operators with which we opened the chapter. If the keypunch job were actually changed along the lines suggested, operators would have continuing responsibility for an identified client or group of clients; they would be permitted to make most decisions about their work procedures and schedules; they would manage their own relationships with clients on a continuing basis; and they would receive direct and regular feedback about their performance effectiveness.

These changes would improve the standing of the job on each of the job characteristics shown to be low in the diagnostic profile for the job (see Fig. 6.2) and should yield gains in the motivation, satisfaction, and performance of the keypunchers. And, in fact, substantial improvements in these outcomes were obtained when the implementing principles discussed above were applied to an actual keypunch job in an insurance company, a job that was originally structured much like the one we have been discussing here (Hackman, Oldham, Janson, and Purdy, 1975).[3]

SUPPORTING AND MANAGING ENRICHED WORK[4]

When appropriately used in a work setting that is hospitable to change, the implementing principles reviewed above can prompt significant improvements in employee work attitudes and behaviors. Unfortunately, these new attitudes and behaviors often fade away over time (Hackman, 1975; Walton, 1977b). We call this the "vanishing effects" phenomenon, and it can compromise the long-term impact of even well-conceived and competently executed changes in jobs.

While many factors can contribute to the vanishing effects phenomenon, prime among them are the *management practices* that determine how people are trained, promoted, compensated, and supervised at work. Typically, these practices are designed to be compatible with traditional, fractionalized jobs. They are often *not* compatible with work on challenging jobs high in motivating potential. The consequence, in many cases, is that new behaviors exhibited by employees on enriched jobs are not supported by existing managerial practices and may even be undercut by those practices. Under such conditions the new behaviors tend to extinguish, and the organization persists pretty much as it was before the work was redesigned.

This state of affairs can often be avoided if attention is given to the redesign of management practices at the same time that rank-and-

---

3   The implementing principles presented in this chapter, although illustrative of the kinds of changes that can be made to improve the jobs of individuals in organizations, obviously are not exhaustive. They were selected for attention here because of the links between the principles and the core job characteristics in the motivational model presented in Chapter 4. Other principles for enriching jobs (many of which are similar to those presented here) are provided by Ford (1969), Glaser (1975), and Herzberg (1974).

4   This section is based on materials from Oldham and Hackman (1980).

file jobs are changed. In this section we examine four management practices that strike us as key to the long-term persistence of work redesign, and we suggest some ways that these practices can be altered to be compatible with work on enriched jobs. They are (1) training practices, (2) career development practices, (3) compensation practices, and (4) supervisory practices.

Training Practices[5]

As noted in Chapter 2, training is a very popular device for attempting to improve the motivation and productivity of organization members. Yet the benefits of time and money spent on training appear to depend substantially on how the work of the persons trained is designed.

The irony is that training is often provided when it isn't much needed and is eliminated in precisely those circumstances when it could have real benefits. Consider employees who work on simple, routinized jobs. Training is unlikely to have beneficial effects for these individuals, since the requirements of the job usually can be mastered very quickly without any special instruction. It has been estimated, for example, that employees can learn most routine jobs within two weeks, simply by proceeding to do the work (O'Toole, 1975). Because training is objectively unnecessary in such circumstances, it may be experienced by employees as an attempt by management to gain even more control over their on-the-job behavior. The result is likely to be no improvement in work performance (the employees knew all they needed to know to do the job already), heightened feelings of frustration and disillusionment with management, and increased organizational vulnerability to the problems that arise when the work force is overqualified for the work being done (see Chapter 2). In effect, training (which is widely viewed as an inherently valuable activity) can actually make things worse rather than better for traditionally designed jobs.

On the other hand, training activities are sometimes completely eliminated after the work has been enriched. The belief, apparently, is that work redesign will solve all problems of job performance, and

---

5   By training practices, we mean instructional processes that are initiated by the organization to improve the job-relevant knowledge, skill, and attitudes of organization members.

that employees will informally provide one another with help in gaining any new knowledge or skill that may be required. These are very optimistic assumptions. The actual consequences of work re-design sans training, in many cases, is an increase in the *motivation* of employees to work effectively (because of the improved design of the work itself) but a decrease in their *capability* to do so (because new skills are required that they do not presently hold).

We know of one example of this in a large transportation organi-zation. The job of reservationist was enriched so that it required a variety of skills and abilities and a good deal of autonomy on the part of the incumbents. However, the organization neglected to provide employees with all of the information and expertise they would need to perform the new, enriched tasks effectively. The result was a group of frustrated reservationists who were not able to take advan-tage of the new opportunities the enriched job provided.

How can such problems be alleviated when jobs are enriched? Two different types of training may be required. First is technical training, to ensure that employees have the knowledge and the skills necessary to execute their enriched tasks competently. If work re-design has been successful, then employees will care more than previously about performing well. They should experience self-reward when they find they have done well and feel displeased with themselves when they fail. A good technical training program for employees on enriched jobs can increase the likelihood that their work experiences are characterized more often by self-reward than by displeasure with their performance.

The second type of training that often is needed when work is redesigned has to do with the management of interpersonal relation-ships and decision-making processes. When work is designed accord-ing to the dictates of the scientific mangement approach, employees have little objective need to coordinate and negotiate with others to get the work done or to make decisions about work processes or scheduling. All such matters are decided by management and speci-fied in clear detail for those who actually perform the work. On enriched jobs, however, a great deal of decision making and coordi-nation may be required, and the prior work experiences of the employees may have provided them with few chances to exercise or hone their skills in carrying out such activities. So even if the em-ployees are competent to execute the technical aspects of their enriched work, problems may develop because of insufficient knowledge and skill about how to *manage* their new and expanded work responsibilities. Training about such matters should be welcomed by the affected employees and could have substantial benefits for work performance, employee attitudes, and the social climate of the work unit. Thus, for the keypunch operator case described earlier, a training program that focused on the management of interpersonal processes could enhance operators' skills in dealing with their new "clients" and thereby improve the chances for individual work effectiveness.

In summary, how training practices are managed after jobs are enriched can substantially affect the persistence of behavioral and attitudinal changes prompted by the redesigned work. The beneficial effects of work redesign may soon vanish if appropriate training is not provided, simply because employees do not have the information or skills necessary to perform the enriched job well. A good training program can increase the chances that employees will be successful on their enriched jobs—and therefore that the effects of work redesign will persist over time.

Career Development Practices

Career development, as used here, refers to the process by which a synthesis is worked out between employee aspirations and the opportunities for mobility that are present in the work environment. Ideally, this synthesis will result in the fulfillment of both individual and organizational objectives (Van Maanen and Schein, 1977). Specific organizational practices having to do with career development include job rotation, various promotional systems, and workshops on life planning and career development.

In this section, we focus on ways career development practices can affect the success and persistence of work redesign activities. Essentially, we examine whether career development practices are appropriately responsive to the variety of experiences different individuals have on enriched jobs. As will be seen, the effectiveness of a work redesign program may be significantly compromised if career development programs do not help individuals respond and adjust satisfactorily to their new on-the-job experiences, problems, and aspirations. We consider separately three types of reactions to enriched work: those of "overstretched" employees, those of "fulfilled" employees, and those of "growing" employees.

The Overstretched Employee.   We suggested in Chapter 4 that work redesign may not be appropriate for certain people, such as employees with weak needs for personal growth and those whose knowledge and skill are not sufficient to deal with the demands of the job. These individuals may find enriched work threatening and may balk at being "pushed" or stretched too far by the work. As a result, adverse consequences may appear both for the persons involved and for their employing organizations (Blood and Hulin, 1967). Examples include an increase in personal anxiety, psychological or behavioral withdrawal from the job, and various counterproductive activities that express employees' displeasure with the newly enriched work.

Typical career development practices (like life-planning workshops and promotional schemes) that are geared to the upwardly mobile employee may be completely out of place in this situation and produce few desirable outcomes. If management is interested in retaining overstretched employees, alternative career development practices that are responsive to their special situation may be in order.

One such approach assumes that the growth aspirations of overstretched employees can and will be "rekindled" by challenging work. The idea is that after experiencing such work, employees may begin to respond positively to it. Under this assumption, then, some form of employee counseling may be sufficient to help overstretched employees begin to take advantage of the opportunities for growth available on enriched jobs. Later, after the work is mastered and the initially overstretched employees are comfortable with it, discussions about further career opportunities could be initiated.

A second approach assumes that overstretched employees are *not* likely to learn to appreciate the demands and opportunities provided by enriched work. In this case, creating alternative, downward career paths that lead to simpler jobs more consistent with the employees' needs may be in order. This might involve creating new, nonchallenging jobs or transferring employees who presently hold lower-level jobs to create additional openings for work on those jobs. In either case, the downward movement of the overstretched employee would require downward transfers to be legitimitized. This would be difficult in many organizations because of strong norms against *any* downward movements. To overcome this norm, it might be necessary to begin by moving downward obviously competent employees who prefer less demanding work (Hall, 1976).

Which assumption is correct—that employees will, or will not, gradually come to value and respond positively to enriched work that initially is psychologically threatening to them? Answers to this question obviously have substantial implications for the career development practices used in an organization. Unfortunately, there is currently little research evidence on the question, and that which does exist is not altogether consistent (e.g., Brousseau, 1978; Hackman, Pearce, and Wolfe, 1978). At this point, then, we can recommend only that considerable thought be given to career development practices for overstretched employees so that they are neither denied opportunities to move beyond their present work attitudes and aspirations nor forced to remain on a job that is psychologically discomforting to them.

The Fulfilled Employee.   A second type of response to work redesign is a state of "fulfillment." By this we mean that individuals are basically satisfied with the responsibilities and challenges of their enriched jobs. Fulfilled persons perform well at work but have no particular desire to move upward in the organizational hierarchy. Instead, they are pleased with their jobs and want to retain the amount of responsibility they currently have. Career development practices designed for the upwardly mobile employee may be inappropriate for the fulfilled individual. Indeed, such practices run the risk of overstretching these employees, which can have adverse consequences, especially if the employees are performing well on their current jobs.

What career development practices may be appropriate for fulfilled employees? What would one do to retain current levels of challenge and responsibility and yet not create conditions where stagnation may develop? Two types of developmental practices may be especially appropriate in these circumstances.

The first is traditional job rotation. In this practice individuals are periodically rotated through jobs where new learnings and skills can be obtained, yet which require little additional responsibility. Movement is short-term, with employees eventually returning to their regular positions.

A second possibility is the formation of *lateral* career paths (Schein, 1978). These paths would allow employees to move into different functional areas (to manufacturing from finance, for instance) at approximately the same horizontal level in the organization. While opportunities for movement would be enriched, there would not be major increases in responsibility. For this reason, lateral paths should be attractive to employees who are basically content with their present level of responsibility.

As with the practice of downward transfer discussed earlier, there may be stigmas attached to job rotation and lateral career paths because historically employees who have moved anywhere but upward have been viewed as "failures." This stigma is not likely to be an easy one to reshape, but formal and public policies that directly legitimatize (and even reward) lateral movement may ultimately create greater acceptance of such practices.

The Growing Employee.   A third possible response to work redesign programs is movement by employees into a "growth cycle." These employees are so stimulated by the enriched nature of their work that they seek even higher levels of responsibility and additional opportunities for on-the-job learnings. After a period of time, even those who were initially challenged and stimulated by an enriched job may find that the job now provides insufficient opportunities for continued growth.

If action is not taken for such employees, stagnation and disillusionment may result. Because they are no longer being stretched by their work, they may feel that their careers are at a standstill. Further, they may come to believe that the organization has little interest in providing the kinds of opportunities they seek and therefore begin to look to other organizations for more challenging work.

Organizations can reduce the likelihood that human resources will be wasted in this fashion by installing career development practices specifically tailored to meet the needs of the "growing" employee. Two such practices are described below.

The first involves reinforcing traditional hierarchical career paths that allow individuals to move upward within their function to levels of leadership and authority (Schein, 1978). Such paths provide persons new growth opportunities simultaneously with increases in responsibility for organizational outcomes, but they usually are restricted in number.

Second, special assignments might be offered to the "growing" employee. These would be short-term, challenging jobs filled with opportunities to exercise authority and creativity. Because opportunities for hierarchical mobility will always be limited by the relatively small number of top positions in organizations, some ingenuity in designing stimulating short-term assignments would seem well worthwhile in organizations where significant numbers of employees have demonstrated increased (rather than diminished) desires for further growth and development after work redesign.

The career development practices suggested in this section clearly are not exhaustive of what might be done to support and follow up work redesign. However, they do indicate the diversity of activities that may be called for if (as predicted) it turns out that different employees respond differently to the enrichment of their work. The absence of appropriate career development practices in organizations where work redesign has been introduced seems certain to erode the long-term benefits of enriched work.

Compensation Practices

How people are paid for their contributions to the organization can also adversely affect the persistence of work redesign activities and can neutralize some of the beneficial effects of enriched jobs. Two aspects of compensation arrangements are dealt with here: (1) the absolute *level* of pay desired by employees after their jobs have been redesigned and (2) the *form* of payment (contingent versus noncontingent on work performance).[6]

Absolute Level of Pay.   One of the controversial issues connected with the practice of work redesign is its impact on employees' views of their pay. Some commentators have argued that enhancing employees' responsibilities through work redesign usually results in demands for more money because people simply *expect* higher pay for greater responsibility (Lawler, 1977). Alternatively, it has been

---

6   Not addressed here is the *focus* of the compensation system. In general, we concur with Lawler (1977) that the appropriate focus of compensation arrangements depends on the amount of interdependence in the work itself. When individuals have their own autonomous jobs, an individually based plan may be most appropriate; when work is designed for groups (see Chapters 7 and 8), a group-based plan is usually preferred; and when there is substantial organization-wide interdependence (or when the contributions of separate individuals or groups to organizational performance cannot be reliably disentangled), a broader plan (such as the Scanlon Plan) may be indicated.

suggested that enriching work only rarely leads to demands for higher pay (Walters and Associates, 1975). This latter view rests on the assumption that responsibility at work and pay demands are basically independent of one another; indeed, it can be argued that an improved job may provide sufficient psychic rewards and that more material rewards would be motivationally superfluous. We know of no systematic research that has contrasted these two viewpoints. Furthermore, we have observed cases where additional money is demanded after work redesign and cases where it is not. Apparently employees view pay and responsibility as connected under some circumstances, while other times they are viewed as separate features of the employment arrangements.

Clearly, however, if some (or all) employees in a work unit become dissatisfied with pay levels, undesirable consequences are likely. As we have suggested in earlier chapters, pay dissatisfaction can distract the attention of employees from enriched work and orient their energy instead toward coping with questions of compensation. The result may be relatively low levels of motivation and performance on enriched jobs.

If such problems are to be avoided, some improvement in the level of pay offered employees following work redesign may be required. One approach is to give all employees in the affected work unit substantial pay increases as a sign that the newly enriched jobs are important and that management is serious about the changes being made (Lawler, 1977). Alternatively, any savings that result from the work redesign program might be shared with employees in the work unit on a proportional basis (Walters and Associates, 1975). Either of these approaches seems likely to reduce pay dissatisfaction that results from work redesign and thereby increase the chances that behavioral changes prompted by the enriched jobs will persist.

Also at issue is the timing of changes in compensation arrangements for employees. One possibility is to design and announce a new pay plan prior to (or simultaneously with) changes in the work itself. Alternatively, several plans might be developed prior to the changes but held in reserve until (and unless) signs of pay dissatisfaction appear following work redesign. The first approach heads off possible problems with pay level before any damage is done and provides employees with an early sign of management's good faith. The advantage of the second approach is that the pay plan that is eventually introduced can be tailored to the particular compensation problems that emerge.

Form of Payment.   When jobs are enriched, how should people be paid? Is it advantageous to use salaries, hourly wages, or some type of incentive or bonus for good performance? There is a good deal of controversy about the matter. On the one hand, some commentators (e.g., Deci, 1975) have argued that contingent rewards (such as bonuses) may be inappropriate for tasks that are intrinsically meaningful and interesting. The reasoning is that employees paid on a contingent basis may conclude that they are performing the task *because* of the external reward, and therefore that the task must not be very satisfying or interesting in and of itself. According to this view, a bonus or incentive system could change employees' perceptions of the reasons for their behaviors and ultimately diminish the motivational benefits of enriched work. Several laboratory investigations support this basic position (see Staw, 1976, for a review).

Advocates of Deci's position argue that noncontingent rewards (such as salaries or hourly wages) are most appropriate for and supportive of enriched work. These rewards are seen as allowing individuals to experience all the benefits of redesigned work. Moreover, salary plans enhance employees' felt freedom and treat them as mature adults. In this sense, salary systems encourage responsibility and trustworthiness among employees, which is compatible in spirit with most work redesign programs.

A contrasting position is that contingent pay plans (such as bonuses and piece-rate systems) are perfectly appropriate for enriched jobs. The notion is that the rewards available from the pay plan and those available from the work itself are *additive* (see Chapter 2). Thus, work motivation should be maximized when employees are paid contingently for good performance on enriched tasks. There is also evidence that supports this view (e.g., Arnold, 1976).

What are we to conclude from these contradictory positions? Is it more appropriate to use noncontingent or contingent payment systems for enriched work? The answer, we believe, depends on the following two factors.

First is the degree to which it is possible to *measure* the output of enriched jobs. Simple quantity of output may not be the most appropriate output measure. As we have previously suggested, *quality* of the work performed is more likely than work quantity to be enhanced through work redesign. To the extent that managers and employees agree about what work outcomes should be measured (and how they should be measured), contingent pay systems may be indicated. When there is no agreement or when measurement is impossible, noncontingent systems may be more appropriate and more motivationally effective.

A second factor is the level of *trust* between management and employees (Lawler, 1971). Contingent reward systems may be incompatible with enriched work if employees perceive the systems as attempts by management to control and manipulate their behavior on enriched jobs. In such cases, any motivational advantages of contingent systems may be more than offset by suspicion of them and salary plans may be more appropriate. If, on the other hand, there is high trust in the organization, employees are more likely to believe that the plans will be administered equitably, and they may see them as a fair and appropriate means of sharing in the gains generated by high work productivity. In such circumstances, contingent payment systems would seem fully congruent with enriched, challenging work.

Supervisory Practices

The final set of management practices to be considered deals with the behaviors of first-line supervisors toward employees whose jobs have been redesigned. Research has demonstrated that enriching employees' jobs can cause serious strains in the relationship that exists between them and their supervisors (Alderfer, 1967), and numerous case reports have shown that such relationship problems can lead to an early and unanticipated demise of even well-conceived change projects.

These strains may be rooted in changes in the *role* of the supervisor that accompany the redesign of rank-and-file jobs. In many cases, autonomy, decision-making responsibility, discretion, and quality control activities are removed from the job of the supervisor and assigned to subordinates when jobs are enriched. Such shrinkage of the responsibilities of the supervisor may result in a substantial (and not necessarily constructive) change in the supervisor's behavior.

This apparently is what transpired when the jobs of telephone operators were redesigned, as reported by Lawler, Hackman, and Kaufman (1973). Many of the responsibilities of first-line supervisors were reassigned to the operators, which resulted in supervisors experiencing large amounts of "free time" after the changes had been made. Most of the supervisors chose to use this time to supervise the operators rather closely as they worked on their newly enriched jobs.

Postchange assessments showed few changes in employee motivation or satisfaction but a substantial *decrease* in operator perceptions of the respect and fair treatment they received from their supervisors. The researchers attributed the failure of the project to generate improvements in motivation or satisfaction to this deterioration in supervisor-subordinate relationships.

The pattern of results obtained in this study is consistent with the more general notion that reducing a supervisor's autonomy and power often prompts overcontrolling, rules-minded, and excessively critical behaviors on the part of the supervisor (Kanter, 1977). Such behaviors can more than offset any positive changes in employee motivation and satisfaction resulting from the enrichment of the work itself.

How might such counterproductive behaviors by supervisors be avoided when work is redesigned? The usual approach, of course, is to send the affected supervisors off to a training program where they would learn how to behave in ways that are constructive and supportive of their subordinates. The problem is that such programs have been shown to be largely ineffective in generating lasting changes in managerial attitudes and behaviors (Campbell, Dunnette, Lawler, and Weick, 1970).

What may be required, then, is to change the duties of the supervisors, so that their own work grows in meaning and responsibility, and so that supporting autonomous work by their subordinates becomes a natural part of their job. Among the tasks that could be folded into supervisory jobs after work redesign are the following (Walters and Associates, 1975):

- Gathering data for charting trends and forecasts in work volume and work-force needs.

- Training employees in their new responsibilities and counseling them about both work-related problems and career opportunities.

- Helping subordinates set performance goals and reviewing with them their performance in attaining those goals.

- Providing increased openness of communication both upwards (sharing employee concerns with higher management) and downwards (sharing with employees information about changes in organizational objectives and policies).

- Developing and testing with subordinates innovations in methods and procedures for executing and coordinating the work.

- Working on aspects of the work context (such as compensation and control systems, opportunity structures, equipment, and space) that may be causing dissatisfaction or impeding employees' work.

- Managing the evolution of the job enrichment process itself.

The focus of these activities is to support subordinates in performing their work effectively; the list does not include such traditional supervisory activities as direct monitoring of subordinates' behaviors, checking their work, or serving as disciplinarian. Many of the tasks listed require that supervisors turn their attention upward and outward in organization—managing the organizational context so that it facilitates high subordinate motivation and effective work performance. Thus, if supervisors are to perform these tasks well, their own jobs must contain considerable responsibility, discretion, and control. Since these qualities would have to be pushed down to the supervisors from higher levels or organizational management, the net effect would be to enrich the supervisors' jobs—just as previously had been done for the subordinates' jobs.

Such changes in supervisory jobs should prompt more supportive and effective behaviors by supervisors for at least three reasons. First, supervisors now would have *more power* to help their subordinates in meaningful ways. For example, the supervisors might have significant influence over the pay system in their units or over the career opportunities that are available to employees. As we have seen, attention to organizational practices such as these can enhance the likelihood that work redesign changes will persist.

Second, because of their new responsibilities the supervisors would have *less free time* to closely supervise. In fact, there might be so many demands for the time of supervisors that they would be forced to give even more freedom and discretion to their employees.

Finally, because the supervisors would be integral members of the management team, they should have a *greater investment* in the success of the redesign effort. This should result in behaviors that directly support the redesigned work, especially if supervisors have been trained in the skill of helping (rather than bossing) their subordinates and if they have been personally involved in the redesign of their subordinates' jobs.

CONCLUSION: WORK REDESIGN AND MIDDLE MANAGERS

In the first half of this chapter we examined several principles for redesigning jobs. These principles are not hard and fast rules, nor do they guarantee success in work redesign. They probably are most appropriately viewed as heuristics for generating a diversity of ideas about how jobs might be improved. Only when those ideas are installed competently in a hospitable organizational context can motivational improvements be expected.

In the second half of the chapter, we highlighted four organizational practices that may compromise the "staying power" of changes in attitudes and behavior that result from enriched work: training, career development, compensation, and supervisory practices. When these practices support the work of rank-and-file employees on enriched jobs, then the effects of job changes should be both strong and lasting. When, however, organizational practices are incongruent with the new attitudes or behaviors, then the benefits of enriched work are unlikely to persist over time, and the "vanishing effects" phenomenon we discussed in earlier pages may be observed.

Throughout this chapter and the last we have emphasized that making substantial changes in jobs that persist over time requires attention to the *systemic* properties of organizations. Job changes made as if they were in an organizational vacuum are almost sure to fail. For this reason it seems essential that work redesign not be construed as a short-term, limited focus "fix" for specific attitudinal and behavioral problems observed among rank-and-file workers. Instead, it appears more appropriate to view changes in how work is structured as involving alterations in how the organization as a whole functions and as something that will both affect and be affected by other aspects of the organization.

One implication of this view is that middle managers may play an especially important role in guiding the installation and follow-up of changes in jobs. Middle managers, more than supervisors or top managers, have direct responsibility for those organizational systems we identified in Chapter 5 as potential constraints on the *potency* of job changes. And it is middle managers who may be best positioned to alter those managerial practices discussed in this chapter as key to the *persistence* of work redesign effects.

What, then, should middle managers do to increase the chances that job changes will be big enough to make a difference and that they will persist long enough to be worth the bother of making them? Three groups of activities, which occur at different stages in the work redesign process, seem particularly important.

Stage 1.   When the transition is made from diagnostic studies to implementation activities, there is risk that the work redesign project will fall victim to the "small change" effect. Are existing organizational systems (particularly the technological, personnel, and control systems) sufficiently flexible to allow for major alterations in job structure? If not, can managers introduce "slack" in those systems, or otherwise change them to increase their hospitality to work redesign? If the answer to these questions is no, then (as suggested in Chapter 5) plans for work redesign should probably be terminated because chances for success are negligible.

Stage 2.   Once it is determined that the organizational context is hospitable to work redesign, the problem becomes one of making sure that substantial changes in the work itself actually get made. This is not so straightforward as it might seem: there are numerous forces, both within and among people, that tilt managers and employees toward safety and conservatism when binding decisions must be made about how "radical" the changes actually will be. The fears and anxieties of those responsible for making the changes (and of those who will be affected by them) sometimes lead to so great a dilution of the original work redesign plans that it is hard to tell what is really different after the changes have been installed. The perceptive middle manager will be watchful for signs of timidity and retreat, and will provide the support and encouragement that is necessary to ensure that planned major changes in jobs are not unintentionally replaced by attractive but substantively trivial window dressing.

Stage 3.   Once changes in jobs have been installed, their congruence with the ongoing managerial practices of the organization comes to the fore. If existing managerial practices support autonomous work on challenging jobs, then little may be required of middle management other than occasional signs of support and approval. If, however, key practices (particularly those having to do with training, career development, compensation, or supervision) undercut the opportunities and challenges provided by enriched work, then those practices must be revised to increase their congruence with the work itself. Interpersonal and intergroup tensions are also likely to emerge at this stage as people struggle to adjust to their new tasks and roles. The middle manager, who is in a position to notice the onset of conflict but relatively less likely to be a party to it, must be ready to consult with those involved and help them accommodate to each other in their new relationships. It is difficult and time-consuming to revise existing managerial practices and to aid in the resolution of social conflict. Yet it seems imperative that middle managers take on these issues as they emerge in Stage 3. Not to do so, in many cases, is to risk losing the considerable investment made in work redesign to the "vanishing effects" phenomenon.

In sum, middle managers have a significant role to play in the design of changes in jobs, in their installation, and in supporting them over time. We have often observed middle managers assume a distant, "wait and see" stance toward work redesign activities undertaken by their subordinate managers or by organizational consultants. In our view, such a stance is decidedly ill-advised. For it is the behavior of middle managers, perhaps more than any other single factor, that ultimately determines whether work redesign turns out to be a success or yet another "good idea that doesn't work in the real world."

FOR ADDITIONAL READING

Ford, R.N. *Motivation through the work itself.* New York: American Management Associations, 1969. A comprehensive report of the pioneering AT&T studies of job enrichment, which were carried out following the dictates of Herzberg's motivation-hygiene theory. Includes practical guides for creating enriching changes in jobs.

Walters, R.W., and Associates. *Job enrichment for results.* Reading, MA: Addison-Wesley, 1975. A how-to-do-it book written by a group of consultants well practiced in work redesign.

Hall, D.T. *Careers in organizations.* Santa Monica, CA: Goodyear, 1976; Schein, E.H. *Career dynamics.* Reading, MA: Addison-Wesley, 1978. Two recent, comprehensive books on organizational careers. Both discuss employee needs at various career stages as well as alternative career development strategies.

Lawler, E.E., III. Reward systems. In J.R. Hackman and J.L. Suttle (eds.), *Improving life at work.* Santa Monica, CA: Goodyear, 1977. An excellent discussion of how reward systems influence individual behavior and organizational productivity. Emphasizes the need for congruence between reward systems and other aspects of the organization, including how work is designed.

Alderfer, C.P. An organizational syndrome. *Administrative Science Quarterly,* 1967, *12,* 440-460. This study highlights the impact of work redesign on interpersonal relationships in organizations, especially relationships with superiors. It shows how "enriching" changes in jobs can sometimes result in a deterioration of superior-subordinate relationships and suggests some reasons for this phenomenon.

PART THREE
DESIGNING WORK FOR GROUPS

7
THE DESIGN OF WORK FOR GROUPS
AND GROUPS FOR WORK

In the previous section of the book we dealt exclusively with the design of work for individuals. We began in Chapter 4 with a theoretical framework that specifies the properties of "motivating" individual jobs and the kinds of people who are likely to prosper on those jobs. Then, in Chapters 5 and 6, we showed how that framework can be used to diagnose the motivational structure of existing jobs and to guide redesign activities intended to enrich those jobs. We ended the section by suggesting that certain managerial practices may have to be revised after work has been redesigned, to support employees in their new work behaviors and to ensure the persistence of those behaviors over time.

We turn now to a different approach to the design of work, one that involves using groups rather than individuals to perform tasks. As noted in Chapter 3, this approach has its roots in systems thinking about organizations, and it requires us to worry not only about organizational tasks and the people who perform them but also about the design of groups as performing units. So we will discuss here both the design of work for groups and the design of groups for work.

USING GROUPS TO DO WORK

Some tasks cannot be done except by a group. How, for example, could an individual build a complete tractor? The weight and complexity of the assembly requires many hands and muscles. Or how could an individual integrate economic, diplomatic, defense, and domestic considerations in reaching an optimal decision about the sale of arms to a particular country? Surely such a decision is better made by a group comprising individuals who are expert in the several relevant specialties than by a single person who knows only a little about all of them. Other kinds of tasks seem to demand individual performance. A group cannot take slides using a photographing microscope; the technology requires a single pair of eyes and a single finger on the shutter release. Nor can a group conduct a symphony orchestra.

Yet there are many tasks in organizations that could reasonably be performed either by individuals or by an interacting team, and it often is unclear which option would be better. In practice, unimportant or routine tasks usually wind up being designed for and assigned to individuals. We tend to think of organizations as being made up of individuals, not groups, and somehow it seems both easier and more appropriate to design jobs to be carried out by individual employees. Besides, people invariably talk about "my job" rather than "our job" when asked to describe their work.

However, the situation is quite different when a piece of work is viewed as especially important to the organization, or when it involves dealing with great complexity or with emotionally tense issues. In such circumstances we seem invariably to form a committee or task force to do the work, in effect, creating a group task.

Why? There are several reasons. One stems from the fact that people who are charged with making tough decisions or who are responsible for ensuring that a piece of critical work gets done well often experience a good deal of personal stress. To deal with this stress, they seek the social and emotional support that a group can provide. It is far easier to acknowledge that "we failed" (and to rationalize why in a group) than it is to live with the cold fact that "I failed." Groups sometimes are formed by managers specifically to protect themselves against the possibility of personal failure and embarrassment.

Moreover, for decision-making tasks, there is general agreement that people more readily *accept* decisions in which they have participated, which prompts managers to form committees as a device for carrying out planning and decision-making activities (Vroom and Yetton, 1973). Finally many people believe that groups perform tasks better than do individuals. More human resources are available for work on the task, and as a result the group may get the job done both quicker and better. Especially widespread is the notion that groups do higher-quality work because of the tendency for group members to check each other's work, and therefore to identify and correct errors as the task is being performed.

Are such assumptions justified? Is it really better to have complex and important work done by groups rather than individuals? The evidence is unclear and sometimes conflicting. It is true that group members sometimes seem to combine their inputs synergistically and come up with a product that is far better than what would have been obtained if an individual had done the work alone—or even if the inputs of individuals had been obtained independently and combined *post hoc* into the best possible group product.

Yet it also is true that groups can perform incredibly poorly, sometimes worse than what would have been accomplished by a randomly selected individual member working alone. The experience of being on committees, for example, is rarely described in glowing terms. Instead, people are frequently heard to report, "What a waste of time. I could have done it better by myself in half the time." Also well documented is the tendency of individuals with different points of view to get into unproductive and destructive conflict in group settings. And the "groupthink" phenomenon described by Janis (1972) shows how even highly cohesive groups of very talented individuals can generate plans or decisions that are wholly inappropriate for the task at hand.

Overall, research findings about task-oriented groups are as hard to systematize as are people's actual experiences in groups (for reviews, see Davis, 1969; Shaw, 1976). If forced to generalize, we would conclude that groups perform many (but not all) tasks somewhat better than individuals, but at a cost in efficiency as measured by productivity per person-hour. However, a far more accurate generalization would be that there is great *variation* in how groups perform, that their effectiveness ranges from awful to wonderful and includes all points in between.

For this reason, the only reasonable answer to the oft-asked question, "Which is better, individuals or groups?" is "It depends." It depends on whether the group and its task are *well designed*. It depends on whether or not it is *feasible* to create well-designed work groups, given the nature of the work to be done and the organization where it will be done. And it depends on whether the group, once formed, is appropriately *managed and supported.* Only after we have achieved a good understanding of these three issues will it make sense to ask whether a group or an individual design for work is indicated in given organizational circumstances.

We begin this chapter by clarifying the kinds of groups we will be discussing. We then propose a conceptual model that specifies how groups and their tasks should be designed for optimum performance effectiveness. The chapter concludes with a review of circumstances when it is and is not feasible to create self-managing work groups. Then, in the next chapter, we explore what is required to support and manage groups at work. These prescriptions turn out to differ substantially from those set forth earlier for the support of *individuals* who hold enriched jobs (see Chapter 6). Finally, at the start of Chapter 9, we return to the individual versus group question. Based on our discussion of work redesign for individuals and for groups in Parts Two and Three of the book, we offer in that chapter some specific guidance about when it is advisable to design enriched jobs for individual employees and when the creation of self-managing work teams is preferable.

Self-Managing Work Groups: A Definition

There are many kinds of work groups in organizations. Probably most common are what are called "coacting" groups. People in coacting groups may report to the same supervisor and work close to one another, but they have individually defined tasks. Even if group members meet together periodically to discuss how the work is going, or occasionally help one another out, it is still a coacting group.

We will *not* be dealing here with coacting groups. Workers' tasks in such groups may or may not be well designed motivationally, and management may or may not give appropriate attention to the social context in which individuals do their work. But in either case the work does not belong to the group as a whole, and groups are not treated as the basic performing units of the organization. Individuals are.

What we *are* dealing with in this chapter can be termed "self-managing work groups" (Hackman, 1978). These are intact (if small) social systems whose members have the authority to handle internal processes as they see fit in order to generate a specific group product, service, or decision. Such groups have the following three attributes.[1]

---

1   These defining characteristics were developed collaboratively with Mary Dean Lee.

1. They are *real* groups. The group must be an intact and identifiable social system, even if small or temporary. At minimum, this requires that members have interdependent relations with one another, that they develop differentiated roles over time, and that the group be perceived as such both by members and nonmembers (Alderfer, 1977).

2. They are *work* groups. The group must have a defined piece of work to do that results in a product, service, or decision whose acceptability is at least potentially measurable. If a group does not generate productive output, then we do not consider it to be a work group.

3. They are *self-managing* groups. Group members must have the authority to manage their own task and interpersonal processes as they carry out their work. If control over who does what when is instead retained by management, then a group would be self-managing in name only.

Only groups that meet all three of these conditions will be dealt with here. This includes groups that sometimes are called "autonomous work groups" (Bucklow, 1972) or "self-regulating work groups" (Cummings, 1978), as well as temporary task forces set up to solve specific problems, decision-making committees, many kinds of management teams, and so on. Excluded are aggregations with loose boundaries whose members have casual rather than interdependent relations with one another; groups that do not perform productive work, such as families and social clubs; and groups that do not have the authority to decide how members will go about working together. In a phrase, we are talking about real groups whose members plan and labor together to generate real group products.

Self-Managing Work Groups at Butler Manufacturing: An Example[2]

A few years ago the management of Butler Manufacturing Company opened a new plant in Story City, Iowa, for the assembly of two-story-high grain driers that sell for about $25,000 each. Assembly of the grain driers is a fairly complicated operation, involving as many as 3000 different parts. Butler management decided that it would set up

---

2   This description is adapted with permission from the *World of Work Report*, November 1977, pp. 124-126, published by Work in America Institute, Inc., Scarsdale, New York.

the work so that teams of workers would have autonomous responsibility for constructing the driers, rather than use a traditional production line.

Members of the Butler work teams can work together pretty much as they wish in getting the driers assembled. Employees change their particular job assignments frequently within the teams, both as part of a formal rotational program and informally with the approval of other work-team members. Typically, operators in their first 18 months on the job master three of five basic tasks: assembly, fabricating, machining, painting, and shipping. In addition, they gain some experience with the other two types of work. At the end of 18 months, most employees are able to build an entire grain drier by themselves.

As part of their work, employee groups participate in the design and development of new products and tools. In some areas they purchase tools and materials on their own, obtaining supervisory approval only for purchases over $200.

Work is not restricted to the plant itself. Employees are also sent out on service calls throughout the region. According to plant manager Larry Hayes, "It teaches them the impact on a farmer's business if a machine isn't working. They also learn more about the technical aspects: how the product is used in the field. And they become more in tune with our customers, our bread and butter."

There are no quality inspectors at Butler, only two engineers, and very few foremen. As a result, there is a substantial team involvement in supervisory functions, including hiring and promotion. Peers help select new team members, and two supervisors were picked by other staff from among the employees. One supervisor described how his functions are different than those of traditional first-line managers: "It's not the traditional scheduling, pushing people, and taking names. My job is heavily counseling people and behavior modification, and that's more interesting. Meanwhile, every night the conference room is filled with people having their team meetings during working hours and carrying on joint supervision."

There are many kinds of meetings. Probably the most important are the weekly team meetings, in which production, quality, tooling, maintenance, and behavioral problems are considered. Leadership of the meetings rotates weekly. A monthly plant-wide meeting is held to discuss financial results and economic trends (productivity data are provided daily to each team). And a plant-wide advisory group of six production workers meets every two weeks with the plant manager, a meeting Mr. Hayes characterizes as the "pop-off valve." A summary of the questions and answers exchanged at this meeting is posted on the plant bulletin board.

With all the teamwork and meetings, it is not surprising that interpersonal skills are seen as critical to the successful operation of the plant. To facilitate development of these skills, a training program involving a 30-hour taped seminar has been developed. In addition, the plant has been searching for someone knowledgeable in sensitivity training and role playing who can teach interpersonal skills.

How is it all working? Most employees seem pleased. Sue Loder reports: "Basically, you are your own boss. We are presented with a challenge: how to get an order out. It is up to us how long it takes. We get satisfaction out of doing better than standard. The team finds out a few days later how we did on any job order. We try to beat the previous month's record."

Absenteeism and turnover data also suggest that employees are, for the most part, responding positively to the team concepts. Absenteeism averages only 1.2 percent, compared to a typical rate of 5 percent or higher for factory employment. Turnover is 10 to 12 percent on an annual basis, compared to an average of about 35 percent for U.S. production workers. Of those who have left, less than 4 percent have been terminated; the rest have resigned, mostly to attend school.[3]

Management also is pleased with the way the plant is operating. According to the plant manager. total plant expenses are considerably lower than they were projected to be when production began. Cost reductions are especially marked in overhead expenses such as tooling and supplies, and in indirect labor costs such as salaries for office, staff, and supervisory functions. In addition, Mr. Hayes likes the way equipment and materials are used by employees. "We have a proprietary feeling about our equipment," he says. "People make it work."

Profits also are excellent. Before the plant opened, Butler projected what its short-term profitability would be. It turned out that

---

3   In interpreting these data, it should be noted that the work force is young and that the plant is located in a rural community where people traditionally have been relatively hardworking and affluent.

profits have run 20 percent higher than projected for the first two years. "In effect," Mr. Hayes says, "we didn't lose what we expected in 1976, and this year we have made more than we expected." Mr. Hayes estimates that "we are probably 10 percent higher in profitability than comparable operations elsewhere which have been in business for 10 years or more.

"If we weren't," he adds, "the Story City plant might be in trouble. After all, there has to be a reason for doing something differently. Butler wants to see if this system, which people here call 'self-managed work teams,' truly affects productivity. We aren't in it for the fun and games; we have lots of competing companies in our marketplace."

A MODEL OF WORK GROUP EFFECTIVENESS[4]

What is it that distinguishes the drier assembly teams at Butler from less effective work groups? What factors are most responsible for their apparent success, and what may be mere window dressing? Before we can deal with such questions we need to agree on what is meant when we say a work group is "effective." Here are the three criteria of group effectiveness that will guide our discussion in the pages to follow.

1. The productive output of the work group meets or exceeds organizational standards of quantity and quality. If the work of the group is not acceptable to those who receive it and use it (grain driers that do not work, or too few of them) then the group cannot be considered effective.

2. The group experience serves more to satisfy than frustrate the personal needs of group members. Sometimes groups develop patterns of interpersonal behavior that are destructive to the well-being of group members. If most members find that their experiences in the group serve to frustrate their needs, and to block them from achieving personal goals, then it would be hard to argue that the group is a successful social unit.

---

4   Material in the remainder of this chapter is adapted from Hackman (1978).

3. The social process used in carrying out the work maintains or enhances the capability of members to work together on subsequent team tasks. Some groups operate in ways that destroy the integrity of the group itself, that is, the group "burns itself up" in the process of performing the task. Even if the product of such a group is acceptable, we would not define as successful a group that generates so much divisiveness and conflict among members that they are unwilling or unable to work together on future occasions.

These criteria are, we believe, modest. They do not demand extraordinary accomplishment or exemplary social processes from group members. Yet neither are they easy to achieve. Just how would one proceed to design a work group that "passes" these three criteria of effectiveness?

It would be lovely if there were a simple and straightforward answer to that question, but unfortunately there is not. It is necessary, therefore, to work backwards from the criteria to understand what group conditions are most closely associated with effectiveness, and then to determine how groups can be set up to satisfy those conditions. In effect, we must build a *model* that specifies what is required for self-managing work groups to be effective.

Intermediate Criteria of Effectiveness

The first step in building the model is illustrated in Fig. 7.1. There we specify three "intermediate" criteria of team effectiveness. While not themselves final indicators of effectiveness, these criteria do relate closely to the ultimate success or failure of a work group. They are: (1) the level of *effort* that group members bring to bear on the task, (2) the amount of *knowledge and skill* applied by group members to task work, and (3) the appropriateness of the *task performance strategies* used by the group in doing its work.

If by some magic we could set all three of these intermediate criteria at an appropriate level, we would be able to help almost any group, working on virtually any task, become effective. We could, for example, ensure that members work hard enough to get the task completed, correctly and on time. We could tinker with the amount of talent in the group, including the mix of skills held by different group members, to make sure that there is ample talent available to meet the demands of the task. We could adjust the performance

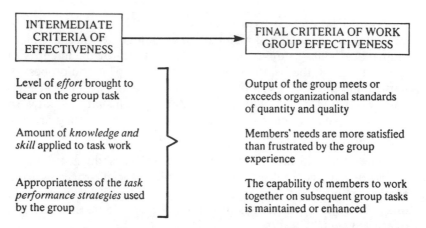

Fig. 7.1 The intermediate criteria of work group effectiveness.

strategies used by the group in its work, the ways members go about working together on the task, to make sure that these strategies are fully appropriate for the kind of work being done and consistent with the personal needs of group members.[5]

The problem, of course, is that such magic cannot be performed: it usually is not possible to manipulate directly the effort, knowledge and skill, and performance strategy that members use in performing a task. What can be done, however, is to create conditions when the work group is designed that favor the achievement of the intermediate criteria. We discuss how this might be accomplished next.

Key Design Features

While the standing of a self-managing work group on the three intermediate criteria is affected by many factors, three features of the basic design of the group warrant special attention. They are: (1) the

---

5   For certain kinds of work, one or two of the intermediate criteria may be particularly salient in determining group effectiveness, and the other(s) less salient. As will be seen later in this chapter, the *work technology* plays an important role in affecting the salience of the intermediate criteria and therefore which aspects of the group design are most critical to effectiveness. In the pages to follow, we will assume that all three intermediate criteria are salient, which is usually the case when complex tasks are assigned to work teams in organizational settings.

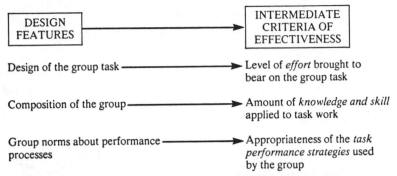

Fig. 7.2 Relationship between the design features and the intermediate criteria.

design of the group task, (2) the composition of the group, and (3) group norms about performance processes. As is shown in Fig. 7.2, each of these design features is especially closely related to one of the three intermediate criteria.

Design of the Group Task.   The motivational structure of the group task affects the amount of effort group members put into their work.[6] Although systematic research on the motivating properties of group tasks is scarce, we can obtain some guidance by examining the attributes of motivating *individual* tasks (see Chapter 4) and translating those properties to the group level. Following this logic, we would expect group members to experience high motivation in their work (and therefore to exert high effort) when the following conditions are met:

1. The group task requires the use of many different skills for successful completion (skill variety).

2. The group task is a whole and meaningful piece of work (task identity).

---

6   It should be noted that member effort also is affected by relationships among members and by aspects of the organizational context (such as the reward system, performance objectives, supervisory expectations, and so on). The present focus is on the *design* of the work group; the roles of interpersonal and contextual factors are addressed in the next chapter.

3. The outcomes of the group's work on the task "make a difference" to other people either inside or outside the organization (task significance).

4. The group task provides substantial latitude for members to decide together how they will carry out the work, including the methods to be used, the assignment of priorities to various subtasks, the pace of the work, and so on (autonomy).[7]

5. The group as a whole receives trustworthy information, preferably from doing the work itself, about the adequacy of group performance (feedback).

To generate ideas for creating a group task high on these properties, one can use the same "implementing principles" discussed in Chapter 6 for enriching individual jobs: combining subtasks into a larger whole, forming natural work units, establishing client relationships, vertically loading the job, and opening feedback channels. However, it is important to make sure that the focus remains on the overall task of the *group,* not on the tasks of individual group members, when these principles are applied.

Similarly, it is essential that members of the group clearly understand that it is a group task that is being performed. Confusion on this point can develop, since only rarely will the task be done in concert by group members. Instead, various individuals typically assume responsibility for different subtasks, and members coordinate with one another to complete the entire piece of work. All members must understand, therefore, that how the subtasks are divided up, how they are assigned to members, and how member activities are coordinated is a *group* decision.

If a group task is well designed according to the criteria set forth above, then members are likely to agree that the work is meaningful; they will understand that they collectively (not individually) are

---

7   Earlier in this chapter we pointed out that a group cannot be considered "self-managing" unless management has given members substantial authority for handling their own affairs. That was definitional. But having formal authority for internal group processes is only the prerequisite for creating high motivation in work groups. The level of autonomy built into the task itself determines the degree to which members will be able to *use* that authority to generate products that they "own" and for which they feel responsible.

responsible for the results of the work; and they will agree that the group as a whole is the proper recipient of feedback about performance effectiveness.

The Butler grain drier teams are a good case in point. Assembling these large devices is a complex and challenging undertaking, and the motivational attributes listed above are all present. Many different skills are required to assemble the drier; the group has responsibility for the whole task; the work is significant, in that how well a drier works is critical to the business of the farmer customers; the group has substantial autonomy for determining who does what, when, and how in carrying out the assembly; and feedback about quantity and quality of performance is either generated directly by group members (through their own inspection of completed driers) or provided to the group by clients (farmers who find that their driers do not work as they are supposed to).

Clearly this design would be expected to foster high motivation among group members and to provide them with built-in incentives for high effort to produce good grain driers. And reports from Butler confirm these expectations. Yet focusing on the design of the group task to create conditions for high work motivation does run counter to traditional wisdom that the effort expended by work teams derives mainly from the personalities of group members or from the norms of the group itself. We frequently hear managers report that ". . . everybody in the fabrication team is just lazy," or that " . . . we've got a bunch of real hard workers in the shipping group," or that there is an "antiproductivity norm" in some other group.

While it is true that individuals differ in energy level and in how hard they typically work on the job, there is not a great deal that anyone can do about people's personalities. And while norms clearly do develop in many groups that encourage especially high or low member effort, any attempts to *directly* alter group norms to improve member effort are probably doomed to failure. The reason is that group norms do not develop by chance. Instead, they are formed and shaped as devices *for dealing with particular problems or opportunities that confront the group.* And one common impetus for the development of norms about effort is the nature of the work the group is doing, that is, the design of the group task.

Consider, for example, a group task that is very low in motivating potential. Members find work on the task boring, frustrating, and generally unpleasant. As they share with one another their private reactions to the work, eventually they may develop an informal agreement that the best way to minimize their shared negative feelings is simply not to work so hard. When members begin to enforce such an agreement, they have developed a group norm that restricts work effort. Any attempt to alter that norm that does not also deal with the *reason* the norm developed probably will be futile and may even backfire.

On the other hand, if a group task is high in motivating potential, such that members find the work exciting, fulfilling, or otherwise rewarding, these experiences also are likely to be shared among group members, and a norm encouraging high effort on the task is likely to emerge. The implication, then, is that altering the design of the group task may be a better way to affect the effort expended by group members than would be direct attacks on productivity norms themselves. To do the latter, in many cases, would be to address the outcropping of the problem rather than the problem itself.[8]

Composition of the Group.   How a group is composed—that is, who is in the group—directly affects the amount of knowledge and skill that can be applied to work on the group task. Four aspects of group composition have particularly strong influences on the amount of talent a group is actually able to use in its task work.

1. *The group should include members who have high levels of task-relevant expertise.*   It is obvious that far and away the most efficient means of increasing the complement of knowledge and skill available for work on a group task is simply to put very talented people in the

---

8   It should be emphasized, however, that high motivation in response to a well-designed task will come about for groups, just as for individuals, *only* if the group is composed of people who collectively have sufficient knowledge and skill to complete the task successfully. If not, the same kind of frustration and withdrawal observed for individuals with insufficient task-relevant skills will be observed for a group. A basketball team is a good case in point: by all standards the task of a basketball team is well designed (that is, it is high on four of the five motivating task characteristics: skill variety, task identity, autonomy, and feedback). And if a team is skilled enough to be competitive with its opponents on the court and to play *together* competently, then motivation invariably is high. But if a team loses almost all of its games because of a lack of skill, then psychological (and sometimes behavioral) withdrawal of team members is a common outcome.

group. As noted in Chapter 2, relatively sophisticated procedures currently are available for assessing the skill requirements of tasks and for measuring the capabilities of people to meet those requirements. Such procedures should be used in staffing work groups just as they are for selecting and placing people on individual jobs.

2. *The group should be large enough to do the work—but not much larger.* If a task requires three pairs of hands for successful completion, then obviously there should be at least three people in the group. Sometimes groups are understaffed, and those responsible for the design of work groups should be alert to this risk.

Far more dangerous, however, is the risk of overstaffing a work group. Indeed, adding additional members to a group sometimes can even decrease the productivity of the group. The reason is illustrated in Fig. 7.3.

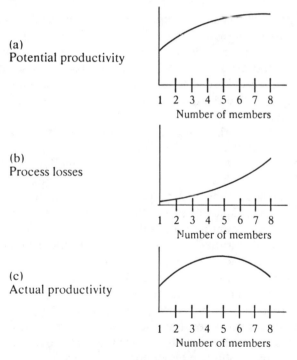

(a)
Potential productivity

1 2 3 4 5 6 7 8
Number of members

(b)
Process losses

1 2 3 4 5 6 7 8
Number of members

(c)
Actual productivity

1 2 3 4 5 6 7 8
Number of members

Fig. 7.3 Illustrative curves showing the relationship between group size and (a) potential productivity, (b) process losses, and (c) actual group productivity. (From Steiner, 1972, p. 96)

Look first at part (a) of the figure. The potential productivity of a group (that is, what the group could produce if member resources were used optimally) increases as size increases. The increase, however, is at a *decreasing rate*. That is, the unique additional contribution made by each new member is less and less. Adding a third person to a dyad may add substantial new resources for task work; but adding one more person to a twenty-person group is unlikely to contribute much to the resource base of the group (Steiner, 1972).

However, groups never perform at their level of potential productivity because of what Steiner calls "process losses." These include motivational problems, difficulties in coordinating member activities, and the inevitable inefficiencies and errors that develop when people attempt to work together. Process losses also increase as size increases—but this time at an *increasing rate,* as shown in part (b) of Fig. 7.3.

The actual productivity of a group, then, is its potential productivity minus its process losses. And, as illustrated in part (c) of the figure, actual productivity can turn downward when a group becomes too large, because the negative consequences of process losses outstrip the resource gains achieved by adding new members. In all, the curves in Fig. 7.3 provide a relatively convincing case for being wary of large work teams.

Nevertheless, large work groups (and especially decision-making committees) are widely used in organizations. The reasons, we believe, have less to do with considerations of group effectiveness than with emotional issues (such as using large numbers to share responsibility and spread accountability) or political considerations (like ensuring that all relevant specialties and functions are represented in the group so they will accept its product). So, in many cases, representatives of various constituencies are appointed to the group one-by-one or even two-by-two, creating a large group, a safe group, a politically "correct" group—and a group that may find itself incapable of generating even a satisfactory outcome, let alone one that shows signs of creativity. In our view, it usually is better to make groups and committees no larger than they absolutely must be to get the task accomplished, and to use alternative means for dealing with concerns about accountability and acceptance.

3. *Group members should have at least a moderate level of interpersonal skill in addition to their task-relevant skills.* As Argyris

(1969) and others have shown, most individuals in organizations are not highly competent in managing complex and anxiety-arousing interpersonal situations. Yet if the group task is challenging and requires high member interdependence, then at least moderate interpersonal skills are needed simply to bring the *task* skills of members effectively to bear on the work of the group. This requirement becomes especially salient when the group is demographically diverse (composed of people who differ in age, gender, race and so on) and when a work group consists of representatives of *other* organizational groups (such as functional departments) who may have a conflicting or competitive relationship with one another.

4. *The group should be composed to balance between homogeneity and heterogeneity of membership.*   On the one hand, if the members are too much alike, some of the special advantages of having a team are lost, including the special expertise and perspectives that different individuals can bring to the task and the chance for people in the group to learn new skills from their co-workers. Yet excessive heterogeneity also can impair group effectiveness, because insufficient "common ground" among members makes communication difficult and provides for less-than-needed interchangeability among members.

Even when the heterogeneity of member skills is at about the right level problems can develop, particularly around the reluctance of members to share their knowledge and skill with one another. Individuals in a work group often have a vested interest in keeping to themselves special expertise they have developed, because their distinctiveness and status at work is based on that expertise. Only if the task of the group is highly motivating and involving are such individuals likely to be willing to sacrifice their "special" status in the interest of the group as a whole.

Composing a self-managing work group so that it meets the four criteria specified above is a complex undertaking. Standard job analysis and selection procedures can be used to ensure that the task-relevant knowledge and skill held by group members is sufficient for competent group performance. And a hard-nosed analysis of how many members are *actually* required to perform the task can reduce the risk that a group too large for good performance will be formed.

It is, however, a much more uncertain business to compose work groups that have the right "mix" of member skills and perspectives, and to ensure that members have a sufficient level of interpersonal skill. How should these issues be handled when work groups are formed, given that there are no off-the-shelf compositional rules for dealing with them?

For one thing, members of work groups should be selected with great care, giving explicit attention to the interpersonal skills as well as the task competence of prospective members. This was done when employees were selected for the new pet food plant of General Foods, where the entire plant was designed around the concept of work teams (Walton, 1972). Fewer than 10 percent of the applicants for work at Topeka were chosen, after an intensive selection process that included five separate screening interviews and extensive psychological testing. The Topeka experiment has been criticized for this process on the grounds that it "stacked the deck" in favor of success (Fein, 1974), but we would argue that the Topeka managers were doing exactly what they should have done to compose the work teams well.

It also is important to think explicitly about the homogeneity-heterogeneity trade-off when work groups are formed. This was done by the managers who designed the grain drier assembly teams at Butler Manufacturing. Before joining their teams, members were trained to mastery on three of the five basic jobs involved in assembling grain driers. Teams were then composed of people who had received different patterns of initial skill training. This provided some commonality of skills within the group (there was always more than one person competent to do each subtask, increasing the group's flexibility in assigning people to work as circumstances changed). At the same time, a moderate level of interteam heterogeneity was established, since no one was initially competent to perform all assembly tasks. This heterogeneity of skill helped encourage members to share expertise with others who had experienced different initial training. Moreover, Butler management developed plans for training activities specifically oriented toward interpersonal skills for both employees and managers. It was hoped that this training would improve group members' skills in working together effectively and increase their competence in managing communications between groups and across hierarchical levels in the organization.

Both the Topeka and the Butler work teams were developed when new plants were built. The difficulties of composing work teams increase when group members must be selected from existing employees who already work on their own, individual jobs. This would be the case, for example, when coacting groups are "converted" into self-managing teams in an ongoing organization. Some such individuals may be unsuited for work in teams, and if the selection rule is simply to "take everyone who is working here now" then it may be exceedingly difficult to compose work groups whose members have an appropriate level and mix of task and interpersonal skills.

Yet if well-composed teams *can* be created within existing organizational units, they can often assume increasing responsibility for the selection and training of members who subsequently join the group. When someone departs, for example, the team might be given responsibility for interviewing possible replacements. And once a replacement is chosen, members could have charge of that person's training and socialization. In many instances, the result will be an improvement in selection decisions since group members often are more knowledgeable than external managers about the special skills that are needed for the work and about the kind of person who is most likely to fit well with other members.

Moreover, group members should experience heightened responsibility for developing the persons that they (not management) chose to join the group. And perhaps most important is the fact that the group would be reaffirmed as a truly self-managing organizational unit. There is little that is more important to the life of a group than decision making about who becomes and remains a member. Being given responsibility for those decisions is a sign of trust from management that is sure to have great significance to group members.

Group Norms about Performance Processes.   As shown in Fig. 7.2, the norms of a group can affect the appropriateness of the performance strategies that are used by a work group in carrying out its task. By performance strategies we mean the choices members make about how they will go about performing a given group task. For example, a group might decide to focus its energy on checking and rechecking for errors, in the interest of a high-quality product. Or members might choose to free associate about ideas for proceeding with work on a new task before starting to perform it. Or the group might decide to divide itself into two subgroups, each of which would do part of the overall task.

All of the above are choices about performance strategy, and those choices can be very important in determining how well a group actually performs. If, for example, successful completion of a certain task requires close coordination among members, with the contributions of each member made in a specific order at a specific time, then a group that has developed an explicit strategy for queuing and coordinating members inputs will probably perform better than a group that proceeds with the task using *ad hoc* or laissez-faire procedures. What specific strategy will work best for a given group task, of course, depends heavily on the particular requirements of that task.

Performance strategies generally are under the control of group norms. Members reach agreement early in their time together about how they will proceed with work on the task. Indeed, for familiar tasks members may not need to talk at all about their strategy, since all are familiar with "standard" procedures for doing the work. A group of senior managers composed to decide who will be selected for a lower-level management position, for example, would be unlikely to talk much about performance processes, simply because all members would have worked in similar groups with similar tasks many times before.

Once a strategy is agreed upon, whether explicitly or implicitly, then members routinely behave according to that strategy and enforce adherence to it. The way the group is working, or what it is attempting to achieve, may never again be addressed by members (Hackman and Morris, 1975). And individuals who deviate from group expectations about how the work is to be done are likely to be brought quickly back into line by fellow members.

The advantage to a group in having clear norms about performance strategies is that the need to manage and coordinate group member behavior on a continuous basis is minimized: everyone knows how things are to be done, and everyone does them in that way with little fuss and bother. More time therefore becomes available to the group for actual productive work.

The risk, of course, is that the performance strategies being enforced may not be terribly appropriate for the group task. Worse, members may be so intent on executing them that no one notices that they are flawed. This is particularly a problem when task requirements or constraints *change* after questions of strategy have been settled. If, for example, the "market" for a group's product were to gradually change from a seller's market to a buyer's market, the group might proceed far too long using its traditional strategy and discover that things had changed only when submerged in products that no one wanted.

The challenge in designing a work group, then, is to help members develop norms that reinforce the use of strategies that are uniquely appropriate to the group task, and that are amenable to change when task requirements or constraints change. How can this be done?

One approach is for an outside agent (such as a manager or consultant) to independently diagnose the requirements of the task and to suggest to the group a way of operating that is particularly appropriate for that task. Group members, presumably, will be grateful for the help provided and (assuming the strategy is in fact workable) adopt it as their own. The problem is that reliance on an "outsider" does not help group members learn to manage their own performance processes or increase their readiness to change how they operate when task or organizational circumstances change. Instead, the group remains dependent on outside guidance and direction.

An alternative approach, and one that is more consistent with group self-management, is to help group members learn how to develop and monitor their *own* norms about performance strategy. When a work group is being formed, the person responsible for designing the group might meet with group members to discuss explicitly how they want to develop their performance strategies. Merely talking through this issue may foster a climate in which strategic questions can be openly discussed—both when initial norms about strategy are developed and in the future when circumstances change. In effect, the manager or consultant would be helping members develop a *general* norm that encourages open and self-conscious discussion of *specific* norms about how group members work together on the task.

There is, of course, no guarantee that such discussions will actually result in particularly innovative or task-appropriate strategies being invented and adopted by the group. All that is being done is to *create conditions* such that questions of performance strategy, which typically are ignored or even suppressed in work groups, are dealt with openly and explicitly. Yet in many cases merely creating these conditions will be sufficient to prompt quantum improvements in the task-appropriateness of the strategies eventually used to guide members' work on the group task (see, for example, Hackman, Brousseau, and Weiss, 1976).

Summary. Three design features have been proposed as useful points of intervention for fostering the effectiveness of self-managing work groups. These design features are viewed as differentially potent in affecting three intermediate criteria of work effectiveness. Specifically:

1. The level of *effort* members bring to bear on the group task is affected primarily by the design of the group task.

2. The amount of *knowledge and skill* available for task work is affected primarily by the composition of the group.

3. The task-appropriateness of the *performance strategies* used by the group in carrying out its work is affected primarily by group norms about performance processes.

It also is true, of course, that each of the intermediate criteria can be affected by design features other than those specified above. Performance strategies, for example, are sometimes affected by cues in the group task or by the composition of the group (through the predispositions about strategy brought to the group by different members) as well as by group norms. Similar effects can be imagined for effort and for knowledge and skill. The point is simply that the most *potent* influences of the design features on the intermediate criteria—and therefore the most useful points of intervention—are those illustrated in Fig. 7.2 and explored in the preceding pages.

THE FEASIBILITY OF DESIGNING WORK FOR GROUPS

In discussing the prechange diagnosis of work systems in Chapter 5, we identified two major diagnostic tasks: first, to assess the need for work redesign; and second, to determine the feasibility of work redesign. That discussion focused primarily on the redesign of individual jobs. The same two diagnostic tasks are appropriate when self-managing work groups are contemplated.

The questions posed in Chapter 5 (see Table 5.2) continue to suffice for establishing the *need* for work redesign. But, as might be expected, questions of *feasibility* are different when one contemplates designing enriched work for groups rather than for individuals. Here, then, are two general questions that we believe to be critical in assessing the feasibility of creating self-managing work groups in organizations.

Question One: Would Self-Managing Work Groups Fit with the People and the Context?

Self-managing work groups are a social form that may or may not fit with the people who would compose them and with the organizational context in which they would function.

Consider first the needs of the group members. When employees have strong needs for *both* personal growth and significant social relationships, a team design would be appropriate. In Chapter 4 we suggested that people with high needs for growth tend to respond more favorably to enriched individual tasks than do people with low growth need strength. Following the same reasoning, it appears that a challenging *group* task (such as those created for self-managing work groups) would be especially attractive to people who are high both in growth and social needs because the group provides an opportunity to satisfy both sets of needs simultaneously as the work is being done.

It would, however, be risky to form work teams if most members were high in social need strength but *low* in growth need strength. In this case, members might use the group experience to obtain desired social satisfactions, but at the expense of work on the task. Similarly, if the prospective group members are high in growth need strength but low in social need strength, then designing enriched work for *individuals* would seem to be the more appropriate alternative. It would be difficult for team members to maintain the considerable energy required to develop an effective group in such circumstances because of individual apathy to working in social situations.

Regarding the organizational context, it should be recognized that self-managing work groups sometimes will clash with the overall climate and managerial style of the surrounding organization. Consider, for example, an organization with a highly "individualistic" climate: personal achievement and interpersonal competition for rewards are paramount, and "group work" is generally viewed by managers as collectivistic nonsense that protects the weak and holds back the strong. Would self-managing work groups prosper in such a setting? Hardly. Nor would they be appropriate in a highly mechanistic organization where organizational rules and procedures are clearly defined and vigorously enforced, with power and authority firmly centralized at the top.

Self-managing work teams are a powerful social invention. In a moderately supportive organizational context they can prompt significant alterations in how work gets done and how the organization itself is managed. But if the people or the managerial climate and style of the organization are clearly unsympathetic to a group design for work, the potential benefits of such groups are unlikely to be realized.

Question Two: How Hospitable are Organizational Systems to Needed Changes?

Sometimes it just isn't possible to form self-managing work groups. It is hard to imagine, for example, how a group of cab drivers, each of whom works alone in response to radioed instructions from a dispatcher, could be formed into a meaningful self-managing group. Or consider a dozen industrial employees strung out at fixed locations on a noisy assembly line, all tending their parts of the machinery. Could work teams be formed in such circumstances that would meet the minimal criteria for self-managing groups we set forth earlier in this chapter?[9] Almost certainly they could not be, and it would be unwise to "force" the creation of self-managing groups in settings such as these.

When organizational circumstances do permit the *formation* of self-managing work groups, the question then becomes whether they can be *well designed* as performing units. To answer this question, it is necessary first to determine which of the design features that we have been discussing in this chapter are most critical for group effectiveness and, second, to assess whether those features can be built into the design of the group.

---

9   Those criteria, it will be recalled, are (1) that the group be an intact and identifiable—if sometimes small or temporary—social system, (2) that the group be charged with generating an identifiable product whose acceptability is potentially measurable, and (3) that the group have the authority to determine how members will go about working together to accomplish their task.

Identifying Critical Design Features.   What features of the design of a self-managing work group are most critical to its effectiveness? This depends on which intermediate criteria are most important for the work being done (see Fig. 7.1). If effort is salient in determining effectiveness, then one would attend especially carefully to the design of the group task; if knowledge and skill are salient, then group composition would receive special attention; and if performance strategies are salient, the focus would be on group norms about performance processes.

Throughout this chapter, we have assumed that all three of the intermediate criteria are of equal importance in determining group effectiveness. In fact, the importance of the intermediate criteria varies from task to task. For some, such as the assembly of grain driers at Butler, all three of the intermediate criteria need to be high. Producing large quantities of high-quality driers requires great effort, a good deal of knowledge and skill, and a relatively sophisticated performance strategy that efficiently sequences and coordinates the work of members.

In other cases, only one or two of the intermediate criteria are salient in determining how effectively the group performs. Consider, for example, a group of park workers who have responsibility for maintaining a specified section of the park grounds. No complex knowledge or skill is required for satisfactory performance, as the work basically involves only picking up debris and raking. Neither is there much room for group decision making about performance strategy: how members go about the task is mostly determined by what needs to be done on a given day. In this case, how well the group performs will be affected mainly by how much effort members expend on their group task.[10]

---

10   The point can be stated more generally as an equation:

$$\text{Overall Group Effectiveness} = S_1 \begin{bmatrix} \text{Level of} \\ \text{effort} \end{bmatrix} + S_2 \begin{bmatrix} \text{Amount of} \\ \text{knowledge} \\ \text{and skill} \end{bmatrix} + S_3 \begin{bmatrix} \text{Appropriateness} \\ \text{of task perfor-} \\ \text{mance strategies} \end{bmatrix}$$

where S_1, S_2, and S_3 are the importances or the *saliences* of the three intermediate criteria in influencing group task effectiveness. How the work technology may affect the saliences of the intermediate criteria is explored in greater detail elsewhere (Hackman, 1978).

What, then, determines how salient each of the intermediate criteria is for a given group task? The nature of the *technology* (equipment, materials, and prescribed work procedures) appears to have a strong effect, as illustrated in our summary model in Fig. 7.4. Usually it is possible to determine which of the intermediate criteria are important in affecting group performance for a given technology simply by asking, "If greater effort (or different levels of knowledge and skill, or different performance strategies) were brought to bear on this task, would group performance effectiveness be likely to change markedly?" If the answer is "yes" for the intermediate criterion being considered, then it is salient in influencing group effectiveness.

Consider a surgical team carrying out a complex operation. Will team effectiveness (defined here as the well-being of a patient after surgery) be influenced by the knowledge and skill brought to bear on the task by team members? Yes, knowledge and skill are salient for this task. Will effort make a difference? Yes, but only moderately so, it's much more a matter of skill. How about strategy? Yes, but also only moderately—the procedures that can be used to carry out the operation are mostly prescribed by the technology, so the latitude the group has to alter its effectiveness by changing how it goes about the work is limited. Thus, we would conclude that all three intermediate criteria help determine surgical team effectiveness, but that knowledge and skill is of greatest salience.

Once the technology has been inspected to determine which of the intermediate criteria are most salient for the work to be done, attention turns to ways of designing the group to increase its standing on those criteria. We would now know which of the design features are most critical to effectiveness, but we would not yet know whether a good design could be achieved, given the constraints of organizational systems already in place.

Testing for Systemic Constraints. Is it possible to build into the design of a self-managing work group those features that are most critical to its effectiveness? If not, the risk is that the group will not be a substantial enough innovation to bring about real alterations in personal or organizational outcomes—the "small change" effect we discussed in Chapter 5.

Once again we direct attention to three key organizational systems: the technological system, the personnel system, and the control

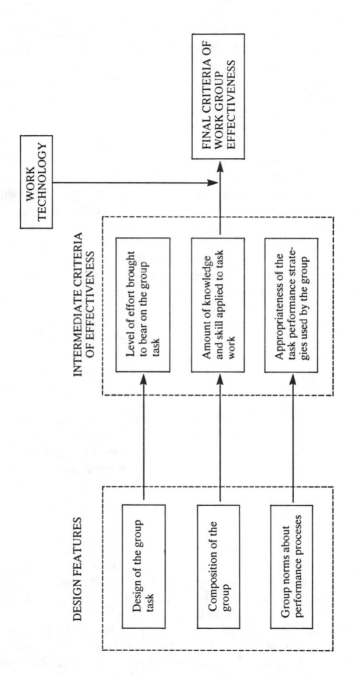

Fig. 7.4 A model of work group effectiveness.

system. The technological system may place constraints on the type of *group task* that can be designed. Would it be possible, given the existing technology, to construct a group task that is high in the motivating characteristics we have been discussing throughout this book (that is, skill variety, task identity, task significance, autonomy, and feedback)? If not, could alterations be made in the technology to allow such a task to be designed?

The personnel system may constrain the *composition of the group*. Given personnel policies and practices, can a task-appropriate "mix" of qualified people be brought together in a group and allowed to exchange specific duties and responsibilities at their own initiative? Could the group be given responsibility for the socialization and training of new members—and, eventually, even for their selection, promotion, and termination? If personnel policies seriously constrain flexibility in composing work groups, can those policies be loosened? Or are they immutable, perhaps because of legal requirements or binding provisions of a labor contract?

Finally, the control system may constrain *norms about performance processes*. To what extent are work processes preprogrammed and enforced by control system measures? How much "room" is there for group members to invent and implement performance strategies that they find uniquely appropriate for the work on the task? For example, could the group devise and implement its own procedures for handling quality control? Could members divide up the work in nontraditional ways? Or would such deviations throw the control system into disarray and control system managers into panic? Are there ways the control system itself could be modified to allow work groups greater latitude in managing their own performance processes?

Summary

We have discussed above two diagnostic questions whose answers bear on the feasibility of creating self-managing work groups in a given organizational setting. The first dealt with how well such groups would fit with the people and the organizational context, and the second with constraints that could make it difficult or impossible to design the work groups well.

The two questions provide a stringent test: only rarely will responses to them signal "full speed ahead" in creating work teams. More often, the answers will indicate that it *may* be feasible to create self-managing work groups in the organization, but that there are aspects of the work or the setting that are cause for caution and careful thought before they actually are put in place.

Occasionally, data gathered about the feasibility of work teams will be clear and negative. In such circumstances, we urge that the idea of creating such teams be abandoned. To "force" self-managing groups in a nonsupportive context, or for work that does not lend itself to a team design, is almost always a bad idea.

CONCLUSION

The conception of self-managing work groups presented in this chapter is both simpler and more complex than other treatments of work group behavior and effectiveness. It is simpler, in that it focuses on three key aspects of the design of the group—task, composition, and norms—each of which is assumed to control considerable variation in group effectiveness, and each of which is potentially open to planned change. It is more complex, in that the three design features are not posited as having consistent effects on performance across all circumstances. What "works" depends on the kind of work that is being done. And whether it makes sense to proceed with the design of work for groups depends jointly on the demands of the work itself, the characteristics of the people, and the properties of the broader organizational context.

Ours is not a model that specifies what "causes" good group performance in the traditional sense of cause-effect relations. Instead, we emphasize how one can *create conditions* that will support high team effectiveness. By creating a motivating group task, a well-composed group, and group norms favoring open discussion of performance strategies, we believe, the *chances* are increased that group members will invest themselves in their work and perform it relatively well. Moreover, we expect that under such conditions group members will find the group experience more satisfying than frustrating and that group processes will be relatively healthy and constructive.[11]

---

11 It must be re-emphasized here that our expectations are *only* expectations. The major tenets of our model are based on existing research findings about task-oriented groups, and we have found the model useful in analyzing self-managing work groups in organizations (and, in some cases, in predicting problems such groups are likely to encounter). But the model itself is new and has not yet been subjected to systematic research testing.

Yet there is still more to the story. So far we have dealt only with the up-front *design* of self-managing work groups. The long-term success of such groups also is affected by how they are supported and managed after they have been formed. In the next chapter, we examine the organizational supports that are needed by self-managing work groups and we suggest some things that managers and consultants can do to help such groups become as task effective and internally healthy as possible.

FOR ADDITIONAL READING

Leavitt, H.J. Suppose we took groups seriously . . . In E.L. Cass and F.G. Zimmer (eds.), *Man and work in society*. New York: Van Nostrand Reinhold, 1975. What if we decided to design and manage organizations using groups rather than individuals as the basic building blocks? Here is a provocative and optimistic view of what might happen.

Bucklow, M. A new role for the work group. Chapter 15 in L.E. Davis and J.C. Taylor (eds.), *Design of jobs*. Middlesex, England: Penguin, 1972. A lucid review of the history of groups in organizations, building toward the "new role" for work groups: the autonomous work group. A good background article.

Cummings, T.G. Self-regulating work groups: A socio-technical synthesis. *Academy of Management Review*, 1978, *3*, 625-634. An excellent current statement in the sociotechnical systems theory tradition about the design and management of work teams in organizations.

Trist, E.L., G.I. Susman, and G.R. Brown. An experiment in autonomous working in an American underground coal mine. *Human Relations*, 1977, *30*, 201-236. An informative report on the formation of self-managing work teams in a coal mine by the consultants who guided the project.

8
SUPPORTING AND MANAGING WORK GROUPS

Once it has been established that it is feasible to create self-managing work teams in an organization, then attention turns to the development of plans for actually installing the teams. Prominent among those plans should be ways the groups will be supported and managed as they go about their work.

When a self-managing group is formed for a specific, short-term task (such as a decision-making committee or temporary task force), then few organizational accommodations may be needed to provide adequate support for the group. Merely making sure that the group is appropriately designed for its work often will be sufficient for the group to get that work done with dispatch.

However, when self-managing work groups are established as a major and continuing innovation in how the work of an organizational unit is done, considerable revision of organizational policies and managerial practices may be required. Work teams usually represent a major deviation from standard organizational arrangements (in which work is designed and managed for individuals who perform on their own or in coacting groups). Organizational practices that have evolved over time to support work by individuals are not likely to be appropriate for self-managing teams, especially if the individual jobs were designed and managed according to the dictates of classical organizational theory and industrial engineering practice.

The implication, then, is that unless special steps are taken to support the work of self-managing teams on enriched tasks, the risk of the "vanishing effects" phenomenon discussed in Chapter 6 is quite high. It is hard to overemphasize the point. Even in new plant situations, where new organizational policies and practices have been instituted side by side with work teams, the beneficial effects of the innovative team designs often erode over time.

The Topeka pet-food plant of General Foods provides a good example. As noted in the last chapter, work teams were a key feature of the design of that plant when it opened in 1971, and those teams were set up skillfully and thoughtfully (Walton, 1972). Moreover, numerous organizational policies and managerial practices were instituted during the start-up phases of the plant specifically to provide support for the team concept. Yet as Walton (1977b) notes in a retrospective account of the experiment, the work groups experienced a good deal of turmoil and some periods of significant erosion during the first six years of plant operation. Many of the difficulties encountered appear to have been rooted in aspects of the organizational context—particularly compensation practices and management continuity.

In this chapter we review some factors that research and theory show to impinge on the effectiveness and persistence of self-managing work groups. These factors fall into two groups: (1) aspects of the *organizational context* in which the groups function and (2) patterns of *interpersonal processes* that emerge within the groups themselves. We will suggest some ways to adjust the organizational context and to consult with groups about their interpersonal processes that may help them become and remain effective as work teams. Toward the end of the chapter we present a summary model of work group effectiveness that integrates the material presented in this and the preceding chapter, and we conclude with a discussion of how managerial behavior must be changed when work teams are created.

CREATING A SUPPORTIVE ORGANIZATIONAL CONTEXT

There are numerous contextual factors that can and do affect work group performance, ranging from mundane items such as the ambience of the workplace to more significant features such as the relationships between a self-managing work group and other groups with which it must deal. A manager or consultant involved with work teams must continuously monitor the organizational context to identify special problems or opportunities that require remedial attention or invite developmental initiatives. The particular focus of these actions, of course, will vary from group to group and setting to setting.

There are, nevertheless, three general aspects of the organizational context that deserve special mention here because they have direct effects on the intermediate criteria of group effectiveness discussed in the previous chapter. These contextual factors can support and reinforce—or counteract and compromise—the impact of the design of the group itself. As shown in Fig. 8.1, the contextual factors are (1) rewards and performance objectives, (2) training and technical consultation, and (3) the clarity of task requirements and constraints.

Rewards and Objectives

As noted in Chapter 6, even well-conceived improvements in the jobs of individuals can be compromised if the reward system is incongruent with how the work is designed. The same is true for self-managing groups. Consider, for example, a work group that has been given autonomous responsibility for accomplishing a meaningful task and that receives regular and trustworthy feedback about how well the group as a whole is performing. What would happen if organizational rewards were provided to individual group members based on managerial perceptions of the relative contributions of those individuals to the group's performance? One possibility is that members would feel they have been set off against one another in a competition for the rewards. Another is that members would find their work on the group task impaired by the fear (or the fact) of pay inequities among members. Group norms that restrict member effort on the task could emerge as members struggle to deal with their competitive feelings and with worries about internal inequities in compensation. And, overall, the group would be unlikely to operate as effectively as it might in the absence of divisive compensation arrangements.

When work is designed for groups, it can be advantageous for rewards to be made contingent on the performance of the group as a whole—or, when that is not feasible, on the performance of even larger organizational units such as the department or section where

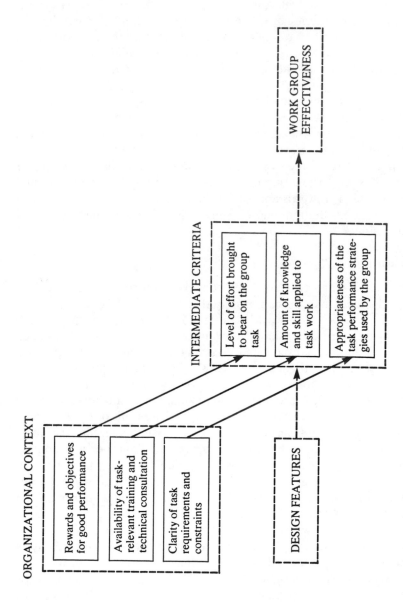

Fig. 8.1 How aspects of the orgniazational context affect the intermediate criteria.

the group is located (Lawler, 1977). A reward system that recognizes and reinforces excellent *group* performance, when well managed, can complement and amplify the motivational incentives that are built into the group task. The result, in many cases, will be an increase in the motivation of members to work hard and work *together* to attempt to obtain recognition and rewards for the group as a whole.[1]

The same line of reasoning applies to performance objectives that are set for self-managing work groups and to organizational control systems that are used to monitor the achievement of those objectives. That is, objectives should be set in collaboration with the group, and control systems should monitor how the group as a unit is doing in accomplishing its objectives. This not only ensures that control devices have the proper focus (the group as a whole, rather than individual members) but also generates some motivational benefits. A number of studies have shown that when a group accepts a moderately difficult performance objective and receives feedback about its progress toward achieving that objective, goal-directed effort is enhanced (Zander, 1971).

Moreover, there may be an important complementary relationship between how the work of a group is designed and group performance objectives. Consider first the situation for individuals at work. We saw in Chapter 4 that enriching jobs has a greater effect on jobholder satisfaction and on the *quality* of the work done than on simple quantity of production. On the other hand, specific and challenging performance objectives (when accepted by the performer) affect on-the-job effort and the *quantity* of the work accomplished (Locke, 1968). So when difficult, specific objectives are set for work on enriched individual tasks, both the quantity and the quality of performance may be improved (Umstot, Bell, and Mitchell, 1976; Umstot, 1977).

---

1   It should be recognized, however, that a group-based reward system does not necessarily solve the problem of pay equity among group members, especially for groups whose members were differentially skilled and differentially paid at the time the group was formed. While it may be possible for managers to help group members devise an equitable means for distributing incentive or bonus compensation among themselves in such cases, this is not an easy consultative task. An alternative is to pay group members on a straight salary basis, perhaps tieing raises to the acquisition of additional task-relevant skills.

Now let us translate this line of thinking from the individual to the group level. If a group has a well-designed task, and if it also sets specific and challenging performance objectives, the result could be well-satisfied group members, high-quality group performance, *and* large quantities of work produced. If, moreover, organizational rewards are provided to the group contingent on excellent performance, then the effort and the effectiveness of a well-designed work group could be further enhanced.

The ideas discussed above are extensions of observations and findings about individuals at work, and most of them await systematic research testing at the group level. For that reason, they should be viewed more as avenues to explore than as proven guidelines for action. We do, however, have considerable confidence in the main point made—namely, that the effort expended by members of a self-managing work group depends not only on how well the group and its task are designed, but also on group performance objectives and organizational rewards for achieving those objectives.

Training and Technical Consultation

We turn now to the second intermediate criterion of effectiveness: the knowledge and skill group members bring to bear on the task. As was pointed out in the last chapter, the capability of the group as a performing unit is most powerfully determined by how the group itself is composed. But a good composition is not enough in many cases. In addition, management must provide special training or technical consultation to group members as they proceed with their work, especially when the group task is complex and challenging.

Too often self-managing work groups are formed, given a large and complex task to perform, and then left to "work things out" on their own. If the knowledge and skill required for effective work on the task are not already available within the group, this can be both frustrating to group members and counterproductive. Worse, since well-designed groups are assured that members have both the authority and the responsibility to manage their own task performance processes, group members may feel that asking for help is a sign that they have failed or that they are not willing to live up to their part of the bargain that was made when the group was formed.

For this reason, it is important to make sure that outside help and expertise about performance-related matters are readily available to group members. In one sales organization, for example, customer service agents were formed into autonomous work groups and given full responsibility (among other things) for compiling and communicating information about the organization's rates and inventory. Such information previously had been the province of a separate department and the agents merely had to quote facts from mimeographed pages they were given. While group members were eager to have the responsibility of preparing their own data sheets (they previously had complained frequently about inconsistent and incomplete information they were provided), the hard fact of the matter was that members did not have the knowledge and expertise needed to perform that part of the group task. The result was frustration, impatience, and a feeling on the part of some managers that the work group idea was a bad one because "the rank-and-file people just can't handle the whole job." In this case, a few hours of training for the agents, had anyone thought of it, would have solved the problem in short order.

In practice, it often is necessary to create new and direct organizational links between work teams and those staff groups that have special information or expertise needed by the teams. Since such staff groups (such as an engineering service group in industry or the legal department in a regulated service organization) typically deal only with managers, it is often necessary for a line manager to help members of *both* the staff group and the work group learn that transactions between the two are not only appropriate but desirable. Similarly, it may be necessary to work with the organization's training department to gain acceptance of the work team as a legitimate "client" of training services.

Once both the work team and the technical or training staff become comfortable working together when consultation is needed, managers can gradually lessen their involvement. But *establishing* the legitimacy of training and technical consultation for the group and creating opportunities for such activities to take place is clearly a management responsibility. Even when group members feel that they badly need help in expanding the pool of task-relevant knowledge and skill available within the group, existing social and organizational constraints may inhibit them from seeking it on their own.

Task Requirements and Constraints

Finally, management must take pains to clarify both the objective requirements of the group task and any constraints that may limit what the group can do in carrying out its work. As suggested in the previous chapter, a well-designed work group has a general norm that encourages active, inventive exploration of strategic alternatives for performing the group task. Such a norm increases the chance that the group will come up with an innovative or especially task-effective way of proceeding.

However, the success a group has in inventing appropriate performance strategies also depends on how clearly members understand what are (and are not) firm task requirements and what the outer-limit constraints are within which the group must function. When, for example, an idea comes up about how group members might carry out their work, members are likely to discuss its feasibility to see if the idea would "work" in practice. That discussion invariably will involve members testing the idea against their perceptions of the requirements and constraints of the group task: "No, we couldn't do that, because we have to provide a continuous flow of output, and that approach would generate output in irregular batches," or "That's a really neat idea, because we would have two different people checking the paperwork, and we know that it is extremely important that our documentation be perfect."

If task requirements and constraints are obscure, then the group will be handicapped in developing uniquely appropriate performance strategies. Indeed, when clear information about these matters is not available to group members, they run the risk of developing and executing performance strategies that are nicely suited to *incorrect* perceptions (or assumptions) about what the task actually requires or what the constraints on group behavior actually are. Often these perceptions are excessively conservative (perceiving constraints that do not exist or task requirements that are merely "the way things have always been done" rather than the way things *must* be done). In such circumstances, team performance will be less than optimal. And member morale is likely to suffer because members feel more hemmed in than they actually are or because what *seem* to be quite task-appropriate performance strategies do not work as expected.

Unfortunately, objective task requirements and constraints are often obscure to group members, either because nobody has taken the trouble to analyze and specify them or because management has neglected to share information about them with the group. If open exploration of strategic alternatives by members of self-managing work groups is to result in real group performance benefits, management must make sure information about the objective properties of the task is provided to the group as clearly and as completely as possible.

FOSTERING HEALTHY INTERPERSONAL PROCESSES

In the preceding pages we have explored some factors that can help provide a supportive organizational context for self-managing work groups. Creating group-level rewards and challenging objectives, providing opportunities for technical consultation and training as needed by the group, and clarifying task requirements and constraints can improve work team effectiveness.

But how about the interpersonal behaviors that take place within the work group itself? Intermember relations in small groups often leave much to be desired. Sometimes members fall too readily into interpersonal competition and conflict, and provide little support and help to one another as they struggle to deal with difficult and anxiety-arousing issues. Other times groups become so oriented toward sharing warmth, support, and good feelings that the task itself is all but forgotten.

It would seem, therefore, that improving the quality of the interpersonal relationships that develop among group members could help them improve their effectiveness. And a number of approaches to group consultation are in fact based on this assumption (Argyris, 1962; Blake and Mouton, 1975). Such approaches often involve experiential sensitivity training and team building with intact groups, and they focus directly on relationships among members rather than on the interface between the group and its task. The goal is to help individual members gain the interpersonal skills required for task effectiveness and to help the group as a whole understand and improve its norms. Ideally, the group develops interpersonal skills and group norms that foster interpersonal openness about ideas and feelings, and that facilitate individual and group risk taking in the interest of better group performance.

In general, research evidence suggests that such interventions can be powerful in changing what transpires in the training groups themselves and in altering member beliefs and attitudes about appropriate behavior in groups. The problem is that such new lessons do not transfer readily from the training setting to "back home" work groups.

Nor do newly learned behaviors persist for long in the absence of ongoing support and reinforcement. Moreover, the actual *task effectiveness* of groups whose members have received interpersonal training is rarely enhanced (and is sometimes impaired). Apparently the link between the interpersonal competence of group members and the task effectiveness of the group as a whole is neither as direct nor as straightforward as one might wish (see, for example, reviews by Campbell and Dunnette, 1968 and by Hackman and Morris, 1975).

For this reason, one would be ill-advised to rely on group process interventions as the sole or primary means of facilitating the performance of self-managing work teams in organizations. An alternative and more focused approach is summarized in Fig. 8.2. As was the case for our discussion of the organizational context, we have selected for special attention three aspects of the interpersonal process that may be especially important in affecting the standing of a group on the three intermediate criteria of effectiveness.

For each of the three aspects of group process addressed, patterns of group interaction that impair effectiveness are referred to as "process losses," and those that enhance effectiveness are called "process gains."

Coordinating Efforts and Fostering Commitment

When effort is salient in determining group effectiveness it is critical for members to coordinate their activities in a way that minimizes the amount of effort that is "wasted." There always is some slippage in how well members coordinate their activities that prevents the group from achieving its potential maximum productivity. And, as noted in the previous chapter, the larger the group, the greater the loss, simply because members functioning together in a coordinated fashion becomes increasingly difficult as size increases.

Thus the manager or consultant should be especially watchful for process losses deriving from faulty coordination when a large group has a task for which effort is important to eventual group effectiveness. Often the views and advice of an "outsider" can be helpful to group members in finding ways to minimize wasted effort and improve intermember coordination so that the group achieves the greatest possible leverage on the contributions of its members.

The effort applied by group members to the task is also affected by how committed members are to the group, and therein lies the

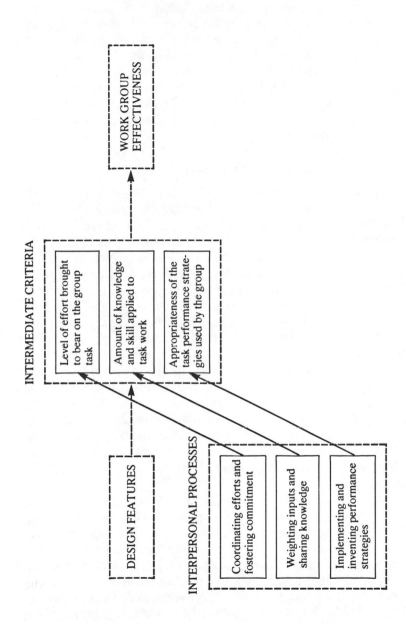

Fig. 8.2 How interpersonal processes affect the intermediate criteria.

potential for creating process gains. When, for example, members greatly value their membership in the group and find working collaboratively with other group members rewarding, the overall level of effort expended by group members working on the task can be considerably increased. Managers can sometimes foster such commitment by helping group members understand the importance of the group's work, or by encouraging the development of a positive group "identity" that is valued by members and consistent with their own needs and goals.

Weighting Inputs and Sharing Knowledge

Consider now tasks for which member knowledge and skills are important in affecting how well the group performs. Probably the greatest risk of process loss for such tasks has to do with the "weighting process" used by group members in combining their inputs to generate a final decision or solution. It is possible in research studies, when one knows relatively precisely the task-relevant knowledge of each group member, to predict how well the group would perform if member talents were combined optimally (Davis, 1969). These predictions often are reasonably accurate. But when they are in error, it almost always is because they overestimate actual group performance. That is, given the prior expertise of group members, groups actually perform less well than they "should" have performed.

Why does this happen? Often the problem is that the inputs of certain members are given extra credence for reasons that have little or nothing to do with their task-relevant knowledge or expertise. Such persons may have especially high status in the group, or they may be known to be powerful and have important "connections," or they may simply present their views to the group especially fluently and persuasively.

A manager or consultant sometimes can help group members improve how they assess and weigh one another's contributions to the work of the group. Members can be encouraged to take time out from their regular work to review how they are using the contributions that various individuals have to make. Or, occasionally, a direct intervention can help the group hear and consider the views of members whose contributions are being overlooked. The problem, of course, is that such consultation risks being seen as "meddling" by members of a self-managing work group, and rightly so. In general, therefore, about all that an outsider can do is to offer the group the opportunity to examine the issue—and to be ready to provide consultation if the invitation is accepted.

It also is possible for managers or consultants to help members of work teams learn better how to share with one another their own special task-relevant skills, and even to work together to gain knowledge or generate skills that previously did not exist within the group. Employees who are accustomed to working more or less on their own, turning to the supervisor (not other employees) when help or information is needed, tend to be neither practiced nor skilled at sharing task-relevant knowledge with one another or at using one another to learn new task skills. Thus, managerial assistance that helps members gain this capability can be very helpful when the group task requires substantial knowledge and skill for effective performance.

Implementing and Inventing Performance Strategies

Since members of self-managing work groups may not have much practice at developing and implementing performance strategies, it is often appropriate for a manager or consultant to help the group assess the task, and develop strategic alternatives that are particularly suited to it. Among the questions that might be posed for the group to consider are: What is the objective of our work on this task? What requirements and constraints are present in the task that limit our options in pursuing that objective? What special talents do we have within the group that can aid in our work, and what are our limitations? Given these objectives, opportunities, and limitations, what alternatives can we think of for how we might proceed with our work? Which of these is likely to be especially effective? How should we choose among them?

If the requirements and constraints of the task being performed are relatively clear, discussion of questions such as these should help a group formulate a way of proceeding with task work that fits well with the objective demands of the task itself. The role of the manager or consultant in such discussions is to pose the right questions and to help group members address them competently.

It also is appropriate at times for the manager or consultant to propose *specific* performance strategies that may help group members avoid process losses or realize potential process gains.

The kinds of process losses that are likely to occur for various types of tasks are, to some extent, predictable. If, for example, the task requires a great deal of close coordination, it is a safe bet that there will be slippage and miscues among group members. Or if long periods of sustained effort are required for certain subtasks, then drops in member motivation probably will be a problem. A knowledgeable manager or consultant can often anticipate the kinds of problems that are likely to develop for the task being performed and suggest performance strategies that will reduce the vulnerability of the group to them.

There are, for example, a number of standard or "off the shelf" performance strategies that sometimes can be used to minimize certain types of process losses. Indeed, standard parliamentary procedure is one such device that can be useful for social decision-making tasks. For tasks requiring group judgments, procedures such as the Nominal Group Technique (NGT) and the Delphi method can be helpful in combining member opinions with minimum distortion (Delbecq, Van de Ven, and Gustafson, 1975).

When NGT is used, for example, members first generate their individual ideas about the task (which has been carefully formulated and phrased beforehand), and then use a structured round-robin technique to record each idea for later consideration by the group. Each idea is then clarified so that all members understand it before evaluative discussion takes place. Actual decision making involves a structured and iterative voting procedure, which gradually narrows the number of ideas being considered and eventually leads to a group consensus.

The Delphi technique structures the group process to an even greater extent. Members make private estimates about the question that has been posed, and subsequently are provided with summaries of the views of the group as a whole. After studying this feedback members make a new set of estimates, and the process continues until an acceptable level of consensus is reached. There is no need for face-to-face interaction at all using Delphi: a "group decision" can be reached with each member communicating only with a central staff and only by mail. In effect, such devices minimize process losses by minimizing process itself.

There are also structured techniques designed specifically to increase the chance that process *gains* will emerge as members work together on the task—that is, to encourage a special "synergy" among members that can result in high group creativity.[2]

One popular example of such a technique is called "brainstorming" (Osborn, 1957). In brainstorming, a group follows three general rules: (1) ideas are expressed as they come to group members, no matter how silly they may seem, (2) members are encouraged to elaborate on one another's ideas and to use a preceding idea expressed by one member as a stimulus for a new idea by someone else, and (3) no ideas can be evaluated until all ideas have been stated. The intent is to separate the process of idea generation from the evaluation process, so that new ideas can emerge in a "storm" of free-thinking without the dampening effect of comments such as, "Yeah, but that wouldn't ever work . . ."

Research on the effects of brainstorming has yielded mixed results. On the one hand, there are numerous case reports of enhanced creativity under brainstorming rules. Moreover, some experimental research has shown that brainstorming instructions do prompt higher creativity, when brainstorming groups are compared to control groups in which no special instructions are given (e.g., Meadow, Parnes, and Reese, 1959). Yet there is reason to question whether gains in creativity obtained using brainstorming are attributable to special features of the group interaction process itself. Some studies have shown that "nominal" groups (in which individuals operate alone under brainstorming instructions with their ideas pooled later by the experimenter) show as much or more creativity than do "real" groups in which members work together interactively under brainstorming instructions (Dunnette, Campbell, and Jaastad, 1963).

While it is clear that group members often "feel more creative" when using special procedural strategies such as brainstorming, it remains an open question just how much of a process gain, if any, actually results from the use of such techniques. For this reason, it may often be better to help group members learn how to invent and test their *own* strategies for going about the task. As members

---

2   A book is available that deals exclusively with techniques for increasing group creativity, including brainstorming, synectics, creative problem solving techniques, and so on (Stein, 1975). For each technique, the author reviews instructions for its use, its theoretical basis, and the present state of evidence regarding its efficacy.

become practiced at assessing task requirements and developing strategic plans based on them, they may come up with ways for proceeding with their work that are considerably more effective (and better tuned to their own group and its work) than would be any of the "off the shelf" strategies that are available.

In sum, the role of managers or consultants in helping a group deal with questions of performance strategy is twofold. First they can assist the group in "reading" the task correctly and in developing or selecting strategies that minimize process losses. And second, they can help the group identify or invent strategies that foster "synergistic" effects in the interactions that take place among group members—thereby creating process gains.

For both activities it is important that the role of managers or consultants be one of helping rather than directing the group in locating, inventing, and adopting performance strategies. To impose strategies on a self-managing work group—even objectively task-appropriate strategies—is to risk compromising the autonomy of the group in managing its own internal processes, which can be a lethal blow to the group's integrity and long-term effectiveness.

Summary

Because there are process losses, and at least the potential for process gains, associated with each of the three intermediate criteria of effectiveness, consultation with members about group process matters can often contribute to group effectiveness. It is, however, important that such consultation be focused on aspects of the group process that are "alive" for the task the group is performing. An intervention that deals with nonsalient aspects of the group process may do more harm than good. It would be inappropriate, for example, to intervene with a program that helps members learn to share their special skills with one another (a fairly common type of team-building intervention) if effort, rather than knowledge and skill, were the only intermediate criterion of importance for the task of the group. In this case, the skill-oriented intervention might succeed in getting members intensely involved in juicy process issues, but steal away time and energy needed for getting the real work of the group accomplished.

A SUMMARY MODEL OF WORK GROUP EFFECTIVENESS

We have now fleshed out a full model that specifies the factors that are most critical to the effectiveness of self-managing work groups. It is summarized in Fig. 8.3. To the extent the model has validity (and it has not yet received systematic research testing), it suggests a five-step process for creating self-managing groups.

Step One: Assessing Feasibility.   As noted in Chapter 7, self-managing work groups should not be formed unless two feasibility tests can be met:

1. Would self-managing groups fit reasonably well with the needs of the people who would be in them and with the climate and managerial style of the organization in which they would function?

2. Are organizational systems reasonably hospitable to the changes that would need to be made to establish such groups? What constraints in the technological, personnel, or control systems might make it difficult to implement needed changes in the design of the group task, in the composition of the group itself, or in the norms of the group about performance processes? Can any such constraints be circumvented or changed?

If responses to either of these feasibility tests are negative, then it is doubtful that well-designed self-managing work teams can be created.

Step Two: Designing the Group.   The next step is to invent a good design for the group. Given the imperatives of the work technology, which of the three intermediate criteria of effectiveness—effort, knowledge and skill, performance strategies—are most salient, and how can the group be set up so it has the best possible chance of achieving them? Is the task well constructed from a motivational point of view? Is the group about the right size, and does it have the right mix of members? Do the norms of the group foster open and inventive formulation of task-appropriate performance strategies?

Step Three: Forming the Group.   When a self-managing work group is formed, it is not enough to merely bring the members together, give them their group task, and suggest that they get down to work.

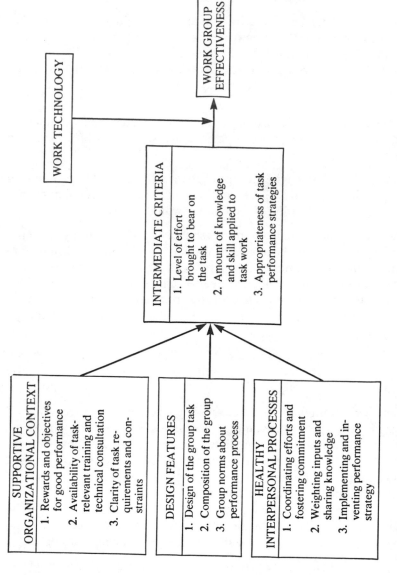

Fig. 8.3 The effectiveness of self-managing work groups: a summary model.

Instead, the group will need some time, and perhaps some outside assistance, to develop its identity and to assume responsibility for its internal processes. In effect, responsibility for the process and performance of the group must be "handed off" from management to group members themselves.

Over time, successful self-managing work groups will seek increasing responsibility for their own affairs. Eventually, members may become both competent and comfortable in monitoring and revising their behavioral norms, in proposing revisions in the group task (or redesigning the task on their own), and in managing issues of group size and composition. In effect, a mature self-managing work group will be involved in managing its own design, not just working within the design initially provided by management.

When a group is first formed, however, it may be necessary to help members get off to a good start by inviting them to participate in some "team-building" activities intended to establish the boundaries and identity of the group and to assist members in coming to grips with their shared authority for managing internal group processes. Then, as the group gains a sense of its identity and begins to develop its own ways of dealing with task and organizational issues, the manager or consultant can gradually withdraw from prominence in group activities.[3]

Step Four: Providing Organizational Supports.   Once the basic design of the group is satisfactory and plans have been laid for proceeding to implement that design, attention turns to the organizational context in which the group will work. Given the intermediate criteria that are salient, are organizational policies and practices likely to support rather than impede group effectiveness? Do organizational rewards and objectives encourage hard, effective work by group members? Is training and consultative assistance available, if needed, to help members hone their task-relevant skills and to aid them in

---

3   As is the case for most organizational innovations, group formation tends to be less difficult when a group is created from scratch, with new people coming together to begin work together on a new task. If group formation involves the redesign of an existing group rather than the creation of a new group, relatively more time and attention will have to be given to matters of interpersonal process when the changes are introduced.

obtaining information they need to perform the task? Are task requirements and constraints clear, so the group can devise performance strategies that are uniquely appropriate to its task?

Step Five: Fostering Good Interpersonal Processes: Finally, after dealing both with the basic design of the group and with the organizational context, attention turns to the interpersonal processes that emerge among group members. Do member relationships and patterns of interaction help or impair group effectiveness? If effort is important for group effectiveness, how are members coordinating their work on the task? Is commitment to the group and its work sufficiently high? If knowledge and skill are salient, how are the talents of different group members weighed and brought to bear on the task? Are the contributions of certain talented or knowledgeable members not getting the attention they deserve (and, perhaps, are the views of high status individuals being taken too seriously)? Are members sharing uniquely held knowledge and skills with one another, and, even better, are they working together to improve the overall level of talent of the group? If performance strategies are salient in determining group effectiveness, how well are members executing their chosen strategies? Do members disagree about how the group should proceed? Are the strategies in use fully appropriate to the task, or should the group be encouraged to reconsider how it is going about its work? Are there any "off the shelf" performance strategies that might usefully be brought to the attention of group members?

The order of the five steps summarized above is deliberate. Too often we have observed a manager or consultant attempt to "fix" a faulty work team by going to work directly on obvious problems that exist in members' interpersonal processes. And, too often, these problems turn out not to be readily fixable because they are only symptoms of more basic difficulties in the design of the group or in its environment. Process is an important thing, but it is not the only thing.

THE ROLE OF THE MANAGER

It should be clear from material in this chapter and the last that self-managing work groups must be provided with substantial authority for decision making about task and interpersonal matters if such groups are to be effective in the long term. Just as a managerial strategy of "pseudo-participation" in organizational decision making may be worse than no participation at all, so it is that work groups must be given *real* authority for managing matters internal to the group. Nothing will demoralize a self-managing work group quicker than a state of "pseudo-authority," in which members are allowed to manage their own affairs so long as things are going well, but authority is withdrawn by managers when problems develop or when there is a crisis that managers feel requires them to "take over."

Yet it must be emphasized that self-managing work groups will not have the capability to deal with all aspects of their work together from the moment the group comes into being. There are numerous challenging issues that members will need to learn how to handle before they are ready to take them on. Organizational managers must be ready both to help a group develop its capabilities to deal with these issues and to negotiate with members about when it is time for them to be given additional responsibilities.

Developmental Tasks for Self-Managing Work Groups

Three arenas in which managers can help work teams increase their readiness for additional responsibility have been identified by Walton and Schlesinger (1979). These arenas, which apply primarily to groups with a long expected life (rather than one-shot committees or task forces), are: handling social and interpersonal issues, managing technical and administrative matters, and analyzing economic trade-offs.

For social and interpersonal matters, for example, relatively undeveloped groups will have only basic capabilities in allocating tasks among members, in sharing work, and in enforcing norms to get the work of the group done. As the group increases in social sophistication, according to Walton and Schlesinger, members will be able to handle much more challenging and anxiety-arousing social problems, such as identifying and diagnosing interpersonal issues that arise in the group, balancing high group cohesion with freedom for member diversity, and developing the capability to allocate pay and other rewards differently within the group.

In the technical and administrative arena, newly formed groups will have only basic knowledge of operational and maintenance requirements. As the group develops, members will gradually gain the capability to diagnose complex technical and administrative problems and to develop solutions to those problems that take account of how the group fits into the broader workflow of the organization.

As a group increases in economic sophistication, members will move from a rudimentary understanding of performance objectives and their economic implications to development of the capability to make complex economic decisions involving trade-offs among competing objectives that have different economic consequences. At the highest level of economic sophistication, for example, a team would be able to evaluate the economic implications of proposals it generates for improvements in the work, including the investment required and the anticipated return on that investment (Walton and Schlesinger, 1979).

Groups do not move inexorably toward increasing sophistication in each of these three arenas as time passes and members gain experience working together. Instead, gains in sophistication are followed by retreats, and different groups in the same organizational unit may "plateau" at different stages in different arenas. Moreover, organizational arrangements that would be ideal for mature or fully developed groups are sure to be inappropriate for new work groups that are just beginning to learn how to operate as self-managing units.

The challenge for managers, then, is to help groups that have different capabilities and different styles of operating increase their sophistication in the three arenas identified above. The process will have more in common with shooing chickens across the barnyard than with planting regular rows of corn in a freshly plowed, rectangular field.

Complications for Managers

Few first-line managers are likely to have all of the skills required to help members of self-managing groups develop themselves into sophisticated performing units. Indeed, the knowledge and skills that characterize fully developed self-managing work groups probably exceed those held by most first-line managers at the time the groups are initially formed. How are managers to help a group learn to do things that they do not know how to do? Worse, when managers do succeed in helping groups assume high levels of responsibility in the social, technical, and economic arenas, they will probably have worked themselves out of a job in the process.

These complications suggest that the design (and evolution) of the role of the first-line manager is a considerable challenge when self-managing work groups are created, and one that must be attended to carefully by those who have responsibility for the change activities. Among the issues identified by Walton and Schlesinger (1979) as key to the design of appropriate supervisory roles in innovative work systems are the following.

1. *The recruitment, selection, training, and support of supervisors.* It takes some special skills to effectively nurture and manage work teams, and neither "veteran" supervisors of traditionally designed jobs nor fresh college graduates without supervisory experience are likely to be fully prepared for the supervisory tasks and challenges they will face. While care should be given to the recruitment and selection of supervisors, then, it is usually necessary to invest organizational resources in supervisory training to help those who are chosen develop and hone their skills at managing groups. The supervisor must learn, for example, how to exercise real authority in dealing with the group as a unit, and simultaneously to serve as a process consultant to it as the group struggles to gain better control of its own social and work behaviors. And supervisors must develop strategies for dealing with the inevitable (and desirable) rise of informal leadership within a work team without either abdicating their responsibility or getting into a leadership struggle with influential group members.

These and other supervisory skills are neither well practiced by most first-line managers, nor are they simple to learn. The organization would be well advised to help supervisors with such matters, both through direct instruction and by providing opportunities for supervisors of different work teams to compare notes and learn from one another. Indeed, it is often useful to form one or more informal "support groups" composed of work team supervisors. Such groups could be used for learning, as a setting for sharing feelings about the tensions in the supervisory role, and even as a vehicle for pressuring higher management to give greater attention to the needs and aspirations of the supervisors.

2. *The development of appropriate evaluation and reward systems for supervisors.* In traditionally designed work systems, supervisors are often held personally responsible for the productivity of their

subordinates. When work is done by self-managing groups, the group is made responsible for its own performance. Therefore, it would not be appropriate to measure and reward the performance of supervisors primarily in terms of the productivity of their work teams. Moreover, such a scheme would provide a great temptation for the supervisor to "get in there and straighten things out," which might indeed enhance short-term group productivity but at potentially great long-term cost to the integrity and self-management capabilities of the work team.

How, then, should supervisory performance be measured and rewarded? Walton and Schlesinger suggest that the appropriate criteria might emphasize the degree to which the supervisors succeed in fostering increased self-management capabilities on the part of the work teams for which they are responsible. Specifically:

> It is appropriate for superiors to work with a supervisor to establish timetables for his or her responsibilities as a developer of a work group, and it is also appropriate to establish benchmarks for determining to what level a group's capabilities have been developed. This strategic aspect of the supervisory role is clearly amenable to some form of goal setting, systematic assessment, and reward. It tends not to be treated this way. It should be (Walton and Schlesinger, 1979).[4]

3. *The development of plans to utilize freed-up supervisory capacity.* If in fact a first-line manager is successful in increasing the breadth and depth of a work team's capacity for self-management, a day will come when there is little left for the supervisor to do. How should this additional managerial capacity be utilized so that the organization will benefit from the increased skill and experience of the supervisors, and so that the supervisors themselves continue to be challenged and stretched? Given that there is insufficient "room" in the management hierarchy for everyone to be promoted, there are no easy answers to this question. Some organizations have increased the supervisor's span of control by adding responsibility for more work groups or by extending supervisory responsibilities across shifts.

---

4   Reprinted from "Do Supervisors Thrive in Participative Work Systems" by R.E. Walton and L.S. Schlesinger, *Organizational Dynamics*, Winter 1979, New York: AMACOM, a division of American Management Associations, p. 34. All rights reserved.

Others have attempted to "pull down" managerial responsibilities that were previously held by members of higher management. Still others have folded into the supervisory role responsibilities that previously belonged to various staff specialists in training, engineering or quality control departments. Each of these "solutions," obviously, serves only to transfer the problem from the supervisory role to other roles, or to delay the reckoning that ultimately must take place—namely, *what is to be done about the fact that the organization is leaner and in fact needs fewer managers than it did before the work was redesigned?* In a period of organizational growth or expansion, this problem can be handled; in a time of zero growth or retraction, the problem may defy resolution in a way that satisfies all groups who are affected by it.

Summary

The manager of a work team has a tough job. When work is designed for self-managing groups, many traditional managerial tasks and responsibilities cease to be appropriate. No longer, for example, do the managers have direct responsibility for the work behavior and productivity of individual employees. The group does. No longer are they initiating, structuring, and directing work processes. The group is.

The kinds of things managers *should* be doing when managing work teams include (1) monitoring the basic design of the group and the organizational context, making alterations as needed for effective group performance, and (2) consulting with the group so that it becomes increasingly capable of managing its own affairs in the social, technical, and economic arenas.

The problem with group and contextual redesign is that most first- and second-line managers simply do not have the power that is needed to adjust how a group is set up or to make substantial changes in the group's work environment (revising compensation arrangements, task design, group compensation, and so on). And the problem with developmental and interpersonal consulting, as discussed earlier, is that the manager may not be skilled or practiced at such activities. Well-intentioned attempts to "help the group over the rough spots" may, for this reason, be seen more as managerial meddling than as help.

The net effect, in many instances, is that groups are not "brought along" as quickly or as well as they might be, group effectiveness remains suboptimal, and managers wind up feeling that their own status has been compromised in the bargain, that the meaningfulness of the managerial job has been stripped away.

There are no easy solutions to these problems. For this reason, it is essential that higher management give special attention to both the *role* and the *person* of the first-line manager when work is designed for teams. Especially important, it seems to us, is to make sure that the managerial role includes sufficient power to do what needs to be done to help the work groups develop into effective teams that fit well with their organizational environment, and to select, train, and support the managers as persons so that they gain the new skills they will need in their new leadership roles.

CONCLUSION

In general, we find much to be said in favor of self-managing work groups as an organizational device. They can be motivationally advantageous, and it is a truism that more task-relevant resources are brought to the work by a group than by an individual performing the same task. Yet the material reviewed in this chapter and the last suggests that the device of the self-managing work group is far from a panacea for the solution of organizational problems. For one thing, such teams are *not* always technologically or motivationally appropriate, and attempting to create them by force in an environment where they do not fit is a sure route to organizational problems. Moreover, it is relatively difficult to create, support, and manage such groups—more difficult, for example, than individual job enrichment, itself a rather substantial undertaking. So, as will be seen in the next chapter, where we explicitly compare work redesign for individuals and for groups, we favor relatively conservative use of self-managing work groups in organizations, at least until more is learned about how most effectively to install and maintain them.

FOR ADDITIONAL READING

Schein, E.H. *Process consultation.* Reading, MA: Addison-Wesley, 1969.
   This short book provides tools and instructions for effective consultation with groups. It identifies things that frequently go wrong in groups

and provides strategies for helping groups deal effectively with these problems and move beyond them.

Zander, A. *Groups at work*. San Francisco: Jossey-Bass, 1977. Written from a social psychological perspective, this readable book offers commentary on important small group phenomena. Included are summaries of research findings on a number of interesting questions about groups and some new hypotheses about why things happen as they do in work groups.

Delbecq, A.L., A.H. Van de Ven, and D.H. Gustafson. *Group techniques for program planning*. Glenview, IL: Scott, Foresman, 1975. A practical guide to the use of the Nominal Group Technique and Delphi approaches to minimizing group process losses. Short, readable, and practical.

Walton, R.E., and L.S. Schlesinger. Do supervisors thrive in participative work systems? *Organizational Dynamics*, Winter 1979, 24-38. What is to be done with the role of the supervisor when self-managing work groups are created? Here is an excellent conceptualization of the problem, based on studies in a number of organizations where work teams were installed. Includes a number of action suggestions.

PART FOUR
IMPLEMENTATION AND CHANGE

9
INSTALLING CHANGES IN WORK SYSTEMS

So far we have dealt primarily with the *content* of changes that are made when work is redesigned and with diagnostic procedures for assessing the appropriateness and feasibility of these changes. We now turn to questions of *process*—what is done when the time comes to actually install job changes in a given organizational setting.

We discuss here five strategic choices that are made, whether deliberately or implicitly, when work is redesigned. While the eventual success or failure of a change project can hinge on these choices, there are few handy, generally applicable ways of dealing with them. Little research has been conducted on the consequences of proceeding one way or the other in installing changes in jobs, and the research that is available is often inconsistent. Moreover, what turns out to be an appropriate installation strategy in some organizational circumstances will not work in others. Installing changes in work systems is a complicated, contingent, and mostly uncharted business.

For these reasons, our discussion will rely more on reasoned conjecture and less on firm results from controlled research than we would like. And while we will attempt to summarize and extend conventional wisdom about the risks and benefits of the choice alternatives considered, this chapter assuredly is *not* a "how to do it" manual for installing changes in jobs.

CHOICE ONE: INDIVIDUAL VERSUS
GROUP DESIGNS FOR WORK

Probably the single most significant choice that must be made when work systems are redesigned is whether to enrich individual jobs or to create self-managing work teams. In Parts Two and Three of the book we pointed out the many differences between individual and team designs, and we discussed the feasibility of both options. However, we did not offer specific guidance about how to choose between them.

Sometimes, as noted in Chapter 7, there isn't much choice: the nature of the work demands either an individual or a group design. But what if there *is* room for choice, if the work is such that either design could be installed? Which should be selected?

Often this choice is determined mostly by the proclivities and talents of change consultants or by the prior preferences of managerial clients. These factors should not be overlooked: it would be silly for a change that nobody wants to be installed with the help of a consultant who doesn't know how to do it. Yet several aspects of the work and the organizational situation also bear on the choice, and we review the most important of these below.

In Table 9.1 we summarize three general steps in planning for the redesign of work. First is to establish whether there is a need for work redesign at all. This is the "appropriateness" question discussed in detail in Chapter 5. If there is no special problem or opportunity in the work setting for which work redesign might be a useful change strategy, then planning for change would terminate before the individual versus group design question is even addressed.

Table 9.1.
Deciding about Redesigning Work

STEP ONE: IS THERE A NEED FOR WORK REDESIGN? (see Chapter 5)

1. Is there a problem or opportunity for which work redesign would be an appropriate change strategy?
2. Does the problem or opportunity centrally involve the motivation, satisfaction, or work effectiveness of the employees?
3. Might the design of the work be responsible for the observed problems or the unexploited opportunities?

4. What specific aspects of the job, as presently structured, most need improving?

STEP TWO: IS WORK REDESIGN FEASIBLE?

A. *The Feasibility of Enriching Individual Jobs* (see Chapter 5)

1. How ready for change are the employees whose jobs would be re-designed? Do they have appropriate knowledge and skill, growth need strength, and satisfaction with the work context?

2. How hospitable are existing organizational systems to the needed changes? Are the technological, personnel, and control systems likely to constrain the changes that must be made to improve the jobs? If so, can these systems be made more hospitable to work redesign?

B. *The Feasibility of Creating Self-Managing Work Groups* (see Chapter 7)

1. Would self-managing work groups fit with the people and with the organizational context? How do employees stand on knowledge and skill, on social as well as growth need strength, and on satisfaction with the work context? Is the overall climate and managerial style of the organization likely to be supportive of self-managing groups?

2. How hospitable are existing organizational systems to the needed changes? Can intact, identifiable groups be formed that have definable products and the authority to manage their own internal processes? Given the nature of the work to be done, what design features are most important in constructing the self-managing groups? Are the technological, personnel, and control systems likely to constrain the creation of groups with these features? If so, can these systems be made more hospitable to self-managing work groups?

STEP THREE: CHOOSING BETWEEN INDIVIDUAL AND GROUP DESIGNS

1. If neither an individual nor a group design is feasible, do not proceed with work redesign.

2. If one alternative is feasible and the other is not, the choice is obvious.

3. If *both* individual and group designs are feasible, opt for the group design only if it is substantially more attractive than the best possible individual design.

Once the need for work redesign is established, it is time to assess the relative feasibility of individual and group design options. The critical questions (taken from Chapter 5 for individual work redesign and from Chapter 7 for group design) are summarized in Table 9.1. The answers to these questions will provide a reading on the likelihood that substantial and meaningful changes can actually be made in the work system, given the nature of the work to be done, the characteristics of the people who do it, and the properties of the organizational context.

Sometimes it will turn out that neither individual job enrichment nor self-managing work groups is feasible for a given work setting. Under such circumstances, we recommend that planning for change be terminated, as shown in Step Three in the table. It is better not to proceed with work redesign if the planned changes would clash badly with the people or the organizational context, or if only token changes in the work itself could be made.

Other times one alternative will be clearly feasible and the other will be infeasible. In a highly competitive, consumer-oriented manufacturing organization, for example, it might turn out that enrichment of the individual jobs of sales personnel would be quite feasible and appropriate, but that creating self-managing teams of salespersons would fit poorly both with the needs and skills of the people and with the overall climate and style of the organization. In such cases the choice between individual and group designs for work is obvious.

Perhaps of greatest interest are situations in which *both* individual job enrichment and the creation of self-managing work groups are feasible alternatives. How should one choose when both are viable?

As indicated in the last entry in Table 9.1, we recommend opting for self-managing work groups only when they appear to offer substantial advantages over enriched individual jobs. Designing, implementing and managing work teams requires a good deal of behavioral science sophistication and managerial talent (see Chapters 7 and 8). One must attend not only to the design of the work, but also to the design of the team that will perform the work. And one must support work on enriched tasks not only by tailoring organizational practices to fit the demands of those tasks, but also by consulting with work group members about their interpersonal relationships.

Moreover, a team design typically requires more pronounced alterations of existing organizational practices and managerial styles than does the enrichment of individual jobs. It may be necessary to substantially redesign reward systems to support productive work by groups. Potentially destructive conflict can develop between work teams, and management must be sensitive to this possibility and competent in dealing with it should it emerge. Personnel selection and career mobility practices may have to be changed substantially to deal with the fact that groups, not individuals, are the primary performing units. And, of course, the assignment of responsibility for work outcomes to groups rather than to individuals can jolt the values and expectations of top managers and require them to seriously reconsider their views about how organizations should function.

For these reasons, we believe that the case for creating self-managing work groups in traditional work organizations should be clear and compelling before this design option is taken. Sometimes, to be sure, the case *is* a strong one. A group design might fit considerably better with the work, the people, and the broader organization than would an individual design. The motivating potential of a well-designed group task might greatly exceed that of the best possible design for individual jobs. Or the management philosophy of top managers might clearly favor groups over individuals as the preferred performing units of the organization.

In such cases, well-designed self-managing work groups can generate beneficial outcomes for the organization and for its employees that far exceed those of enriched individual jobs. But unless the case for self-managing work groups is compelling, it may be more prudent in traditional organizations (if not as adventuresome) to opt for the less radical alternative of enriching the jobs of individual employees.

CHOICE TWO: THEORY-BASED
VERSUS INTUITIVE CHANGES

In Chapter 3, we reviewed several theoretical approaches to work redesign, including activation theory, motivation-hygiene theory, job characteristics theory, and sociotechnical systems theory. We have drawn heavily on job characteristics theory in developing the ideas and recommendations set forth in this book. Had we based our thinking on other theoretical models, our conclusions would no doubt have been somewhat different. So just what is the role of theory in carrying out work redesign? Is it better to follow the dictates of one or another conceptual approach to changing jobs, or is a more intuitive approach preferable?

There are good reasons for basing the implementation of work redesign on *some* theoretical approach. For one thing, a theory-based change strategy increases the likelihood that the project will focus on the structure of the work itself. It is quite unlikely, for example, that attention will slip away from work-focused questions in a project where the aim is to increase the standing of a job on the five core dimensions of job characteristics theory. The same is true if one is attempting to build more "motivators" into a job using Herzberg's motivation-hygiene theory.

A theory also provides direction regarding the kinds of data that are needed to plan and evaluate changes in jobs, and can alert implementors to special problems and opportunities that may develop as the change activities unfold. Finally, use of an explicit theory of work redesign can help practitioners identify likely *causes* of work redesign successes and failures, and can be of use in diffusing the changes to other organizational settings (Tichy and Nisberg, 1976).

Despite these advantages, it may not always be desirable to rely heavily on theory in carrying out work redesign. One reason is that the particular theory selected may not be fully appropriate for the kinds of changes that most need to be made. If, for example, one relies on a theory that focuses exclusively on the design of *individual* jobs (like motivation-hygiene theory) and the changes that are most appropriate for the work system involve the restructuring of *group* tasks, then the theory is not likely to be of much help in planning and executing the changes, and may even direct planners toward changes that would be unnecessary or inappropriate (Frank and Hackman, 1975).

Reliance on a single theoretical approach also tends to "blind" change agents to phenomena that are not explicitly addressed by the theory, sometimes including phenomena that have major effects on the long-term success of work redesign. Basing change activities solely on motivation-hygiene theory, for example, could result in insufficient attention being paid to the compensation system or to individual differences in how people respond to enriched work. Or reliance on job characteristics theory could lead a practitioner to overlook aspects of the organization-environment relationship that affect the impact of the planned changes, something that would be in the forefront of attention if sociotechnical systems theory were used to guide the change activities.

These concerns suggest that in some circumstances a highly flexible and essentially atheoretical approach to changing jobs may be appropriate. A practitioner following such an approach would simply determine that improvements are needed and then proceed to design specific changes based on his or her intuition and personal experience, perhaps supplemented by data from open-ended interviews or observations.

The advantage of an intuitive, atheoretical approach is that change agents can attend to *all* aspects of the work and organization that are germane to the hoped-for improvements in jobs. The risk is that the plans for change can become rather diffuse and emphasize matters that have little to do with the work itself. If the design of the work is indeed the major source of problems in the organizational unit, this could result in changes that do not make much of a difference in employee attitudes, behavior, or work effectiveness.

What, then, is the appropriate choice? Should one elect a theoretical or an atheoretical approach to change? The answer may turn largely on the competence of the change agents who have primary responsibility for the redesign activities. When these individuals, be they consultants or managers, are knowledgeable and experienced in work redesign, then deliberate use of a theory-based change strategy may not be necessary. Such persons are likely to draw routinely on numerous theories of work design and derive from them principles for change that are uniquely suited to the particular work system being redesigned.

If, however, change agents are *not* especially knowledgeable in the practice of work redesign, then it may be preferable to begin a change project using a single theoretical approach, one that seems to be a good *a priori* fit with the work unit and one with which the change agents are personally comfortable. This approach can help focus attention on critical aspects of the work itself as plans for change are laid, and can provide criteria for assessing the probable effects of various job changes that are contemplated. Yet eventually it will be necessary to move beyond the bounds of whatever theory is used to guide initial planning for work redesign. No theory, no matter how well conceived or how extensively tested, can deal with all of the factors that affect how change activities unfold and what their eventual impact will be. There are simply too many idiosyncracies in work systems designed and populated by humans for a single theory to be able to handle them all.

For this reason, we believe that theories of work redesign, including our own, are best viewed as *aids* in planning for change rather than as blueprints that specify in detail how those changes should be installed. Theories can help order the complexities and idiosyncracies that characterize all attempts to change work systems. But they in no way reduce the need for knowledgeable and skilled change agents who are sensitive to unexpected and unique events that emerge when jobs are redesigned, and who are able to respond appropriately to those events.

CHOICE THREE: TAILORED VERSUS BROADSIDE INSTALLATION

In the section above, we suggested that changes in work systems, whether or not they are guided by a specific theory of work redesign, must be tailored to the idiosyncracies of the organizational unit where they are installed. Should the changes also be tailored to the needs, talents, and readiness for change of individual employees in the work unit, or should they be provided in equal measure to all employees?

As noted earlier in this book, employees' reactions to their work are affected not only by the work itself but also by their own characteristics—specifically, their job-relevant knowledge and skill, their level of growth and social need strength, and their satisfaction with the work context. Since employees in most work units differ in these (and other) characteristics, it would seem a good idea to install job changes following what Ford (1969) calls the "deskside" model. Enriching changes in jobs would be introduced for each employee only when the person was known to be able to handle increased responsibilities, and when he or she was psychologically ready for them. Indeed, "deenriching" changes might even be introduced for employees whose skills or needs were not appropriate for existing jobs. At any given time, then, different individuals within the same work unit would have jobs of differential scope and challenge. The situation would not be static. As employees changed as a function of their work experiences, so would their jobs. Throughout, the aim would be to be as responsive as possible to the needs, attitudes, and talents of the people—consistent with Lawler's (1974) idea of the "individualized organization."

There are, of course, problems with an individualized approach to the design and management of work. For one thing, it is expensive.

It would be costly, both in dollars and management time, to tailor jobs to every person within a work unit. It would be even more costly if individualized work redesign were carried out on a more or less continuous basis. Yet the very idea of individualizing work systems demands at least occasional, if not continuous, revision of jobs as people change.

Moreover, individualizing the design of jobs risks creating feelings of competitiveness and inequity among work unit members. Employees are certain to compare jobs with one another and may begin to view their own jobs as substantially "better" or "worse" than those held by their colleagues. The result of such comparisons may be low satisfaction and poor-quality work, even among employees who are objectively well suited to their jobs (Oldham and Miller, 1979).

The alternative to an individually tailored approach is to install changes "broadside." In this approach, one would first identify the "modal" or most typical individuals in the work unit and then design the work to fit the needs and skills of these individuals as well as possible. Some people would wind up underchallenged and underutilized by their work, and the reverse would be true for other people. But it would be taken as a fact of organizational life that not everyone can have a well-fitting job: people must accommodate to organizational requirements if even moderately efficient collective action is to be possible.

There is merit to a "broadside" approach. For one thing, changes are made once (not continuously), and after the redesign process is over employees and managers alike can concentrate on the numerous other problems that must be resolved to get the work unit functioning efficiently. Management style, once adjusted to the new demands and opportunities in managing enriched work, can once again become more uniform and predictable than would be possible under an individualized model, which should both save money and keep ambiguity and anxiety at tolerable levels.

Moreover, the *need* for an individualized approach to work redesign has not yet been well established. As noted in Chapter 4, research on the role of individual differences in determining how people react to their work is inconsistent: predicted moderating effects rarely are of substantial magnitude and sometimes they fail to appear at all. One possible reason for such findings—and yet another argument in favor of a "broadside" approach to work redesign—is that people may *adapt* to their work (whether it provides more or less complexity and challenge than they presently seek) in relatively short order (see Chapters 1 and 6). If this is true, then "broadside" changes, sensitively installed and supported, might be just as effective in the long term as changes that are tailored to the skills and needs people happen to have at the time the changes are made.

So what is the appropriate choice: tailored or "broadside" changes? While the appropriate choice once again will vary from project to project, three factors warrant attention when the choice is made. First is the nature of work technology. If it would be very difficult to individualize jobs (as might be the case for fixed mechanical production lines), then any attempt to fit jobs to individual workers would be only marginally successful. In other cases, it would be *possible* to individualize jobs within a given technology, but prohibitively *expensive* to do so. In this circumstance, too, the choice seems clear.

Second is the amount of variation among employees in psychological readiness for enriched work and in the knowledge and skill required to do such work well. If there are great differences among job incumbents on such factors, then an individualized approach might be called for because unreasonable amounts of adaptation would be required of employees under the "broadside" model. If, however, employees are relatively homogeneous in their personal characteristics (a not uncommon state of affairs, given organizational selection, employee self-selection, and informal socialization processes), then few employees would be excessively "stretched" if work were redesigned to fit well with the most typical employees in the unit.

Finally, the management philosophy of those responsible for the organizational unit bears importantly on the choice. The risks of tailoring changes to the people are confusion, complexity, and inconsistency—with all the spin-off problems that these phenomena bring. The risks of "broadside" changes are rigidity, forced uniformity, and poor person-job fits—with all of the spin-off problems that *these* phenomena bring. Given that it is almost certain, when jobs are changed, that one will err in one direction or another, it is incumbent upon management to consider explicitly which type of error is more acceptable and to plan for the installation of job changes accordingly.

CHOICE FOUR: PARTICIPATIVE VERSUS
TOP-DOWN CHANGE PROCESSES

Most work redesign projects provide jobholders with increased opportunities for autonomy and self-direction in carrying out the work of the organization. Employees are allowed to do their work with a minimum of interference, and they are assumed to have the competence and sense of responsibility to seek appropriate assistance when they need it. To what extent should the *process* of implementing job changes be congruent with these intended end-states?

At least at first glance, a highly participative process for planning and installing job changes would seem called for. Participation assumes that employees are responsible, mature adults with a good deal to contribute to the organization—just as does work redesign. Should not employees therefore be involved in the process of work redesign, from the collection of diagnostic data to the postchange evaluation of the project?

Those who advocate making employees full collaborators in the redesign of their own jobs point to a number of possible advantages of a participative approach. First, the quality of the diagnostic data that employees provide may be improved. If people know that changes in their own work will be made partly on the basis of their responses to the diagnostic instruments, they may try especially hard to provide valid and complete data. Second, suggestions made by employees may be especially constructive. Since employees are very familiar with their jobs, they may come up with ideas for substantive alterations in the work content that would escape the attention of detached observers.

Third, employees may feel increased ownership of their newly enriched jobs and heightened commitment to the entire work redesign program. These attitudes, which are well-established benefits of participation, can prompt employees to work hard to ensure that meaningful changes are actually made in their jobs and that the work redesign program as a whole succeeds.

Finally, participation increases the chance that lessons will be learned from the change activities that can be used to good effect in future work redesign projects. The involvement of people from a diversity of organizational roles in diagnostic and change-planning activities should make it easier to piece together a complete picture of the change project, including the reasons that various changes were tried, what went wrong (and what went right), and what might be done differently next time.

Some support for these arguments is provided in a study by Seeborg (1978). She investigated the impact of work redesign on individuals attending a two and a half day simulation of an organization. Two installation processes were compared: participative (in which groups redesigned the jobs of their own members) and supervisor-controlled (in which each supervisor unilaterally redesigned the jobs of group members). A greater number of positive changes in job characteristics were found in the participative condition, and members of participative groups subsequently reported higher job satisfaction.

Nevertheless, several commentators have argued that employee participation in the redesign of their own jobs is inappropriate and, indeed, detrimental to the long-term effectiveness of work redesign. It has been suggested, for example, that direct participation by employees in the redesign of their jobs risks a change of focus from "motivators" in the work itself to "hygiene factors" such as compensation, supervision, and workplace amenities (Herzberg, 1968). Moreover, because of their limited perspective on the work system as a whole, employees may be unable to invent or appreciate innovative changes in jobs that would actually be among the most impactful ways to enrich their own work. And any positive attitudes that might develop because of involvement in the *process* of work redesign would be only transitory since long-term motivational benefits depend on the content of jobs after they are restructured, not on the process used to make job changes.

Involving job incumbents in the redesign process can also be a time-consuming business, with much time spent away from productive work in planning sessions. This, of course, is expensive and can disrupt unit productivity while the changes are being planned and installed (Walters and Associates, 1975). Finally, employees may have little desire for such activities and might even find them unpleasant and anxiety arousing. Why, they might inquire, are *they* being asked to take on chores that are *management's* responsibility?

According to those who criticize employee participation in work redesign, a more appropriate strategy is a top-down, management-controlled approach. Initial planning for work redesign, including decision making about what jobs will be selected for change and what alterations will be made, is carried out privately by managers and consultants. Diagnostic work, if done at all, may involve use of an innocuous cover story, such as telling employees that they are being interviewed "as part of our regular program of surveying employee attitudes." Eventually, managers appear with a fully determined set of changes that are installed in traditional top-down fashion.

This approach does away with many of the potential problems with participation noted above. Changes are designed privately, efficiently, and without the fuss and bother of dealing with the emotions and the possibly irrelevant agendas of rank-and-file employees. While one must assume that managers do have the knowledge and expertise needed to generate appropriate changes in employee jobs, a case reported by Paul, Robertson, and Herzberg (1969) provides reassurance on this point. These researchers found that personnel specialists who were asked to suggest changes in their own jobs came up with fewer than 30 minor changes, whereas their managers compiled a list of over 100 much more substantial ideas for job improvements.

Yet just as one can find fault with a participative process, there are significant potential problems with a top-down approach as well. Employee acceptance of the changes may be difficult to obtain, precisely because the change process and the change objectives are incongruent. As one disappointed manager reported when signs of employee resistance appeared after management-developed changes in jobs were announced: "I don't understand why they did not respond more enthusiastically. Don't they realize how we are going to make their work a lot more involving and interesting?" Apparently this individual did not see the lack of consistency between "what we want to achieve" and "how we are going to achieve it."

Moreover, the assumption that employees have few good ideas about how to restructure their own jobs may be wrong. Indeed, it is widely believed—and is probably true—that employees more than their managers know what is wrong with the way their jobs are set up and what is constraining productivity. But merely asking employees for suggested changes may not elicit those ideas, especially if their relationship with management has historically been strained or if employees do not themselves have a good idea of what kinds of changes are sought. Thus, while pro forma participation by employees may be as ineffective as those who argue for a top-down approach suggest, *informed* participation (that is, when employees are full partners in the redesign process and as informed as their managers about the purposes and processes of work redesign) might well yield ideas for change whose quality would surprise and please even skeptical managers and consultants.

There are, then, both risks and potential benefits associated with both a participative and top-down approach to installing work redesign. When should one tilt one way and when the other?

While existing research is far to sketchy to allow us to make firm recommendations, three of the questions posed by Vroom and Yetton (1973) in their theory of leadership and decision making can provide some guidance. First, *who possesses information needed for making decisions about job changes?* If there is a great deal of ambiguity about the job and possible changes in it, or if consultants and managers do not have at hand all of the information needed to assess the feasibility and desirability of contemplated changes, then a participative process may be more appropriate.

Second, *are job changes developed and installed by managers more likely to be accepted or resisted by the job incumbents?* If the climate of the organizational unit is such that employee acceptance of management-installed work redesign will not be a problem, then a top-down approach might be favored on simple grounds of cost and efficiency. If, however, acceptance is not assured then a more participative process may be called for to enhance the commitment of employees to the changes that are made.

Third, *can employees be trusted to generate suggestions for change that will be both substantial in magnitude and focused on the structure of the work itself?* If it is anticipated that employees would contribute constructively and competently to the change process (were they fully involved in that process and well informed about it), then the balance swings toward a more participative approach. If, however, there are good reasons to believe that employee suggestions would focus on relatively trivial or work-irrelevant matters, then it may be preferable for managers to proceed with top-down installation—with the understanding that they may have to deal later with problems of employee acceptance and commitment.

Sometimes the answers to these three questions will clearly signal that a participative, or a top-down, approach is more appropriate. Other times the answers will be ambiguous, and the decision will be a judgment call influenced perhaps more by the values of those responsible for the change project than by any compelling facts of the matter. And still other times considering the trade-offs between participative and top-down installation of job changes may lead to a decision that work redesign is premature or inappropriate for the work unit, that neither the employees nor the managers are, at the moment, ready for the stresses and challenges that would be involved in planning, installing, and supporting significant changes in the way work is structured and managed.

CHOICE FIVE: CONSULTATION VERSUS COLLABORATION WITH STAKEHOLDERS

When work is redesigned, the effects of the changes extend far beyond the individual employees whose jobs are restructured. Invariably, other people and groups have a "stake" in what happens, even if they are not directly involved in the planning and installation process. Prominent among such stakeholders are union representatives and first-line supervisors. Others may include employees in organizational departments whose work will be affected by the changes (such as the personnel department or the quality control department), units that supply work to the focal unit (or receive work from it), or even the community in which the organization is located.

How should relations with these stakeholders be managed when work is redesigned? We assume that *ignoring* people and groups who will be significantly affected by the changes (and who will often be in a position either to support or to undermine those changes) is a generally bad idea. But just how involved should they be, and how should that involvement be structured and managed?

We suggest below two general models for managing relations with stakeholders: a "consultative" model, which involves only limited involvement by the potentially affected parties, and a "full collaboration" model. We will use union-management relationships, which provides perhaps the richest and most challenging example of stakeholder issues in work redesign, to explore the two models.

One reason why the case of organized labor is challenging is that unions have generally been less than enthusiastic about what work redesign has to offer their members. While a number of union leaders have spoken out vigorously in favor of work redesign and quality of worklife programs, questions of job content have only rarely been brought by unions to contract negotiations (White, 1977). Indeed, research findings show that relatively few rank-and-file union members want their representatives to bargain actively for improvements in job content (Giles and Holley, 1978; Kochan, Lipsky, and Dyer, 1974). Given that work redesign has sometimes been the guise for antiunion activities by management, or as a means for trying to improve productivity at workers' expense, this is an understandable view.

Yet organized labor is in a position to either facilitate or obstruct changes in how work is designed in many organizations, and when jobs are changed the worklives of union members can be substantially affected. How, then should work redesign be managed so that the views of union representatives can be brought to bear on the project, and so that the risk of across-the-board opposition to work redesign by the union is reduced?

In the *consultative* model, management designs, implements, and directs the work redesign activities, informing union representatives about project purposes and plans, and inviting reactions from them when they feel that the plans may infringe on the rights of members or violate provisions of the labor contract. This approach maintains the traditional adversarial model of union-management relations, and it has some inherent advantages. There is, for example, little chance that the change process will result in the union being co-opted by management. Instead, workers' rights and interests are likely to be sturdily defended by their unions. Moreover, unions minimize the risk that they will be perceived by their members as too "cozy" with management, or (worse) as yet another tool used by management to manipulate workers. And since both union leaders and managers are likely to be familiar and comfortable with the consultative-adversarial style, problems that might arise in trying to develop a new kind of working relationship can be avoided.

There are, of course, some costs and risks associated with the consultative model as well. One is the possibility that misunderstandings will arise about the work redesign program and its implications, and that these misunderstandings will be difficult to correct because of the adversarial climate of the relationship between the groups. It may be difficult for everyone to understand that *both* workers and the organization can gain from work redesign because of a history of negotiations in which one party's gain has always been viewed as the other's loss.

In addition, there is little opportunity for unions to contribute directly to the design and installation of changes under the consultative model, which risks the loss of some good ideas and valuable information. And the commitment of union leaders to the success of the program may be limited: because the changes are seen as "owned" by management, union representatives may not be motivated to provide the extra push that often is needed to get the changes installed (for example, when managers start to back off from the more substantial and risky of the planned changes as implementation time nears).

Many of these problems are circumvented under a *full collaboration* model, in which union and management representatives are full partners in the design and installation of job changes. This model involves both greater commitment to the project and greater investment in it by organized labor. It is understood that both parties will contribute substantially to the changes and that they are jointly responsible for whatever successes and failures materialize.

The full collaborative model is frequently employed in projects aimed at improving the quality of working life in organizations. In such projects, joint labor-management committees serve as the basic forum and decision-making vehicle for generating and implementing changes.[1] This committee, rather than management acting alone, has both responsibility and authority for deciding what is to be done and for seeing that changes are installed as planned (Nadler, 1978).

While there are obvious advantages to the collaborative approach, there are some significant disadvantages. For one, the union does not play a "watchdog" role as it does in the consultative model. Because the union does not observe the process by which changes are implemented from a somewhat skeptical, arms-length stance, workers' personal interests may be overlooked in the interest of getting the changes installed. And difficulties in the change process itself may be missed (or even suppressed) as union and management representatives enthusiastically charge ahead to execute their jointly conceived plans.

Moreover, responsibility for work redesign failures that develop under fully collaborative conditions can be legitimately attributed in part to the union, and therefore "taint" the union in the eyes of its members. Finally, full collaboration legitimizes the structure of work

---

1   For a provocative essay on how the principles of sociotechnical systems theory can be applied to the design and management of labor-management quality of worklife committees, see Shea (1979).

as an issue of joint union-management concern, something that could constrain the latitude of the union in future contract negotiations. For these reasons, union leaders might find themselves holding back from full partnership and participation in the enterprise, even if the project were explicitly defined as a fully collaborative undertaking. And this, of course, could place stresses on the union-management group charged with designing and executing the change program, with predictable and unhappy consequences for the long-term effectiveness of that group.

There is, then, no single "right answer" about whether a consultative or collaborative relationship with organized labor is preferable when work is redesigned. The same is true when one considers how to structure relationships with other groups that have a stake in work redesign projects.

How should the decision between these two models be made? For starters, it makes good sense to talk about the matter with representatives of significant stakeholders, to obtain their views about what would be the most appropriate and desirable role for them to play. Beyond such discussions, there are at least four factors that might tilt the decision toward either a consultative or a collaborative relationship.

First is the *size of the stake* held by the other party. If stakeholders will be only marginally affected by the changes (for example, members of a staff department who only occasionally have dealings with the work unit where job changes are planned), then simply informing group representatives about the project, and perhaps offering them the chance to make suggestions or give reactions to tentative plans, should suffice. If, however, the work or well-being of the stakeholders is likely to be seriously affected by the contemplated changes a more major role is called for.

Consider, for example, first-line supervisors of the focal jobs. As we have seen throughout this book, both the person and the role of the first-line supervisor is affected, usually powerfully and often negatively, when rank-and-file jobs are redesigned. Clearly a collaborative relationship would be appropriate for these significant stakeholders. Yet we have observed numerous instances in which planners failed to recognize the significance of the stake of supervisors in the project and therefore did not involve them collaboratively in it. Almost without exception the result has been resistance to the changes by the supervisors, and occasionally we have seen supervisors subtly undermine the changes after they were installed.

Second is the *relative strength* of the two parties. If truly colla-borative relationships are to prosper between representatives of two intact groups, then both groups need to be relatively strong and perceived that way by each other. Strong, well-organized unions, for example, have been known to demolish disorganized managerial groups, and vice versa. It may be better to forego the potential advantages of collaboration if there are radical differences in the strength of the groups that would have to work together to plan and install the changes in jobs.

Third is the level of *trust* that exists between the two parties. If management and stakeholder groups are prepared to assume that the motives of the other are more constructive than exploitative, then the feasibility of the collaborative model increases. But if the relationship is ridden with fears, suspicions, and mistrust about "what they might do," the obstacles to true collaboration are so great that it might be better not to attempt it.

Last, is the *efficiency* of the redesign process. The more full partners there are in an organizational change undertaking, the more cumbersome and difficult to manage that undertaking becomes. To involve as full collaborators representatives of all significant stake-holders could, in many instances, result in a group of change planners that is so large and so heterogeneous that little concerted action will be possible. Simple consultation, on the other hand, can be done relatively efficiently even with a fairly large number of stakeholders.

In sum, there are advantages to both the consultative and col-laborative models for managing relations with parties who have a stake in what happens when jobs are changed. We do not find one or the other model generally preferable. But we do mean to signal the importance of the choice between them. Too often a work redesign project comes to be experienced as "ours" by those assigned initial responsibility for project planning. The fact that there are other groups who have a legitimate stake in how the project unfolds is not appreciated and this oversight invariably returns later to haunt the change-planners.

CONCLUSION: DOING IT RIGHT VERSUS GETTING IT DONE

While the five choices discussed above seem to us especially impor-tant in affecting the process and effects of work redesign, there are many other choices about implementation strategy that also must be made when jobs are changed. These choices too are difficult ones, and can spell the difference between a successful and an unsuccessful work redesign project. For example:

- Where to begin. Should initial work redesign activities take place in a particularly well-managed and smoothly functioning organizational unit or in a difficult unit that has many problems? If a "star" unit is chosen, the chances for early success increase, but the change processes used and the results obtained may not diffuse readily to other parts of the organization. If a "problem" unit is selected, a great deal may be learned from the ups and downs of the change project, and diffusion of the innovation may be eased—if it is successful. The problem is that it may not be.

- How far ahead to plan. Should elaborate contingency plans be developed for dealing with the "spin-offs" of work redesign (such as plans for revising compensation arrangements, management style, mobility opportunities, training programs, and so on) before job changes actually are installed? Or is it better to wait until postchange problems and opportunities emerge? If plans are drawn up ahead of time, change agents will be ready to deal with almost anything that comes up after the work is restructured, but the change process may become excessively structured, rigid, and "by the book." If a more reactive stance is taken, there may be greater responsiveness to issues that emerge after jobs are changed, but change agents may find themselves scrambling to try to keep up with a multitude of fast-breaking problems that they are not quite prepared to deal with.

- How to manage participants' expectations about the probable outcomes of the design project. Should great optimism about anticipated benefits be encouraged, or is a more cautious and conservative stance advisable? If high expectations are created, they may serve as a kind of "flywheel" to maintain momentum when the project encounters problems, but the risk of disillusionment is great if outcomes turn out to be less positive than advertised. If expectations are kept low, participants will be more realistic about the limitations of work redesign as a change strategy, but some may conclude that it simply isn't worth the considerable investment required to competently develop, install, and support job changes.

- How heavily to rely on outside expertise. Should consultants with great experience and expertise in work redesign be engaged to design and install the changes, or should managers and employees in the work unit assume near-total responsibility for the project? If expert outside consultants are relied upon, the project will benefit from the special knowledge and skills of these individuals, but they may not be as responsive as "insiders" to special features of the people and the organization where the changes are to be installed. Moreover, personnel in the work unit may not feel much ownership of the project or responsibility for its success. If changes are managed by insiders, ownership, commitment, and responsiveness to unit idiosyncracies will be high, but errors of judgment and technique deriving from participants' inexperience with work redesign may compromise the effectiveness of the project.

• How to evaluate project outcomes. Should project outcomes be evaluated formally, using systematic measuring devices, or should results of the changes be assessed on a more informal and ad hoc basis? The use of systematic procedures, such as our Job Diagnostic Survey or the behavioral-economic measures developed by Macy and Mirvis (1976), can provide relatively reliable and valid assessments of a number of important outcomes of work redesign. But systematic assessment procedures also risk creating a "guinea pig" effect among project participants, and can tempt decision makers to conclude (often incorrectly) that *more* of whatever is being measured is *better* (see Staw and Oldham, 1978). Informal evaluations of project outcomes lend themselves to summary "bottom line" assessments of project successes and failures (something often sought by top managers), but because they are based on data of dubious reliability and validity these conclusions may be untrustworthy.

These trade-offs, and the ones reviewed in more detail earlier in the chapter, suggest that decision making about changing jobs is much like trying to walk on a slippery log: not only is it easy to fall off, but one can fall in either direction with equally unpleasant consequences.

Yet there is one general issue that lies just beneath many of the more specific alternatives we have discussed. This is the tension between installing changes in jobs as competently as possible and getting them installed at all. To redesign work well involves a great deal of prework, planning, and negotiating. Key stakeholders must be identified, and appropriate relationships with them negotiated. A design for prechange diagnostic activities must be invented, and data collection procedures and instruments developed. The readiness of the organization for changes in job structure must be assessed, and the commitment of top management and union leadership tested. Decisions must be made about the level of involvement of job incumbents in the change process, and (if they are to participate significantly) they must be coached in the theory and practice of work redesign. Structural, social, and political problems and opportunities that are idiosyncratic to the work must be identified, and plans laid for dealing with them. The criteria to be used in judging the success or failure of the project must be determined, and appropriate evaluative measures found or devised. The list is long, and the tasks are difficult.

The problem is that so much time and energy may be required to competently perform all of the desired prechange planning and negotiating that the changes themselves may never get made. New organizational priorities may emerge before installation begins that require work redesign to be placed on indefinite "hold." Or key managers may depart, requiring reeducation of their replacements and risking that the new managers will abandon work redesign in favor of their own preferred strategy for organizational improvement. Or significant "snags" may develop as tough questions of feasibility and cost are addressed during change planning, snags so severe that they cast doubt on the advisability of proceeding with the project. Or people may simply run out of energy.

So trying to do work redesign right can sometimes compromise getting it done at all. For this reason, individuals responsible for work redesign projects often choose to get the project "sold" and started as expeditiously as possible, and only then begin work on the difficult problems that must be solved for the project to develop as planned and have its intended effects. The idea is to plunge ahead, to plan on putting out a lot of brush fires that develop because of inadequate prework, and to hope that no insurmountable obstacles to effective change appear after the project is underway.

Which is better: to confront the tough problems early and systematically and risk not getting the project off the ground, or to do whatever has to be done to get the project accepted and started and risk a failure rooted in problems that could have been anticipated (and possibly dealt with) beforehand?

By now the refrain should be familiar: there are potential costs and benefits on both sides, and the best way to proceed depends both on the nature of the organization where the changes will be installed and on the proclivities and assumptions of those who are responsible for guiding the change process. Our view is that it usually is better to risk not doing a project for which the tough issues cannot be resolved beforehand than to do one under circumstances that require compromise after compromise to keep the project alive after it has begun. And we would recommend passing up some opportunities for work restructuring if doing so would also reduce the number of projects pushed to a conclusion that actually were not worth starting in the first place. We favor *better* work redeisgn activities—thoughtfully planned and executed changes that are fully appropriate for their organizational settings—even if that means we will see *fewer* of them.

FOR ADDITIONAL READING

Sirota, D., and A.D. Wolfson. Job enrichment: What are the obstacles? *Personnel,* May-June 1972, 8-17; *and* Job enrichment: Surmounting the obstacles. *Personnel,* July-August 1972, 8-19. This pair of articles presents some of the major stumbling blocks encountered in implementing work redesign and suggests some specific strategies for overcoming these difficulties.

Tichy, N.M., and J.N. Nisberg. When does work restructuring work? *Organizational Dynamics,* Summer 1976, 63-80. The authors present a framework for evaluating work redesign and other organization improvement programs, and then use that framework to analyze two quality of work-life projects and to show why one succeeded and the other failed.

Macy, B.A., and P.H. Mirvis. Measuring the quality of work and organizational effectiveness in behavioral-economic terms. *Administrative Science Quarterly,* 1976, *21,* 212-226. This paper describes the development and implementation of a standardized set of definitions, measures, and costing methods for behavioral outcomes of change projects. The assessment package can be readily applied to the evaluation of work redesign programs.

White, B.J. Innovations in job design: The union perspective. *Journal of Contemporary Business,* 1977, *6,* 23-35. The response of U.S. labor unions to the issue of work redesign is explored in this essay, and explanations for this response are offered.

Walton, R.E. Successful strategies for diffusing work innovations. *Journal of Contemporary Business*, 1977, *6*, 1-22. This paper presents an in-depth analysis of three work restructuring programs. Based on these cases, the author offers some insights about the conditions under which such programs will diffuse to other organizational units.

10
WORK REDESIGN IN ORGANIZATIONAL
AND SOCIETAL CONTEXT

Throughout this book we have explored in some detail ways that work can be redesigned to improve the motivation, satisfaction, and performance of rank-and-file organization members. In concluding the book, we address the design of work in broader perspective. How useful is work redesign as a point of departure for initiating broad-scale organizational changes? Given present trends in society, what will be the shape of work in the future? And to what extent are future directions amenable to influence by those who favor a more "humanistic" than "scientific" approach to the design and management of work systems?

WORK REDESIGN AS A TECHNIQUE OF
PLANNED ORGANIZATIONAL CHANGE

There are reasons both for optimism and pessimism about the use of work redesign as a device for organizational change. When meaningful improvements in jobs can actually be made and supported over time, their effects can be powerful. Yet significant restructuring of work is very difficult to accomplish, especially under "normal" circumstances when organizational systems are operating relatively smoothly. Just how feasible is it to use work redesign as a point of leverage for planned change in organizations?

An Optimistic View

Work redesign has some special advantages in dealing with three key change problems. The first is simply *getting behavior to change*. Many change attempts are based on the hope that if people's attitudes change, or if they learn better what they are supposed to do and how to do it, or if they are helped to understand better the non-obvious causes of their and others' behavior in organizations, then behavioral changes will "naturally" follow.

Research evidence forces us to be skeptical about such hopes. People do not always behave consistently with their attitudes or with what they cognitively "know" they should do. People who have high job satisfaction do not always work hard and effectively. And, in most organizations, vast amounts of task-relevant knowledge and skill are untapped either because people choose not to use their talents in organizational work or because they do not have the opportunity to.

On the other hand, people *do* perform the tasks they have accepted. How well they perform them depends on many factors, including how the tasks are designed. But people perform them. Redesigning jobs, then, is almost certain to result in changes in the overt behavior of the people who hold those jobs. If the changes require people to know more than they now know, then they may become motivated to increase their on-the-job skills. And if the changes turn out to prompt hard, task-oriented work, the people may, over time, develop beliefs and attitudes that support these new work behaviors.

Work redesign, then, does not rely on getting beliefs or attitudes or skills changed first (such as by inducing a worker to "care more" about work outcomes, as in zero defects programs) and hoping that such changes will generalize to work behavior. Instead, the thrust of the change is to alter behavior itself. Attitudes, beliefs, knowledge, and skills will follow these behaviors and gradually become consistent with them.

The second problem of planned change is *getting behavior to stay changed*. After jobs are changed it is difficult for jobholders to slip back into old ways of behaving. The old ways are just not appropriate for the new tasks. Moreover, the requirements and reinforcements built into the new tasks support the new ways of behaving. So one need not worry too much about the kind of "backsliding" that occurs so often after training or attitude change activities, especially those that take place away from the job itself. The stimuli that direct and constrain the person's behavior are experienced right on the job, day after day. And once those stimuli have been changed, they are likely to stay that way until the job is once again redesigned.

The third organizational change problem is *getting the changes to spread* to other organizational systems and practices. What happens in an organization is complexly and redundantly determined. A change in any single organizational system or practice, no matter how competently carried out, cannot be expected to result in a basic reorientation of how an organization operates. If overall organizational change is desired, then eventually the initial changes must spread to and affect other structures, systems, and practices.

As seen in Chapters 6 and 8, changes in jobs invariably place strains on other aspects of the organization—ranging from personnel practices and reward systems to the style of orgnizational management. These pressures, if followed up with vigor and competence, can serve as points of entry for broad-scale organizational improvements. Even organizational practices that previously may have defied all attempts at planned change (such as compensation arrangements or control systems) may now become amenable to change because everyone agrees that they *need* to be changed to fit with the new ways the work is being done. And behavioral science professionals may find themselves freed from the old difficulty of selling their wares to skeptical managers who are not really sure anything is wrong—or, if there is, that they want to hear about it.

Much is required for competent organizational change and for following up and diffusing changes that are made. There are many more "change problems" than the three listed above. But for initiating far-reaching changes, these three—getting behavior to change, getting it to stay changed, and getting the changes to spread—are critical. And for these problems work redesign has some special advantages in comparison to other organization development approaches.

A Pessimistic View

Work redesign has now been available as a device for organizational change for many years. If it is such a good point of leverage for broad-scale organizational change, why do we not see more organizations that have been "turned around" through the redesign of work? There are, we believe, at least three reasons for the limited impact of work redesign. Taken together, they call into question the efficacy and permanence of planned organizational change that begins with the redesign of tasks and jobs.

First, as we pointed out in Chapter 5, managers often anticipate negative effects of job changes on other organizational systems as plans for work redesign are being made. This can prompt numerous small compromises from the ideal design for work in that setting to minimize the anticipated disruptiveness and cost of the planned changes. The result is what we called the "small change" effect, in which the job changes that actually get made are much less pronounced than those originally contemplated and not substantial enough to generate meaningful alterations in employee behavior, let alone set in motion forces for improving other organizational systems.

Second, if substantial changes in work design actually are made, then the resultant stresses and strains on other organizational systems may be viewed simply as "unfortunate problems" that must be corrected. (This is, perhaps, a more likely view than the alternative suggested earlier—namely, that such stresses provide special opportunities for initiating developmental changes in the affected systems.) In many cases, the result is that the innovations in work design are slowly chipped away and rendered impotent. This is the "vanishing effects" phenomenon discussed in Chapter 6: work design comes up against established organizational systems and managerial practices— and loses.

The third reason for pessimism about work redesign as a strategy for far-reaching organizational change has more to do with how the redesign process takes place than with the content or consequences of the changes themselves. Managers are familiar with, and practiced in dealing with, various kinds of prepackaged programs that can be adopted to "fix" defined problems or accomplish specific objectives. Many technological solutions to production problems are of this type, as are certain kinds of marketing and sales programs. There is a tendency for work redesign to be dealt with in the same general way, for changes to be made using essentially a mechanistic installation process.

The problem, of course, is that behavioral science changes such as job redesign tend not to work if they are treated as something that can be simply plugged in and turned on (see Chapter 9). Thus, if managers view work redesign as yet another program that can be bought, installed, and then left to generate all manner of beneficial effects, those effects are most unlikely to appear. In fact, the redesign of work is much more a *way of managing* than it is a prepackaged "fix" for problems of employee motivation and satisfaction. Unless managers understand this, and are prepared to alter how they run their organizations after the work itself is changed, then the prospects for broad-scale improvements in organizational functioning are quite dim.[1]

Mechanistic use of work redesign, while often observed in practice, at least does not run much risk of covert manipulation of the work motivation and attitudes of employees. It is hard to conjecture how giving a person (or a group) meaningful work, autonomous responsibility for the work outcomes, and task-based knowledge of results would be very effective as a manipulative tactic. If, in fact, these conditions are created, then the manager who created them is much more at the mercy of the employee (who may or may not choose to work hard and well) than vice versa. The work situation becomes one that allows and encourages *proaction* rather than requires *reaction*. So it is more likely, when a manager carries out work redesign mechanistically, that he or she simply will fail to create the appropriate conditions for internal work motivation. And the result will be yet another "failure of work redesign" rather than a success in using the device to covertly manipulate the people whose jobs were changed.

---

1   We are acutely aware of the risk of mechanism, for it is precisely the risk of this book. It would be possible to treat the guidelines that have been provided here as recipes for improving work in organizations and to mechanically apply what we have said to any and all organizational situations where motivational problems are observed. Our emphasis throughout on the importance of pre-change diagnosis and on the interdependencies between work design and other organizational systems is an attempt to counter the temptation that some may experience to simply "follow the recipe." We know, however, that whenever tools (such as the Job Diagnostic Survey) and models (such as those for individual job enrichment or for self-managing work groups) are provided, some will rely too much on those aids and too little on their own intelligence and their own analysis of what is *really* going on in the work system being addressed.

The Case for Caution

How do the optimistic and pessimistic views summarized above balance out? That is a question readers will have to address on their own. Our view is a fairly conservative one. While we find the advantages of work redesign as an "organization development" technique to be real and important, the conditions required to secure and retain these advantages in relatively stable, ongoing organizations appear to be present only occasionally.

To redesign work halfheartedly or to use flawed change processes is, in most cases, to assure failure. And it is *hard* to do work redesign well. It requires highly skilled managers and change agents to carry out diagnostic and implementation processes competently and to avoid the "mechanistic installation" problem. It requires a good deal of vision, commitment, and risk taking on the part of those responsible for the changes to ensure that the "small change" effect does not so compromise what is done that nobody notices that anything is different afterwards. And it requires that existing organizational structures, systems, and practices be supportive of the changes (or, alternatively, themselves be amenable to redesign to make them more supportive) to avoid the "vanishing effects" phenomenon.

These requirements often present significant obstacles to change, especially in organizations where work has traditionally been designed and managed according to the tenets of industrial engineering and classical organization theory. Indeed, one critic of job enrichment dismisses our diagnostic, system-focused approach by suggesting (perhaps with some justification) that our "recipe for success is such an amalgam of wisdom and decency that it would seem to require a managerial class of supermen and saints to use it properly" (Florman, 1976, p. 18).

In sum, it appears that only organizations that are already relatively well designed and well managed are likely to meet the conditions required for successful use of work redesign as a strategy for planned change of intact and relatively stable organizational systems. What we may have, then, is yet another case in organizational life where the rich get richer, and the poor—if they try to make the leap—are likely to fail.

We must emphasize, however, that what we have been discussing here is relatively radical and far-reaching change of existing organizations, with work redesign used as an organization development technique to get things underway. As will be seen below, this is far from the only appropriate use of the principles of work redesign.

ALTERNATIVE USES OF WORK REDESIGN

Our suggestion that work redesign can only occasionally be used to "turn around" intact work systems could be taken as an occasion for great pessimism. Indeed, one conclusion could be that we should give up on job redesign as a change strategy. This appears to be the view of Dr. Harry Levinson, a well-known management psychologist, as reported in the *New York Times* article reproduced in Exhibit 10.1.

Lest we be misunderstood, let us emphasize that we do *not* concur with what Dr. Levinson seems to be saying—namely, that the cause is hopeless, that work redesign should be abandoned as a point of leverage for personal and organizational change. For one thing,

Exhibit 10.1
Giving Up on Redesigning Jobs: One Consultant's View

If you're a boss and grumbling employees cause you sleepless nights, forget it. That's the advice of Harry Levinson, a management psychologist. Reporting in a recent issue of his *Levinson Letter,* Dr. Levinson says that most employees eventually get sick of their jobs and that there is really nothing anyone can do for them.

"The quality of work life can be improved in small ways," Dr. Levinson says, "but flextime, worker participation and improved working conditions don't change the basic nature of the work. Most work is repetitive, routinized and boring. No job can be endlessly enriched."

One of the principal tasks of any good manager, Dr. Levinson advises, is to help employees "accept the realities of their job limitations." He cites a study by Herbert Greenberg, president of the Marketing Research Corporation, which purports to show that 80 percent of all American workers in every job category have jobs for which they are unsuited. . . .

"They are," says Dr. Levinson, "simply stuck." A good boss, he contends, will help such employees reconcile themselves to the fact that they are stuck. "But," he concludes, "boredom is a reason, not an excuse, and when dissatisfied employees cannot shape up, they must go."

From *The New York Times.* December 7. 1978. p. D2. © 1978 by The New York Times Company. Reprinted by permission.

sometimes organizational circumstances are such that it *is* possible to use work redesign to initiate substantial changes in work systems. When this is the case, we endorse such applications with enthusiasm. Moreover, as we have emphasized throughout this book, beginning with the case of Ralph Chattick on page 1, how work is structured powerfully affects both organizational productivity and the lives of organization members. These effects, in our view, are far too consequential for the principles of work redesign to be blithely abandoned merely because they cannot be used routinely for radical change of intact work systems.

What, then, are the alternatives to using work redesign as an "organization development" technique? Three possibilities are reviewed below.

Designing New Organizational Units

As noted above, our conservatism about the use of work redesign as an organization development technique stems primarily from the difficulty of getting changes in jobs to take root and prosper in relatively stable, ongoing organizational units. The changes often just do not have a good enough chance against the "big guys"—the interdependent operating systems, organizational structures, and management practices that give the organization its stability.

When, however, new organizations are designed (or when there is a *major* reorganization of an existing unit), it is possible to design organizational systems, structures, and practices from the ground up, and to design them in a way that supports rather than undermines nontraditional work structures. The result can be substantial innovations in the design of work that have powerful and beneficial effects (Lawler, 1978).

Yet even when new organizations are designed (or old ones are redesigned top to bottom) questions of priority and precedence emerge. Consider, for example, how decisions are made about the structure of an organization. By structure, we mean those arrangements often expressed by boxes and lines on organizational charts that divide up and coordinate authority, responsibility, and information in an organization. Decisions about structure include choices about how centralized authority will be, whether the organization will be arranged along functional or product lines, how staff and line relationships will be structured and coordinated, and so on.

At minimum, an organizational structure provides the following:

- Means for managing organization-environment relations, including responses to environmental changes (in the labor market, the competitive environment, or regulatory context).

- Means for coordinating organizational units and assuring an appropriate flow of information and influence—both up and down the organizational hierarchy and laterally across different functional and substantive areas.

- Means for supporting and managing the work activities of organization members—providing direction, information, supplies, technical assistance, and so on, to those who are actually generating the goods or services that the organization exists to produce.

Traditional wisdom about organizational design suggests that the structure of an organization should be responsive to (1) the imperatives of the core technology of the organization, (2) the demands and opportunities in the environment (including how stable and predictable the environment is), and (3) the strategic directions for the organization that have been selected by top management. Thus, the shape of an organization that produces inexpensive furniture for a stable mass market using production line technology would be quite different from that of an organization that produces hand-crafted custom furniture in response to special customer orders.

Decisions about the design of work usually are made within the limits imposed by these presumably more basic decisions about how the organization as a whole is structured. The problem is that after all structural decisions are made there may be few realistic options remaining for how the work can be designed. This can be true even in new organizational units if decision making about the design of work comes only after most other questions of organizational design have been settled.

An alternative approach to the design of organizations would give design of work considerations greater priority, even placing them ahead of decisions about the shape and structure of the organization itself. How this might be done in setting up a new organization is illustrated in the following four-step process.[2]

---

2   The steps below are written as if the organization in question were an industrial firm. The same logic, albeit with different words, can be applied to other types of organizations, including those in the public and nonprofit sectors.

First, the strategy of the organization would be determined by top management. Based on the properties of the organizational environment, the position of the organization in its market, and the goals and values of management, the major aspirations and performance objectives of the organization as a whole would be specified.

Second, designers would identify those special resources and constraints in the organization and its environment that bear on the accomplishment of these strategic objectives. These might include the availability of special work technologies, regulatory constraints, the supply of capital, the character of the labor market, the level of managerial talent available, and so on.

Third, explicit consideration would be given to how the *work* should be arranged to contribute most directly to the accomplishment of strategic objectives given any special resources of the organization (such as a readily available pool of skilled workers) and any constraints within which it must operate (that only a single type of technology is viable for the kind of work that is to be done, for example).

Finally, attention would turn to alternative structures for supporting and managing key work activities, for coordinating and controlling organizational units, and for managing organization-environment relationships. Decisions about these matters would follow from, and be responsive to, the three issues highlighted above: the strategy of the organization, special resources and constraints, and the design of core work activities.

This approach obviously gives greater precedence to design of work considerations than they usually receive when organizations are designed. And it is close to what actually has been done in many successful "new plant" experiments involving innovative work structures (like the Topeka plant of General Foods, discussed earlier in the book). Indeed, as noted in Chapter 5, at the Kalmar plant of Volvo even the core technology of the organization (which usually is considered an immutable given) was redesigned to make possible a design for work that would be consistent with the strategic objectives set by management about the organization's product and its use of human resources.

In sum, the design of a new organization (or the major reorganization of an old one) offers many opportunities for use of the principles of work redesign that we have been discussing in this book. However, even in these relatively benign circumstances one must be careful not to put design decisions having to do with the work itself last, among those issues that are dealt with when all of the "important" organizational design questions have been settled. For to do so risks exactly the same kinds of "small change" and "vanishing effects" problems that often compromise attempts to redesign work within intact, ongoing organizational units.

Seizing Opportunities

The chance to wholly redesign an organization comes only rarely. Yet there are many other occasions when the principles of work redesign can be used appropriately and with considerable impact, particularly when those "stable" organizational systems that make planned change so difficult become temporarily *unstable*. During such periods of turbulence, the defenses of an organization against change are down. And therefore it may be possible both to introduce meaningfully large changes in jobs and to work out an appropriate fit between those innovations and the surrounding organizational systems before things settle down again.

This is precisely the strategy used by a middle manager in a large bank who more than once had tried, and failed, to get certain jobs redesigned in her department. On this occasion, virtually all organizational systems were thrown into disarray as plans were laid for introducing new data processing equipment into the department and, as a by-product, reducing staff size by almost one-third. The manager had responsibility for figuring out how to set up the workflow using the new equipment, and she took that opportunity to create a set of jobs that were quite well designed from a motivational point of view.

She began by conducting a diagnosis of the existing jobs to identify motivational strengths and weaknesses in how the work presently was designed. She then convened her staff to generate ideas for how the new jobs might be structured so they would be higher in motivating potential. The new ideas that the managers came up with were then tried out with some of the people who would fill the redesigned jobs and were further revised based on their reactions and suggestions. Finally, when the basic workflow and set of job descriptions were almost ready, she examined each of the operating systems of the unit and made changes where necessary to make sure that those systems would support the work and the employees as fully as possible. When, eventually, members of top management came around to see how the new data-processing system was operating, they discovered that more than they had anticipated had been changed. But it was all working quite nicely, and they were pleased.

The "opening" for work redesign in this case was provided by a technological change. Because new work technologies invariably require some adjustment of jobs and workflows, they can provide excellent opportunities for reviewing and revising the motivational structure of the work and for improving the design of organizational systems and practices that support the work. And line managers sometimes can have a good deal of influence over how work is restructured in response to technological innovations.

The increasing use of microprocessing technologies in secretarial and clerical functions is a good case in point. Consider, for example, word processing. State-of-the-art word-processing equipment offers the chance for great increases in the efficiency and quality of secretarial work. But the technology itself is relatively neutral about how jobs and organizations are designed to take advantage of these opportunities. So managers who tilt toward a scientific management view of organizations have capitalized on word-processing technology to create secretarial jobs that are highly simplified, specialized, and routinized. A pool of data entry personnel is often formed, whose members do nothing but enter into the machinery materials supplied by word-processing users. Other staff members serve reception and telephone functions for a large group of users, and still others specialize in travel arrangements and administrative chores. Nobody has a motivationally well-designed job, and users of the word-processing service often feel that they have lost their secretaries in the bargain.

Alternatively, the same technology can be used to create secretarial jobs that are both efficient and well designed motivationally. By providing secretaries with remote word-processing terminals, it remains possible for them to have their desks near those of their clients and to maintain special relationships with them. At the same time, the variety of tasks that are performed using the terminals increases, the amount of routine retyping is reduced, and the net effect can be both greater productivity *and* a motivationally improved secretarial job.

For word processing, then, there is a good deal of discretion about how work will be designed to take advantage of a technological advance. In other cases, however, it will be nearly impossible to create well-designed jobs within the limitations imposed by a new technology. Sometimes, for example, line managers are presented with an intact, highly efficient and motivationally disastrous package of equipment and work procedures that is the product of literally years of careful work by engineer's and systems analysts. There will be nothing the managers can do but plug in the technology and then attempt to deal with the resulting motivational and organizational problems however they can. (Work design consultants are sometimes called in for advice about the emergent "people problems" in such circumstances, but they are not likely to be of much help: the problems are rooted in the technology, and the technology cannot be changed.)

The forward-looking manager, then, will keep in close contact with those groups who are developing equipment and procedures for future use in the manager's organization. This will usually be difficult, since research and development, systems, and engineering groups are often both functionally and geographically remote from the line manager. But unless influence can be wielded at the time work technologies are designed and developed, line managers may later find themselves with serious motivational problems on their hands— problems for which no immediate remedies are apparent.

We have focused above on the "openings" provided by technological changes in work organizations. There are numerous other kinds of changes and instabilities that also can be used by watchful managers and consultants as occasions for revising the way jobs and work systems are structured.

One such occasion is a change of managers. Most new managers are interested in using their "honeymoon" period in their new positions to make some changes to improve unit functioning. This is one reason why the arrival of a new manager is a time for concern about the continuation of a preexisting work redesign program: as noted earlier, the new manager may favor a different approach to organizational change. But for precisely the same reason a management change can provide an opportunity for some fresh thinking about how the work of the unit is structured and supervised. Work redesign, in these circumstances, can be viewed as an interesting "new broom" for use by the new management team in making change, rather than as a not necessarily desirable legacy of the departed managers.

Similarly, the introduction of a new product or service can provide an occasion for restructuring work systems, as can periods of rapid growth (or shrinkage) in the size of an organizational unit. Other opportunities for work restructuring may develop as a function of changes in the economy, in the market for the goods or services provided by the organization, in the legislative or regulatory context within which the organization operates, or in the labor market. These environmental changes are often not perceived to have implications for the design of work, but they all can provide good openings for rethinking how the organization structures and manages its key work activities.

In sum, organizations regularly move back and forth between periods of relative stability and periods of transition and instability. Rather than use work redesign to try to change an organization when things are relatively stable (for example, by sending human resource staff members around the organization to sell their wares to whatever management groups will provide an audience), it may be better for human resource professionals to lie in wait for those times when the organization is (for whatever reasons) particularly receptive to the possibility of change in how work is structured. The wait rarely will be long.

Local Changes

When planned, developmental changes in organizations using work redesign are infeasible, and when there are not naturally occurring "openings" for change, must work redesign simply be set aside until more favorable conditions prevail? No, there is yet another option. Individual managers often can proceed on their own initiative to make enriching changes in the work of the people they supervise. Managers can release some of their own decision-making responsibilities to subordinates; they can place subordinates in direct contact with the "clients" of their work; they can encourage sharing and rotation of responsibilities on an informal basis; they can combine fragmented tasks into more meaningful jobs; and so on (Oldham, 1976b).

No complex diagnosis of the work system is involved in such undertakings, no planning groups sit down to "greenlight" possible changes, and there is no outside evaluation of how the jobs were changed and with what effects. The manager simply decides that he or she is going to do everything that can be done to create conditions for high internal motivation and personal growth at work within his or her own domain. Sometimes there is quite a lot that can be done (for example, in decentralized, low-technology units where the manager has considerable discretion); other times the manager has less latitude. But there almost always are *some* changes that can be made, in the work or in the manager's own behavior, to improve the motivational properties of subordinates' jobs.

As we noted earlier, work redesign is really more a way of managing than it is a formal intervention technique, and the potential payoffs to people and to organizations from "local" changes in how jobs are designed should not be underestimated. Indeed, there is probably more job enrichment going on at local initiative today than there are "seized opportunities" and planned change programs combined.

Summary

In this section we have reviewed three alternatives to the use of work redesign as a device for planned, developmental change of intact organizational systems. Each of these—designing new organizational units, seizing serendipitous opportunities for change, and informal change at the initiative of local management—offers the chance to bring the principles of work redesign to bear on the life and work of people in organizations.

Yet whether any or all of these approaches will be used to good effect depends heavily on what managers *want* to do and on what they are *able* to do. What does the future portend for work redesign in U.S. organizations? Will we decide that we want to create jobs high in complexity, challenge, and autonomy? And, if so, will we become more competent than we are at the moment in designing such jobs and managing people who work on them? As will be seen in the section to follow, we may be very near the point at which such questions will be decided.

THE DESIGN OF WORK IN THE FUTURE

In the preceding pages we have provided an assessment of where organizational change through the redesign of work stands at present. While we could not be terribly optimistic about using work redesign to reorient entire organizations, we did see many useful alternative applications of the approach.

What of the future? How is work likely to be arranged in the decade to come? Will the idea of enriched, internally motivating work catch on and become dominant in how organizations are managed? Or do we have here a passing fad that, like so many other behavioral science interventions, soon will be laid to rest in favor of the next new idea to come along?

Here are two possible scenarios for the future, two routes that could be followed in designing work for the 1980s. The first route involves fitting jobs to people and is consistent with enriched work and personal growth. The second emphasizes fitting people to jobs and attempts to maximize technological and engineering efficiency. As will be seen below, what work will look like in organizations in the next decade greatly depends on which route is chosen.

Route One: Fitting Jobs to People

Route One builds directly on the ideas in this book. The basic notion is that by designing work so that people can be *internally* motivated to perform well, gains will be realized both in the productive effectiveness of organizations and in the personal well-being of the work force.

Under Route One, work would sometimes be designed to be done by individuals working more or less autonomously, and other times it would be set up to be performed by self-managing work groups. But in either case the aspiration would be to arrange things so that employees (1) experience the work as inherently meaningful, (2) feel personal (or collective) responsibility for the outcomes of the work, and (3) receive, on a regular basis, trustworthy knowledge about the results of the work activities.

Assuming we follow Route One, and do so competently and successfully, here are some speculations about how work might be designed and managed by the late 1980s.

1. Responsibility for work will be clearly pegged at the organizational level where the work is done. No longer will employees experience themselves as people who merely execute activities that "belong" to someone else (such as a line manager). Instead, they will feel, legitimately, that they are both responsible and accountable for the outcomes of their work. Moreover, the resources and the information needed to carry out the work (including feedback about how well the work is getting done) will be provided directly to employees without being filtered first through line and staff managers. As a result, we will see an increase in the personal motivation of employees to perform well and a concomitant increase in the quality of the work that is done.

2. Questions of employee motivation and satisfaction will be considered explicitly when new technologies and work practices are invented and engineered (just as intellectual and motor capabilities are presently considered). No longer will work systems be designed solely to optimize technological or engineering efficiency, with motivational problems left for managers to deal with after the systems are installed. Moreover, there will be no single "right answer" about how best to design work and work systems. In many cases work will be "individualized" to improve the fit between the characteristics of an employee and the tasks that he or she performs. Standard managerial practices that apply equally well to all individuals in a work unit will no longer be appropriate. Instead, managers will have to become as adept at adjusting jobs to people as they now are at adjusting people to fit the demands and requirements of fixed jobs.

3. Organizations will be viewed as places where people grow and learn new things. Organizations will support and nurture employees' aspirations for personal development, and will provide a buffet of means for these aspirations to be pursued. As a result, people will tend more to see themselves as having personal control of their careers (rather than as pawns moved about by their employers), and most will find work a fulfilling part of their lives. This kind of fulfillment, it should be noted, goes far beyond simple "job satisfaction." People can be made "satisfied" at work, as Ralph Chattick was in Chapter 1, simply by paying them adequately, keeping bosses off their backs, putting them in pleasant work spaces with pleasant people, and arranging things so that the days pass without undue stress and strain. The kind of satisfaction we will see in the late 1980s is different: it is a satisfaction that develops when people are stretching and growing as human beings and increasing their feelings of self-worth as productive organization members.

4. Organizations will be leaner, with fewer hierarchical levels and fewer managerial and staff personnel whose jobs are primarily documentation, supervision, and inspection of work done by others. This will require new ways of managing people at work, and will give rise to new kinds of managerial problems. For example, to the extent that significant motivational gains are realized by enriched work in individualized organizations, managers will no longer have the problem of "how to get these lazy incompetents to put in a decent day's work." Instead, the more pressing problem may be what to do *next* to keep

people challenged and interested in their work. For as people become accustomed to personal growth and learning on the job, what was once a challenge may eventually become routine, and ever more challenge may be required to keep frustration and boredom from setting in. How to manage an organization so that growth opportunities are continuously available may become a difficult managerial challenge, especially if, as predicted, there is shrinkage in the number of managerial slots into which employees can be promoted.

5. Finally, if the previous predictions are correct, there eventually will be a good deal of pressure on the broader political and economic system to find ways to use effectively human resources that no longer are needed to populate the bowels of work organizations. Imagine that organizations eventually do become leaner and more effective and, at the same time, the rate of growth of society as a whole is reduced to near zero. Under such circumstances, there will be large numbers of people who are "free" for meaningful employment outside traditional private and public sector work organizations. To expand welfare services and compensate such individuals for not working (or for working only a small portion of the time they have available for productive activities) would be inconsistent with the overall thrust of Route One. What, then, is to be done with such individuals? Can we imagine groups of public philosophers, artists, and poets compensated by society for contributing to the creation of an enriched intellectual and aesthetic environment for the populace? An interesting possibility, surely, but one that would require radical rethinking of public decision making about the goals of society and the way shared resources are to be allocated toward the achievement of those goals.

Route Two: Fitting People to Jobs

If we take Route Two, the idea is to design and engineer work for maximum economic and technological efficiency, and then do whatever must be done to help people adapt in personally acceptable ways to their work experiences. No great flight of imagination is required to guess what work will be like in the late 1980s if we follow Route Two, as the sprouts of this approach are visible at present. Work is designed and managed in a way that clearly subordinates the needs and goals of people to the demands and requirements of fixed jobs. External controls are employed to ensure that individuals do in fact behave appropriately on the job. These include close and directive supervision, financial incentives for correct performance, tasks that are engineered to minimize the possibility of human mistakes, and information and control systems that allow management to monitor the performance of work systems as closely and continuously as possible. And, throughout, productivity and efficiency tend to dominate quality and service as the primary criteria for assessing organizational performance.

If we continue down Route Two, what might be predicted about the design and management of work in the late 1980s? Here are our guesses.

1. Technological and engineering considerations will dominate decision making about how jobs are designed. Technology is becoming increasingly central to many work activities, and that trend will accelerate. Also, major advances will be achieved in techniques for engineering work systems to make them ever more efficient. Together, these developments will greatly boost the productivity of individual workers and, in many cases, result in jobs that are nearly "people proof" (that is, work that is arranged to virtually eliminate the possibility of error due to faulty judgment, lapses of attention, or misdirected motivation). Large numbers of relatively mindless tasks, including many kinds of inspection operations, will be automated out of existence.

Simultaneous with these technological advances will be a further increase in the capability of industrial psychologists to analyze and specify in advance the knowledge and skills required for a person to perform satisfactorily almost any task that can be designed. Sophisticated employee assessment and placement procedures will be used to select people and assign them to tasks, and only rarely will individuals be placed on jobs for which they are not fully qualified.

The result of all of these developments will be a quantum improvement in the efficiency of most work systems, especially those that process physical materials or paper. And while employees will receive more pay for less work than they presently do, they will also experience substantially less discretion and challenge in their work activities.

2. Work performance and organizational productivity will be closely monitored and controlled by managers using highly sophisticated information systems. Integrated circuit microprocessors will provide

the hardware needed to gather and summarize performance data for work processes that presently defy cost-efficient measurement. Software will be developed to provide managers with data about work performance and costs that are far more reliable, more valid, and more current than is possible with existing information systems. Managers increasingly will come to depend on these data for decision making and will use them to control production processes vigorously and continuously.

Because managerial control of work will increase substantially, responsibility for work outcomes will lie squarely in the laps of managers, and the gap between those who do the work and those who control it will grow. There will be accelerated movement toward a two-class society of people who work in organizations, with the challenge and intrinsic interest of key managerial and professional jobs increasing even as the work of rank-and-file employees becomes more controlled and less involving.

3. Desired on-the-job behavior will be elicited and maintained by extensive and sophisticated use of extrinsic rewards. Since (if our first prediction is correct) work in the late 1980s will be engineered for clarity and simplicity, there will be little question about what each employee should (and should not) do on the job. Moreover (if our second prediction is correct), management will have data readily at hand to monitor the results of the employee's work on a more or less continuous basis. All that is required, then, are devices to ensure that the person *actually* does what he or she is *supposed* to do. Because many jobs will be routinized, standardized, and closely controlled by management, it is doubtful that employee motivation to perform appropriately can be created and maintained using intrinsic rewards (people working hard and effectively because they enjoy the tasks or because they obtain internal rewards from doing them well). So it will be necessary for management to use extrinsic rewards (such as pay or supervisory praise) to motivate employees by providing such rewards contingent on behavior that agrees with the wishes of management. The most sophisticated strategy for accomplishing this, and one that is wholly consistent with increased management control of organizational behavior is "behavior modification" (see Chapter 2). If Route Two is followed, we predict that behavior modification programs will be among the standard motivational techniques used in work organizations by the late 1980s.

4. Most organizations will sponsor programs to help people adapt to life at work, including sophisticated procedures for assisting employees and their families in dealing with alcohol and drug abuse problems. Such problems will become much more widely offered (and needed) than they are at present because of unintended spin-offs of the movement toward the productive efficiencies promised at the end of Route Two.

Consider, for example, a man currently working on an undemanding, repetitive, and routine job. It might be someone who matches checks and invoices, and then clips them together to be processed by another employee. The job is low in motivating potential, and the outcomes from hard work probably have more to do with headaches and feelings of robothood than with any sense of meaningful personal accomplishment from high on-the-job effort. Clearly, there is a lack of any positive, internal motivation to work hard and effectively.

Now let us transport that employee via time machine to the mid-1980s, and place him on a very similar job under full-fledged Route Two conditions. The work is just as routine and undemanding as it was before. But now there is greater management control over hour-by-hour operations, and valued external rewards are available, but only when the employee behaves according to explicit management specifications. How will our hypothetical employee react to that state of affairs?

At first, he is likely to feel even more like a small cog in a large wheel than before. Whereas prior to the introduction of the new management controls he could get away with some personal games and fantasies on the job, that is now much harder to do. Moreover, the problem is exacerbated, not relieved, by the addition of the performance-contingent rewards. The negative intrinsic outcomes that were contingent on the hard work before are still felt, but they have been supplemented (not replaced) by a set of new and positive *extrinsic* outcomes. So the employee is faced with contingencies that specify, "The harder I work, the more negative I feel about myself and what I'm doing, the more likely I am to get tired and headachy on the job, *and* the more likely I am to get praise from my supervisor and significant financial bonuses." As noted in Chapter 2, this state of affairs—having strong positive and strong negative outcomes contingent on the same behavior—prompts some people to engage in maladaptive behaviors such as drug usage and alcoholism, and to exhibit signs of "craziness."

So if we move vigorously down Route Two, we should expect an increase in behavioral problems among employees. However, only a small proportion of the work force will show signs of serious "sickness," even under full-fledged Route Two conditions. The reason, as suggested in Chapter 1, is that people have a good deal of resilience and usually can adapt to almost any work situation if given plenty of time and a little support. So although we can predict that numerous individuals will feel tension and stress in adjusting to work in the 1980s, and that their aspirations for personal growth and development at work may be significantly dampened, major overt problems will be observed infrequently.

Yet because *any* "crazy" employee behavior is an anathema to management (and clearly dysfunctional for organizational effectiveness), managers will attempt to head off such behaviors before they occur. When they do occur, management will deal with them as promptly and as helpfully as possible. So we should see in the late 1980s a substantial elaboration of organizational programs to help people adapt in healthy ways to their work situations. All will applaud such programs because they will benefit both individual human beings and their employing organizations. Few will understand that the need for such programs came about, in large part, as a result of designing work and managing organizations according to the technological and motivational "efficiencies" of Route Two.

At the Fork in the Road

Which will it be in the 1980s—Route One, or Route Two? Actually, there will be no occasion for making an explicit choice between the two. Instead, the choice will be enacted as seemingly insignificant decisions are made about immediate questions such as how to design the next generation of a certain technology, how to motivate employees and increase their commitment to their present jobs, or how best to use the sophisticated information technologies that are becoming available.

Our view, based on the choices that we now see being made, is that we are moving with some vigor down Route Two. That direction, moreover, seems unlikely to change in the foreseeable future for at least two reasons.

What Is Known.   We know *how* to operate according to Route Two rules, while we tend to fumble when we try to redesign work according to Route One. The issue is not that we are lacking theories about what makes a good job or a good work group. We have presented ideas about that in this book, and if they do not satisfy there are plenty of good alternatives available (e.g., Cherns, 1976; Cummings, 1978; Davis and Trist, 1974; Herzberg, 1976). The problem, instead, is that our knowledge about how to *use* those theories is still rather primitive, particularly regarding the process by which changes in jobs and work systems are installed, and strategies for supporting them once they are in place. As seen in Chapter 9, present knowledge allows little more than specification of some choices that must be made when work systems are redesigned. That is not enough for either a theory of organizational intervention through work redesign or for the development of guidelines that specify how best to proceed to change jobs under various organizational circumstances.

Moreover, scholars are only just beginning to develop procedures for carrying out robust evaluations of the economic costs and benefits of innovative work designs (see, for example, Macy and Mirvis, 1976) and for reconciling the dual criteria of efficiency and quality of worklife in designing work systems (Lupton, 1975). These are particularly important tasks, given the understandable propensity of managers to ask about the "bottom line" in considering whether and how to redesign work systems. The challenge is considerable. It is now generally agreed that simple measures of job satisfaction are not adequate for assessing work redesign activities (see Chapter 1). Neither do simple measures of productivity do the trick (that is, quantity of production as a function of labor cost). Yet other outcomes, including many that are perhaps among those most appropriate for assessing the results of work redesign activities, are currently extremely difficult to measure. What is the cost of poor quality work? Of "extra" supervisory time? Of redundant inspections? Of absenteeism, soldiering, and sabotage? Until we are able to measure the effects of work redesign on such outcomes, it will continue to be nearly impossible to determine unambiguously whether job changes "pay off" for organizations or to specify with certainty what kinds of benefits should and should not be anticipated from this change strategy.

Finally, we currently know very little about the conditions that are required for innovations in work design to persist across time and to diffuse across organizational units. Even when clearly successful changes in jobs have been made they often fail to diffuse throughout the larger organization where they were developed—let alone to different organizations where the same kind of work is done (Walton, 1975b).

What Is Valued.   Even if we did know more about how to design, manage, and diffuse work structured according to Route One, our guess is that most organizations would decide not to use that knowledge very extensively. There are many reasons why. For one, Route One is heavily dependent on behavioral science knowledge and techniques, whereas Route Two depends more on "hard" engineering technology and traditional economic models of organizational efficiency. If behavioral science has ever won out over an amalgam of engineering and economics, the case has not come to our attention. Moreover, Route One solutions, if they are to prosper, require major changes in how organizations themselves are designed and managed; Route Two solutions, on the other hand, fit nicely with traditional hierarchical organizational models and controlling managerial practices. Again, it seems not to be much of a contest.

But perhaps most telling is the fact that Route Two is more consistent with the behavioral styles and values of both employees and managers in contemporary organizations. Experienced employees know how to adapt and survive on relatively routine, unchallenging jobs. Would individuals such as Ralph Chattick, who are comfortable and secure in their worklives, leap at the chance for a wholly different kind of work experience in an organization designed according to the principles of Route One? Some would, to be sure, especially among the younger and more adventurous members of the workforce, but many would not. Learning how to function within a Route One organization could be a long and not terribly pleasant process, and it is unclear how many would be willing to tolerate the upset and the anxiety of the change process long enough to gain a sense of what work in a Route One organization might have to offer.

Managers, too, have good reasons to be skeptical about Route One and its implications. The whole idea flies in the face of beliefs and values about people and organizations that have become well learned and well accepted by managers of traditional organizations (for example, that organizations are supposed to be run from the top down, not from the bottom up; that many employees have neither the competence nor the commitment to take real responsibility for carrying out the work of the organization on their own; that organizational effectiveness should be measured primarily, if not exclusively, in terms of the economic efficiency of the enterprise; that more management control of employee behavior is better management).

Reversing Directions

Are we being too pessimistic? Perhaps. There are documented instances, including a number reported in this book, where employees and managers alike have responded with enthusiasm to work redesign activities that had many of the trappings of Route One.

Yet if one suspects that current trends in management tend to favor Route Two (which we do), and doesn't like that idea (which we don't), what is to be done about it? For one thing, better understanding of organizational changes that involve redesigning work is needed. As noted above, there is a pressing need to know more about (1) the process of carrying out planned change of work systems, (2) strategies for conducting informative evaluations of work redesign activities that account for the multiplicity of their effects, and (3) factors that affect the persistence and diffusion of innovations in the design of work.

Such knowledge, however, would merely improve our capability to begin moving down Route One. It would not make us *want* to go that direction. Providing the social "push" for a reversal of direction, we believe, will require some combination of the following.

1. Organized labor decides to make improvement in the quality of life at work a high-priority item. At present, some union leaders find their members to be uninterested in job enrichment or quality of worklife issues; other labor spokespersons argue that such issues ought to be high on the list of objectives of the labor movement, and are providing leadership in bringing these matters to the attention of their members. Which set of views will dominate in the years to come? What, indeed, are the rewards and risks for unions and for union leaders if they take the lead on this issue?

2. Significant numbers of managers in major corporations, or in large public bureaucracies, decide that work redesign pays off in coin they value. Managers, generally, are adept at identifying indicators of organizational performance that "count" in the eyes of significant

others (such as stockholders, members of congress, or high-level managers) and then managing their organizational units so that the performance indicators are favorable. What kinds of data would it take to convince results-oriented managers that their own objectives would be well served by introducing and supporting innovative designs for work? Or are fundamental changes in organizational control systems and accounting practices required before this can happen? Are such changes likely? Who might initiate them?

3. Government decides to require or encourage organizations to improve the quality of worklife of their employees. Some commentators (e.g., Lawler, 1976) have argued that government might wish to legislate improvements in the quality of worklife, even to the extent of fining organizations that persist in providing a poor quality of worklife for their employees. Others (e.g., Locke, 1976) find government regulation in this area a perfectly awful idea. Would such an approach be politically feasible? Would it work? Are there other ways the government could encourage innovation in work design? How about financial encouragement of organizational experimentation with new ways of designing work? Or, perhaps most significantly, could the present economic incentives that favor capital utilization (through the investment tax credit, which encourages the purchase of technology that often eliminates or routinizes jobs) and that discourage labor utilization (through social security and unemployment taxation) be tilted somewhat more in favor of effective use of human resources?

4. The cultural climate changes to support the idea that work experiences should be more fulfilling and growth enhancing. Will the large numbers of people whose jobs are currently far beneath their qualifications begin to speak with a common voice and demand more personally meaningful work? Will the continued exposure of successful organizational innovations in the media gradually engender a positive cultural value for enriched and challenging work? Will people start to *care* more about the quality of their own and others' experiences on the job?

5. The national economy collapses or enters a period of significant crisis. While not a change strategy that many would wish to actively pursue, in fact an economic crisis might provide a once-in-a-lifetime opportunity to significantly alter how work is designed and how

organizations are run. If those who favor Route One solutions were ready with an attractive vision and a road map for making that vision reality when the present system quits working, then *real* change just might be achieved.

All five of these possible forces for change have one thing in common: they involve changes in what people want or what they need. They deal with the reward contingencies that others have created for us or that we have created for ourselves. For that reason, they deal with power—and, as always is the case for power, they ultimately deal with values.

To the extent that as managers, as consultants, or as scholars we have a bit of power to change how work is designed, how do we want to use it? *What kind of life do we want to create for the people who do the productive work of our society—and how much are we willing to pay for it?* The answer to that question, far more than the answers to questions about how much we do or don't know about organizational change, will determine how work actually is designed in organizations—now, and in the years to come.

FOR ADDITIONAL READING

Lawler, E.E. III. The new plant revolution. *Organizational Dynamics,* Winter 1978, 2-12. Is there an impending revolution in how new organizations are designed? Here is a description of how multiple innovations, including reward systems, physical layouts, personnel policies, and designs for work have been installed simultaneously in new plants. If these experiments are sucessful (as Lawler thinks they will be) their implications could be profound.

Bluestone, I. Decision making by workers. *The Personnel Administrator,* July-August 1974, 26-30; *and* Winpisinger, W.W. Job enrichment: A union view. *Monthly Labor Review,* April 1973, 54-56. Here are the views of two national labor leaders who disagree about what the stance of organized labor should be toward work redesign and quality of worklife innovations in the years to come.

Lawler, E.E. III. Should the quality of work life be legislated? *The Personnel Administrator,* January 1976, 17-21; *and* Locke, E.A. The case against legislating quality of work life. *The Personnel Administrator,* May 1976, 19-21. These two authors lay out the arguments for and against government involvement in improving the quality of worklife in organizations through legislative action.

Kanter, R.M. Work in a new America. *Daedalus,* Winter, 47-78. This article reviews trends in the meaning of work and views about individual rights at work, with special attention to the perceptions of various demographic subgroups. The changing perceptions documented here have numerous implications for the design and management of organizations in the future.

APPENDIXES

APPENDIX A
THE JOB DIAGNOSTIC SURVEY

This appendix reproduces the Job Diagnostic Survey (JDS), an instrument designed to measure the key elements of the job characteristics theory. The survey measures several job characteristics, employees' experienced psychological states, employees' satisfaction with their jobs and work context, and the growth need strength of respondents. For a complete description of the job characteristics theory and the variables measured by the JDS, see Chapter 4 of this volume.

The JDS was designed to be completed by the incumbents of the job or jobs in question—not by individuals outside the job. An instrument designed for the latter purpose is entitled the Job Rating Form (JRF) and is reproduced in Appendix B. Instructions for scoring the JDS and JRF may be found in Appendix C. JDS norms for several job families are provided in Appendix E and may be used for comparison purposes with JDS data collected from many jobs.

The JDS is not copyrighted and therefore may be used without the authors' permission. However, prior to using the JDS, one should carefully read the users' guide for administering and interpreting the instrument (see Appendix D).

A short form of the JDS has also been developed. It excludes measures of the experienced psychological states and uses fewer items to measure other key variables in the job characteristics theory. The JDS short form and its scoring key may be found in Hackman and Oldham (1974).

JOB DIAGNOSTIC SURVEY

This questionnaire was developed as part of a Yale University study of jobs and how people react to them. The questionnaire helps to determine how jobs can be better designed, by obtaining information about how people react to different kinds of jobs.

On the following pages you will find several different kinds of questions about your job. Specific instructions are given at the start of each section. Please read them carefully. It should take no more than 25 minutes to complete the entire questionnaire. Please move through it quickly.

The questions are designed to obtain *your* perceptions of your job and *your* reactions to it.

There are no trick questions. Your individual answers will be kept completely confidential. Please answer each item as honestly and frankly as possible.

Thank you for your cooperation.

SECTION ONE

This part of the questionnaire asks you to describe your job, as *objectively* as you can.

Please do *not* us this part of the questionnaire to show how much you like or dislike your job. Questions about that will come later. Instead, try to make your descriptions as accurate and as objective as you possibly can.

A sample question is given below.

A. To what extent does your job require you to work with mechanical equipment?

1 - - - - - 2 - - - - - 3 - - - - - 4 - - - - - 5 - - - - - ⑥ - - - - - 7

Very little; the job requires almost no contact with mechanical equipment of any kind.

Moderately

Very much; the job requires almost constant work with mechanical equipment.

You are to *circle* the number which is the most accurate description of your job.

If, for example, your job requires you to work with mechanical equipment a good deal of the time—but also requires some paperwork—you might circle the number six, as was done in the example above.

f you do not understand these instructions, please ask for assistance. If you do understand them, turn the page and begin.

1. To what extent does your job require you to *work closely with other people* (either "clients," or people in related jobs in your own organization)?

1 ------ 2 ------ 3 ------ 4 ------ 5 ------ 6 ------ 7

| Very little; dealing with other people is not at all necessary in doing the job. | Moderately; some dealing with others is necessary. | Very much; dealing with other people is an absolutely essential and crucial part of doing the job. |

2. How much *autonomy* is there in your job? That is, to what extent does your job permit you to decide *on your own* how to go about doing the work?

1 ------ 2 ------ 3 ------ 4 ------ 5 ------ 6 ------ 7

| Very little; the job gives me almost no personal "say" about how and when the work is done. | Moderate autonomy; many things are standardized and not under my control, but I can make some decisions about the work. | Very much: the job gives me almost complete responsibility for deciding how and when the work is done. |

3. To what extent does your job involve doing a *"whole" and identifiable piece of work?* That is, is the job a complete piece of work that has an obvious beginning and end? Or is it only a small *part* of the overall piece of work, which is finished by other people or by automatic machines?

1 ------ 2 ------ 3 ------ 4 ------ 5 ------ 6 ------ 7

| My job is only a tiny part of the overall piece of work; the results of my activities cannot be seen in the final product or service. | My job is a moderate-sized "chunk" of the overall piece of work; my own contribution can be seen in the final outcome. | My job involves doing the whole piece of work, from start to finish; the results of my activities are easily seen in the final product or service. |

4. How much *variety* is there in your job? That is, to what extent does the job require you to do many different things at work, using a variety of your skills and talents?

1 - - - - - - - 2 - - - - - - - 3 - - - - - - - 4 - - - - - - - 5 - - - - - - - 6 - - - - - - - 7

Very little; the job requires me to do the same routine things over and over again.	Moderate variety.	Very much: the job requires me to do many different things, using a number of different skills and talents.

5. In general, how *significant or important* is your job? That is, are the results of your work likely to significantly affect the lives or well-being of other people?

1 - - - - - - - 2 - - - - - - - 3 - - - - - - - 4 - - - - - - - 5 - - - - - - - 6 - - - - - - - 7

Not very significant; the outcomes of my work are *not* likely to have important effects on other people.	Moderately significant.	Highly significant; the outcomes of my work can affect other people in very important ways.

6. To what extent do *managers or co-workers* let you know how well you are doing on your job?

1 - - - - - - - 2 - - - - - - - 3 - - - - - - - 4 - - - - - - - 5 - - - - - - - 6 - - - - - - - 7

Very little; people almost never let me know how well I am doing.	Moderately; sometimes people may give me "feed-back"; other times they may not.	Very much: managers or co-workers provide me with almost constant "feedback" about how well I am doing.

To what extent does *doing the job itself* provide you with information about your work performance? That is, does the actual *work itself* provide clues about how well you are doing—aside from any "feedback" co-workers or supervisors may provide?

1 - - - - - 2 - - - - - 3 - - - - - 4 - - - - - 5 - - - - - 6 - - - - - 7

Very little; the job itself is set up so I could work forever without finding out how well I am doing.	Moderately; sometimes doing the job provides "feedback" to me; sometimes it does not.	Very much; the job is set up so that I get almost constant "feedback" as I work about how well I am doing.

SECTION TWO

Listed below are a number of statements which could be used to describe a job.

You are to indicate whether each statement is an *accurate* or an *inaccurate* description of *your* job.

Once again, please try to be as objective as you can in deciding how accurately each statement describes your job—regardless of whether you like or dislike your job.

Write a number in the blank beside each statement, based on the following scale:

How accurate is the statement in describing your job?

1	2	3	4	5	6	7
Very Inaccurate	Mostly Inaccurate	Slightly Inaccurate	Uncertain	Slightly Accurate	Mostly Accurate	Very Accurate

_____ 1. The job requires me to use a number of complex or high-level skills.

_____ 2. The job requires a lot of cooperative work with other people.

_____ 3. The job is arranged so that I do *not* have the chance to do an entire piece of work from beginning to end.

_____ 4. Just doing the work required by the job provides many chances for me to figure out how well I am doing.

_____ 5. The job is quite simple and repetitive.

_____ 6. The job can be done adequately by a person working alone—without talking or checking with other people.

_____ 7. The supervisors and co-workers on this job almost *never* give me any "feedback" about how well I am doing in my work.

_____ 8. This job is one where a lot of other people can be affected by how well the work gets done.

_____ 9. The job denies me any chance to use my personal initiative or judgment in carrying out the work.

_____ 10. Supervisors often let me know how well they think I am performing the job.

_____ 11. The job provides me the chance to completely finish the pieces of work I begin.

_____ 12. The job itself provides very few clues about whether or not I am performing well.

_____ 13. The job gives me considerable opportunity for independence and freedom in how I do the work.

_____ 14. The job itself is *not* very significant or important in the broader scheme of things.

SECTION THREE

Now please indicate how you personally feel about your job.

Each of the statements below is something that a person might say about his or her job. You are to indicate your own personal *feelings* about your job by marking how much you agree with each of the statements.

Write a number in the blank for each statement, based on this scale:

How much do you agree with the statement?

1	2	3	4	5	6	7
Disagree Strongly	Disagree	Disagree Slighlty	Neutral	Agree Slightly	Agree	Agree Strongly

_____ 1. It's hard, on this job, for me to care very much about whether or not the work gets done right.

_____ 2. My opinion of myself goes up when I do this job well.

_____ 3. Generally speaking, I am very satisfied with this job.

_____ 4. Most of the things I have to do on this job seem useless or trivial.

_____ 5. I usually know whether or not my work is satisfactory on this job.

_____ 6. I feel a great sense of personal satisfaction when I do this job well.

_____ 7. The work I do on this job is very meaningful to me.

_____ 8. I feel a very high degree of *personal* responsiblity for the work I do on this job.

_____ 9. I frequently think of quitting this job.

_____ 10. I feel bad and unhappy when I discover that I have performed poorly on this job.

_____ 11. I often have trouble figuring out whether I'm doing well or poorly on this job.

_____ 12. I feel I should personally take the credit or blame for the results of my work on this job.

_____ 13. I am generally satisfied with the kind of work I do in this job.

_____ 14. My own feelings generally are *not* affected much one way or the other by how well I do on this job.

_____ 15. Whether or not this job gets done right is clearly *my* responsibility.

SECTION FOUR

Now please indicate how *satisfied* you are with each aspect of your job listed below. Once again, write the appropriate number in the blank beside each statement.

How satisfied are you with this aspect of your job?

1	2	3	4	5	6	7
Extremely Dissatisfied	Dissatisfied	Slightly Dissatisfied	Neutral	Slightly Satisfied	Satisfied	Extremely Satisfied

_____ 1. The amount of job security I have.

_____ 2. The amount of pay and fringe benefits I receive.

_____ 3. The amount of personal growth and development I get in doing my job.

_____ 4. The people I talk to and work with on my job.

_____ 5. The degree of respect and fair treatment I receive from my boss.

_____ 6. The feeling of worthwhile accomplishment I get from doing my job.

_____ 7. The chance to get to know other people while on the job.

_____ 8. The amount of support and guidance I receive from my supervisor.

_____ 9. The degree to which I am fairly paid for what I contribute to this organization.

_____ 10. The amount of independent thought and action I can exercise in my job.

_____ 11. How secure things look for me in the future in this organization.

_____ 12. The chance to help other people while at work.

_____ 13. The amount of challenge in my job.

_____ 14. The overall quality of the supervision I receive in my work.

SECTION FIVE

Now please think of the *other people* in your organization who hold the same job you do. If no one has exactly the same job as you, think of the job which is most similar to yours.

Please think about how accurately each of the statements describes the feelings of those people about the job.

It is quite all right if your answers here are different from when you described your *own* reactions to the job. Often different people feel quite differently about the same job.

Once again, write a number in the blank for each statement, based on this scale:

How much do you agree with the statement?

1	2	3	4	5	6	7
Disagree Strongly	Disagree	Disagree Slightly	Neutral	Agree Slightly	Agree	Agree Strongly

_____ 1. Most people on this job feel a great sense of personal satisfaction when they do the job well.

_____ 2. Most people on this job are very satisfied with the job.

_____ 3. Most people on this job feel that the work is useless or trivial.

_____ 4. Most people on this job feel a great deal of personal responsibility for the work they do.

_____ 5. Most people on this job have a pretty good idea of how well they are performing their work.

_____ 6. Most people on this job find the work very meaningful.

_____ 7. Most people on this job feel that whether or not the job gets done right is clearly their own responsibility.

_____ 8. People on this job often think of quitting.

_____ 9. Most people on this job feel bad or unhappy when they find that they have performed the work poorly.

_____ 10. Most people on this job have trouble figuring out whether they are doing a good or a bad job.

SECTION SIX

Listed below are a number of characteristics which could be present on any job. People differ about how much they would like to have each one present in their own jobs. We are interested in learning _how much you personally would like_ to have each one present in your job.

Using the scale below, please indicate the _degree_ to which you _would like_ to have each characteristic present in your job.

NOTE: The numbers on this scale are different from those used in previous scales.

10
Would like
having this
extremely
much

9

8
Would like
having this
very much

7

6

5

4
Would like
having this
only a
moderate
amount
(or less)

_____ 1. High respect and fair treatment from my supervisor.

_____ 2. Stimulating and challenging work.

_____ 3. Chances to exercise independent thought and action in my job.

_____ 4. Great job security.

_____ 5. Very friendly co-workers.

_____ 6. Opportunities to learn new things from my work.

_____ 7. High salary and good fringe benefits.

_____ 8. Opportunities to be creative and imaginative in my work.

_____ 9. Quick promotions.

_____ 10. Opportunities for personal growth and development in my job.

_____ 11. A sense of worthwhile accomplishment in my work.

SECTION SEVEN

People differ in the kinds of jobs they would most like to hold. The questions in this section give you a chance to say just what it is about a job that is most important to *you*.

For each question, two different kinds of jobs are briefly described. You are to indicate which of the jobs you personally would prefer—if you had to make a choice between them

In answering each question, assume that everything else about the jobs is the same. Pay attention only to the characteristics actually listed.

Two examples are given below.

JOB A
A job requiring work with mechanical equipment most of the day

JOB B
A job requiring work with other people most of the day

1 - - - - - - - - 2 - - - - - - - - (3) - - - - - - - - 4 - - - - - - - - 5

| Strongly Prefer A | Slightly Prefer A | Neutral | Slightly Prefer B | Strongly Prefer B |

If you like working with people and working with equipment equally well, you would circle the number 3, as has been done in the example.

* * * * * * * * * * * * *

Here is another example. This one asks for a harder choice—between two jobs which both have some undesirable features.

JOB A				JOB B
A job requiring you to expose yourself to considerable physical danger.				A job located 200 miles from your home and family.
1--------	--------2--------	--------3--------	--------4--------	--------5
Strongly Prefer A	Slightly Prefer A	Neutral	Slightly Prefer B	Strongly Prefer B

If you would slightly prefer risking physical danger to working far from your home, you would circle number 2, as has been done in the example.

Please ask for assistance if you do not understand exactly how to do these questions.

1. A job where the pay is very good.

JOB A				JOB B
				A job where there is considerable opportunity to be creative and innovative.
1--------	--------2--------	--------3--------	--------4--------	--------5
Strongly Prefer A	Slightly Prefer A	Neutral	Slightly Prefer B	Strongly Prefer B

JOB A

JOB B

2. A job where you are often required to make important decisions.

A job with many pleasant people to work with.

```
1 -------- 2 -------- 3 -------- 4 -------- 5
```

| Strongly Prefer A | Slightly Prefer A | Neutral | Slightly Prefer B | Strongly Prefer B |

3. A job in which greater responsibility is given to those who do the best work.

A job in which greater responsibility is given to loyal employees who have the most seniority.

```
1 -------- 2 -------- 3 -------- 4 -------- 5
```

| Strongly Prefer A | Slightly Prefer A | Neutral | Slightly Prefer B | Strongly Prefer B |

4. A job in an organization which is in financial trouble—and might have to close down within the year.

A job in which you are not allowed to have any say whatever in how your work is scheduled, or in the procedures to be used in carrying it out.

```
1 -------- 2 -------- 3 -------- 4 -------- 5
```

| Strongly Prefer A | Slightly Prefer A | Neutral | Slightly Prefer B | Strongly Prefer B |

JOB A   _JOB B_

5. A very routine job.

A job where your co-workers are not very friendly.

1 - - - - - - - - 2 - - - - - - - - 3 - - - - - - - - 4 - - - - - - - - 5

Strongly   Slightly   Neutral   Slightly   Strongly
Prefer A   Prefer A   Prefer B   Prefer B

6. A job with a supervisor who is often very critical of you and your work in front of other people.

A job which prevents you from using a number of skills that you worked hard to develop.

1 - - - - - - - - 2 - - - - - - - - 3 - - - - - - - - 4 - - - - - - - - 5

Strongly   Slightly   Neutral   Slightly   Strongly
Prefer A   Prefer A   Prefer B   Prefer B

7. A job with a supervisor who respects you and treats you fairly.

A job which provides constant opportunities for you to learn new and interesting things.

1 - - - - - - - - 2 - - - - - - - - 3 - - - - - - - - 4 - - - - - - - - 5

Strongly   Slightly   Neutral   Slightly   Strongly
Prefer A   Prefer A   Prefer B   Prefer B

JOB A   *JOB B*

8. A job where there is a real chance   A job with very little chance to ɔ
you could be laid off.   challenging work.

1 - - - - - - - 2 - - - - - - - - 3 - - - - - - - - 4 - - - - - - - 5

Strongly   Slightly   Neutral   Slightly   Strongly
Prefer A   Prefer A   Prefer B   Prefer B

9. A job in which there is a real chance   A job which provides lots of vaca-
for you to develop new skills and   tion time and an excellent fringe
advance in the organization.   benefit package.

1 - - - - - - - 2 - - - - - - - - 3 - - - - - - - - 4 - - - - - - - 5

Strongly   Slightly   Neutral   Slightly   Strongly
Prefer A   Prefer A   Prefer B   Prefer B

10. A job with little freedom and   A job where the working conditions
independence to do your work in the   are poor.
way you think best.

1 - - - - - - - 2 - - - - - - - - 3 - - - - - - - - 4 - - - - - - - 5

Strongly   Slightly   Neutral   Slightly   Strongly
Prefer A   Prefer A   Prefer B   Prefer B

JOB A   *JOB B*

11. A job with very satisfying team-   A job which allows you to use your
    work.   skills and abilities to the fullest
                                          extent.

1 - - - - - - - - 2 - - - - - - - - 3 - - - - - - - - 4 - - - - - - - - 5

Strongly   Slightly   Neutral   Slightly   Strongly
Prefer A   Prefer A   Prefer B   Prefer B

12. A job which offers little or no   A job which requires you to be
    challenge.   completely isolated from co-workers.

1 - - - - - - - - 2 - - - - - - - - 3 - - - - - - - - 4 - - - - - - - - 5

Strongly   Slightly   Neutral   Slightly   Strongly
Prefer A   Prefer A   Prefer B   Prefer B

SECTION EIGHT

Biographical Background

1. Sex: Male_____   Female_____

2. Age (check one):

_____under 20   _____40-49

_____20-29   _____50-59

_____30-39   _____60 or over

3. Education (check one):

_____ Grade School

_____ Some High School

_____ High School Degree

_____ Some Business College or Technical School Experience

_____ Some College Experience (other than business or technical school)

_____ Business College or Technical School Degree

_____ College Degree

_____ Master's or Higher Degree

4. What is your brief job title? _____

APPENDIX B
THE JOB RATING FORM

This appendix reproduces the Job Rating Form (JRF). This is a companion instrument to the Job Diagnostic Survey and is designed to be used by supervisors of the focal job (or by outside observers) in rating job characteristics. The JRF provides measures of the key job dimensions; none of the scales measuring affective reactions to the job or work context are included. Scoring procedures for the JRF are included in Appendix C.

JOB RATING FORM

This questionnaire was developed as part of a Yale University study of jobs and how people react to them. The questionnaire helps to determine how jobs can be better designed, by obtaining information about how people react to different kinds of jobs.

You are asked to rate the characteristics of the following job:

Please keep in mind that the questions refer to the job listed above, and *not* to your own job.

On the following pages, you will find several different kinds of questions about the job listed above. Specific instructions are given at the start of each section. Please read them carefully. It should take no more than 10 minutes to complete the entire questionnaire. Please move through it quickly.

SECTION ONE

This part of the questionnaire asks you to describe the job listed above as *objectively* as you can. Try to make your description as accurate and as objective as you possibly can.

A sample question is given below.

A. To what extent does the job require a person to work with mechanical equipment?

1 ------- 2 ------- 3 ------- 4 ------- 5 ------- (6) ------- 7

Very little; the job requires almost no contact with mechanical equipment of any kind.

Moderately

Very much; the job requires almost constant work with mechanical equipment.

You are to *circle* the number which is the most accurate description of the job you are rating.

If, for example, the job requires a person to work with mechanical equipment a good deal of the time—but also requires some paperwork—you might circle the number six, as was done in the example above.

*   *   *

1. To what extent does the job require a person to *work closely with other people* (either "clients," or people in related jobs in the organization)?

1 ------- 2 ------- 3 ------- 4 ------- 5 ------- 6 ------- 7

Very little; dealing with other people is not at all necessary in doing the job.

Moderately; some dealing with others is necessary.

Very much; dealing with other people is an absolutely essential and crucial part of doing the job.

2. How much *autonomy* is there in the job? That is, to what extent does the job permit a person to decide *on his or her own* how to go about doing the work?

1 - - - - - 2 - - - - - 3 - - - - - 4 - - - - - 5 - - - - - 6 - - - - - 7

| Very little; the job gives a person almost no personal "say" about how and when the work is done. | Moderate autonomy; many things are standardized and not under the control of the person, but he or she can make some decisions about the work. | Very much; the job gives the person almost complete responsibility for deciding how and when the work is done. |

3. To what extent does the job involve doing a *"whole"and identifiable piece of work?* That is, is the job a complete piece of work that has an obvious beginning and end? Or is it only a small *part* of the overall piece of work, which is finished by other people or by automatic machines?

1 - - - - - 2 - - - - - 3 - - - - - 4 - - - - - 5 - - - - - 6 - - - - - 7

| The job is only a tiny part of the overall piece of work; the results of the person's activities cannot be seen in the final product or service. | The job is a moderate-sized "chunk" of the overall piece of work; the person's own contribution can be seen in the final outcome. | The job involves doing the whole piece of work, from start to finish: the results of the person's activities are easily seen in the final product or service. |

4. How much *variety* is there in the job? That is, to what extent does the job require a person to do many different things at work, using a variety of his or her skills and talents?

1 - - - - - 2 - - - - - 3 - - - - - 4 - - - - - 5 - - - - - 6 - - - - - 7

| Very little; the job requires the person to do the same routine things over and over again. | Moderate variety. | Very much; the job requires the person to do many different things, using a number of different skills and talents. |

5. In general, how *significant or important* is the job? That is, are the results of the person's work likely to significantly affect the lives or well-being of other people?

1 - - - - - - 2 - - - - - - 3 - - - - - - 4 - - - - - - 5 - - - - - - 6 - - - - - - 7

Not at all significant: the outcomes of the work are *not* likely to affect anyone in any important way.	Moderately significant.	Highly significant; the outcomes of the work can affect other people in very important ways.

6. To what extent do *managers or co-workers* let the person know how well he or she is doing on the job?

1 - - - - - - 2 - - - - - - 3 - - - - - - 4 - - - - - - 5 - - - - - - 6 - - - - - - 7

Very little; people almost never let the person know how well he or she is doing.	Moderately; sometimes people may give the person "feedback"; other times they may not.	Very much; managers or co-workers provide the person with almost constant "feedback" about how well he or she is doing.

7. To what extent does *doing the job itself* provide the person with information about his or her work performance? That is, does the actual *work itself* provide clues about how well the person is doing—aside from any "feedback" co-workers or supervisors may provide?

1 - - - - - - 2 - - - - - - 3 - - - - - - 4 - - - - - - 5 - - - - - - 6 - - - - - - 7

Very little; the job itself is set up so a person could work forever without finding out how well he or she is doing.	Moderately; sometimes doing the job provides "feedback" to the person; sometimes it does not.	Very much; the job is set up so that a person gets almost constant "feedback" as he or she works about how well he or she is doing.

SECTION TWO

Listed below are a number of statements which could be used to describe a job.

You are to indicate whether each statement is an *accurate* or an *inaccurate* description of the job you are rating.

Once again, please try to be as *objective* as you can in deciding how accurately each statement describes the job—regardless of your own *feelings* about that job.

Write a number in the blank beside each statement, based on the following scale:

How accurate is the statement in describing the job you are rating?

1	2	3	4	5	6	7
Very Inaccurate	Mostly Inaccurate	Slightly Inaccurate	Uncertain	Slightly Accurate	Mostly Accurate	Very Accurate

_____ 1. The job requires a person to use a number of complex or sophisticated skills.

_____ 2. The job requires a lot of cooperative work with other people.

_____ 3. The job is arranged so that a person does *not* have the chance to do an entire piece of work from beginning to end.

_____ 4. Just doing the work required by the job provides many chances for a person to figure out how well he or she is doing.

_____ 5. The job is quite simple and repetitive.

_____ 6. The job can be done adequately by a person working alone—without talking or checking with other people.

_____ 7. The supervisors and co-workers on this job almost *never* give a person any "feedback" about how well he or she is doing the work.

_____ 8. This job is one where a lot of other people can be affected by how well the work gets done.

_____ 9. The job denies a person any chance to use his or her personal initiative or discretion in carrying out the work.

_____ 10. Supervisors often let the person know how well they think he or she is performing the job.

_____ 11. The job provides a person with the chance to finish completely any work he or she starts.

_____ 12. The job itself provides very few clues about whether or not the person is performing well.

_____ 13. The job gives a person considerable opportunity for independence and freedom in how he or she does the work.

_____ 14. The job itself is *not* very significant or important in the broader scheme of things.

GENERAL INFORMATION

1. What is your name? _____

2. What is your own job title? _____

3. What is your age? (Check one)

    _____ under 20   _____ 40-49

    _____ 20-29   _____ 50-59

    _____ 30-39   _____ 60 or over

4. How long have you been in your present position? (Check one)

    _____ 0-½ yr.   _____ 3-5 yrs.

    _____ ½-1 yr.   _____ 5-10 yrs.

    _____ 1-2 yrs.   _____ 10 or more yrs.

In the space below, please write down any additional information about the job you rated that you feel might be helpful in understanding that job. Thank you for your cooperation.

APPENDIX C
SCORING KEY FOR THE JOB DIAGNOSTIC SURVEY
AND THE JOB RATING FORM

The scoring manual for the Job Diagnostic Survey (JDS) and the Job Rating Form (JRF) is presented below. For each variable measured by the JDS, the questionnaire items that are averaged to yield a summary score for the variable are listed.

Sections One and Two (the measures of the job characteristics) are identical for the Job Diagnostic Survey and the Job Rating Form, and therefore the same scoring key is used for both instruments.

A computerized scoring service for the JDS is provided by the Roy W. Walters and Associates consulting firm (Whitney Industrial Park, Whitney Road, Mahwah, NJ 07430). The Walters organization also provides printed copies of the JDS.

         *   *   *

I. JOB CHARACTERISTICS (for both the JDS and the JRF).

    A. *Skill variety*. Average the following items:

        Section One: #4
        Section Two: #1
                    #5 (reversed scoring—i.e., subtract the number entered by the respondent from 8)

B. *Task identity.* Average the following items:
   Section One: #3
   Section Two: #11
                 #3 (reversed scoring)

C. *Task significance.* Average the following items:
   Section One: #5
   Section Two: #8
                 #14 (reversed scoring)

D. *Autonomy.* Average the following items:
   Section One: #2
   Section Two: #13
                 #9 (reversed scoring)

E. *Feedback from the job itself.* Average the following items:
   Section One: #7
   Section Two: #4
                 #12 (reversed scoring)

F. *Feedback from agents.* Average the following items:
   Section One: #6
   Section Two: #10
                 #7 (reversed scoring)

G. *Dealing with others.* Average the following items:
   Section One: #1
   Section Two: #2
                 #6 (reversed scoring)

II. EXPERIENCED PSYCHOLOGICAL STATES. Each of the three constructs are measured both directly (Section Three) and indirectly, via projective-type items (Section Five).

   A. *Experienced meaningfulness of the work.* Average the following items:
      Section Three: #7
                      #4 (reversed scoring)
      Section Five: #6
                      #3 (reversed scoring)

   B. *Experienced responsibility for the work.* Average the following items:
      Section Three: #8, #12, #15
                      #1 (reversed scoring)
      Section Five: #4, #7

C. *Knowledge of results.* Average the following items:
Section Three: #5
             #11 (reversed scoring)
Section Five: #5
             #10 (reversed scoring)

III. AFFECTIVE OUTCOMES. The first two constructs (general satisfaction and internal work motivation) are measured both directly (Section Three) and indirectly (Section Five); growth satisfaction is measured only directly (Section Four).

A. *General satisfaction.* Average the following items:
Section Three: #3, #13
             #9 (reversed scoring)
Section Five: #2
             #8 (reversed scoring)

B. *Internal work motivation.* Average the following items:
Section Three: #2, #6, #10
             #14 (reversed scoring)
Section Five: #1, #9

C. *Growth satisfaction.* Average the following items:
Section Four: #3, #6, #10, #13

IV. CONTEXT SATISFACTIONS. Each of these short scales uses items from Section Four only.

A. *Satisfaction with job security.* Average items #1 and #11 of Section Four.

B. *Satisfaction with compensation (pay).* Average items #2 and #9 of Section Four.

C. *Satisfaction with co-workers* Average items #4, #7, and #12 of Section Four.

D. *Satisfaction with supervision.* Average items #5, #8, and #14 of Section Four.

V INDIVIDUAL GROWTH NEED STRENGTH. The questionnaire yields two separate measures of growth need strength, one from Section Six (the "would like" format) and one from Section Seven (the "job choice" format).

A. *"Would like" format* (Section Six). Average the six items from Section Six listed below. Before averaging, subtract 3 from each item score; this will result in a summary scale ranging from one to seven. The items are:
#2, #3, #6, #8, #10, #11

3. *"Job choice" format* (Section Seven). Each item in Section Seven yields a number from 1-5 (i.e., "Strongly prefer A" is scored 1; "Neutral" is scored 3; and "Strongly prefer B" is scored 5). Compute the need strength measure by averaging the twelve items as follows:

#1, #5, #7, #10, #11, #12 (direct scoring)
#2, #3, #4, #6, #8, #9 (reversed scoring—i.e., subtract the respondent's score from 6)

Note: To transform the job choice summary score from a 5-point scale to a 7-point scale, use this formula: $Y = 1.5X - .5$.

C. *Combined growth need strength score.* To obtain an overall estimate of growth need strength based on both "would like" and "job choice" data, first transform the "job choice" summary score to a 7-point scale (using the formula given above), and then average the "would like" and the transformed "job choice" summary scores.

VI. MOTIVATING POTENTIAL SCORE.

$$
\text{Motivating potential score (MPS)} = \left[\frac{\text{Skill variety} + \text{Task identity} + \text{Task significance}}{3} \right] \times \text{Autonomy} \times \text{Feedback from the job}
$$

APPENDIX D
GUIDELINES AND CAUTIONS IN USING THE
JOB DIAGNOSTIC SURVEY

The Job Diagnostic Survey is intended for use (a) in diagnostic activities to determine whether (and how) existing jobs can be improved to increase employee motivation, performance, and satisfaction; and (b) in evaluation studies of the effects of work redesign. This appendix provides guidelines and cautions in using the instrument.[1] In the first section, a number of issues that should be addressed before the instrument is administered are examined. Then we turn to procedures for collecting JDS data, including prototype instructions to respondents. Finally, we examine a number of limitations of the instrument and cautions regarding its use. For guidance in interpreting JDS results, see Chapter 5 of the text and Appendix E (which provides JDS means and standard deviations for several "families" of jobs).

PLANNING TO ADMINISTER THE JDS

1. What are the kinds of jobs and organizations for which the JDS is intended?

The JDS can be used for most jobs in almost any kind of organization. It has been used with blue-collar, white-collar, professional, and lower-level managerial personnel, and in business, service, and public organizations. It is less appropriate for middle- and upper-level managers, whose jobs are much more strongly defined by *role* relationships than by concrete tasks to perform.

---

1   Our work in validating the Job Diagnostic Survey was funded in part by the Manpower Administration, U.S. Department of Labor (Research and Development Grant No. 21-09-74-14 to Yale University), whose support we gratefully acknowledge.

Also, respondents must be moderately literate. Use of the JDS is not recommended for individuals with an eighth grade education or less, or for individuals who do not read and understand English well.

2. How should a "job" be defined when using the JDS?

Since JDS results for individual respondents are almost always grouped into job categories, it is very important how job groups are defined. Each job should refer to a number of people who do essentially the same thing at work. Examples could be "keypuncher in accounts payable," "quality control inspector," "Grade II social worker," "customer service representative," "manufacturing foreman," or "pediatric nurse."

Care should be taken not to define jobs too broadly. If a job group includes people who actually do different things at work (like all "manufacturing workers at the Rock Creek plant") then it will not be possible to draw conclusions about the strengths and weaknesses of specific jobs within that large, heterogeneous group.

Because of the importance of the matter, it is recommended that users write down a brief title for each specific job to be analyzed *before* the JDS is administered. If you find that you have some people left over (those who do not fit into any of the job categories you select), they may be lumped together in a final "miscellaneous" job group, but results for that category may be hard to interpret.

3. Who should administer the JDS?

The person who actually gives the JDS to the respondents should not be an immediate supervisor of the respondents. It is very important that respondents have a sense of privacy and know that their answers will be kept confidential. It is difficult to create such conditions when one's boss is handing out the questionnaires. Therefore, it usually is advisable to have an "outsider" (a staff member from the personnel department or an internal or external consultant) responsible for actual administration of the instrument.

It is also true, of course, that both line managers and relevant union officials should be fully informed beforehand about the purposes of any diagnostic study, what the respondents will be asked to do, and what the results will be used for. The cooperation of managers and union leaders is essential, especially when action steps may be taken on the basis of the results. But these individuals should not be directly involved in administering the JDS.

4. Where and when should the JDS be administered?

It generally is most convenient and efficient to administer the JDS to small groups of respondents—from three or four up to about fifteen at a time. Above fifteen, things start to get cumbersome, and it is difficult for one person to respond to questions as they arise.

It is preferable for the questionnaire to be administered during regular working hours in a room separate from the usual work place. The room should be quiet and private. Employees should not take the JDS at their work stations, because distractions invariably arise and because it frequently is tempting for employees to discuss the instrument and compare answers with people around them. Since employees sometimes have questions as they fill out the JDS, the person who administers it should stay in the room with them while they take the questionnaire. Respondents should not be allowed to take the JDS home with them to complete it.

The instrument takes most people 20 to 25 minutes to complete. Because there are always a few people who take longer, successive groups should be scheduled at no less than 45-minute intervals. If groups of respondents are especially large (fifteen or more), allow an hour between groups.

5. Should taking the JDS be voluntary?

Yes. It is better to have no data at all from an individual than to have data from an unwilling respondent.

6. Must people take the JDS anonymously?

Yes, except in special circumstances. In many uses of the instrument, names are not actually needed: the intent is to learn how all people who work on a given job perceive that job and react to it. In such cases, the answers of respondents can be averaged, and there is no need for names.

In other applications of the JDS some kind of identification may be required. When jobs are to be changed, for example, it may be desirable to examine the growth need strength scores of specific individuals, or there may be plans to compare the JDS scores of individuals prior to the change with their scores afterwords. This can be accomplished by asking each respondent to put a unique identifying mark on the first questionnaire that can be matched to the same mark on the re-test questionnaire. (Asking respondents to identify their questionnaires with their mother's maiden name is useful for this purpose: it preserves anonymity, and will not be forgotten in the time between the first and second testing.)

Finally, it is sometimes necessary to know the actual name of each respondent—for example, when research is being carried out that requires information to be obtained from organization records (absenteeism, productivity, or employment data). In such cases it is imperative that the JDS be administered by someone who does not have managerial authority over the respondents, and who can be trusted by the respondents to preserve the confidentiality of the information they provide. Under these circumstances, even an "outside" person must be prepared to spend considerable time with the respondents providing assurances of confidentiality and explaining how the results will be used.

GIVING INSTRUCTIONS TO THE RESPONDENTS

1. How should I introduce the JDS to the people who will be taking it?

The way the JDS is initially introduced to respondents can strongly affect how carefully and candidly they complete the instrument. Therefore, you should carefully plan your opening remarks (and perhaps rehearse them a couple of times) before encountering your first group of respondents.

You might begin by introducing yourself and explaining what your own job is and why you are asking them to take the JDS. Then move to a discussion of the following points:

a) That you are asking them to take a questionnaire about their job and how they react to it.

b) Why this is being done, and how their answers will be used.

c) Why it is important that they complete the instrument, and that they provide honest and candid responses. Help them understand how the eventual benefit to themselves will be increased the more accurate and candid their answers are. (If this cannot be said with honesty, then it is probably unwise to use the instrument.)

d) What arrangements have been made to protect the confidentiality of their individual responses and to ensure that the results will in fact be used as you have said.

At this point, there usually are questions about the purposes of the study. After questions have been dealt with, emphasize that participation is voluntary, and give individuals the opportunity to leave if they wish. Then distribute the questionnaires.

2. What special instructions should I provide?

When all respondents have the questionnaire, you should cover the following specific points in whatever order is most comfortable to you.

- They should give their first reaction to each item and move through the questionnaire quickly. The items are straightforward, and there are no "trick" questions.

- They should fill in all blanks, even if they are unsure about a specific question. Explain that if someone has to guess on an item, it is better that they do it than a computer.

- They should not talk or compare answers while taking the questionnaire. Explain that the important thing is their own, *personal* response to each question.

- You will remain in the room to answer any questions they have while taking the questionnaire. Ask that they signal when they have a question, and you will come to them to keep from disturbing other respondents.

- The questionnaire will take about 20 to 25 minutes to complete.

Respond to any additional questions of a general nature, and then ask the respondents to begin. After a few minutes, you might walk around the room to see if everyone is underway and moving through the JDS without difficulty.

3. Should everyone leave at the same time?

No, it usually is better if individuals are allowed to leave as soon as they have finished. This also will give you the opportunity to thumb through the completed questionnaire as each individual leaves to check for pages that may have been left blank. Respondents frequently skip pages by accident, and a quick check as the person leaves can prevent the data from that peson from being entirely lost.

4. What questions am I likely to be asked?

Listed below are a number of questions that respondents sometimes have, and some ways you might respond to them.

Q: What does this question (or word) mean?

A: (Explain by using a synonym or by expanding on the language of the question. Do not give an example of a specific incident from the work setting, as this may influence the respondent's answer to the item. For example, if someone does not understand what "feedback" means, explain in your own words that it has to do with finding out how one is doing on the job, but refrain from saying, "You know, it's like when your foreman tells you that your day's work is below quality standard.")

Q: I'm not finished (or I want to think about it). Can I take it home and bring it back tomorrow?

A: As I said before, your best answers are your first reactions to each question. So I'd appreciate it if you would go on through it now. I'll stay until you are finished. If there are any specific questions that you are having trouble with, I'd be happy to see if I can explain them in more detail.

Q: Some of the questions seem to repeat what other questions asked. Why is that?

A: The people who made up the questionnaire tried to get at the most important matters in two or three different ways to make sure that they are covered from all possible angles. Therefore, some of the specific items may seem similar. Please try to answer each question as it is asked, and don't worry about making each answer match what you may have said for a previous question.

Q: This question (or section) doesn't apply to my job. Can I leave it blank?

A: No, please try to answer each question as best you can.

Q: Will we get a summary of the results from our questionnaires?

A: (Answer honestly, avoding the temptation to placate the respondent by answering affirmatively if in fact it is not certain that they will receive feedback.)

Q: Why should I have to take this questionnaire? It's not part of my job.

A: (Explain again how the results are to be used, and emphasize why it is important to have each person's own views. If the respondent persists or becomes loud, it usually is best to suggest that you step outside the room to discuss it further. A single hostile respondent can be very disruptive to the entire group, so you should get such a person outside fairly quickly. Then you can try to deal with the person's concerns, and (if unsuccessful) can allow the person to return to his or her work station with minimal disruption to others. Never allow yourself to be drawn into an argument with a single respondent in the presence of others who are taking the instrument.)

Q: Is everybody in the division (or section, or plant) taking this question-naire? Why not?

A: (The specific content of questions such as this [and the preceding one] may not be as important as a more general concern or mistrust lying beneath the question. Often individuals who are mistrustful of the whole activity [e.g., they fear being exploited, or are worried about a hidden purpose of the questionnaire] express their mistrust indirectly by asking question after question about details of the project. Usually the best policy is to be truthful and complete in responding to the question as initially asked. But when you begin to sense that no answer ever will be fully satisfactory, you may wish to ask the respondent directly what his or her greatest concerns about the project are so you can try to deal with the root difficulty. Sometimes [not always] this will bring out material that the respondent had been unable or afraid to say before and that you can then deal with directly. Other times nothing will meet the concerns of the respondent, and the best course of action will be to give the respondent the option of leaving without completing the questionnaire. Again, it is better for a hostile or mistrustful respondent to be given a genuinely free option of leaving than for his or her concerns to be swept under the rug or suppressed, because in such circumstances the concerns invariably resurface in the form of invalid or deliberately misleading responses to the questionnaire itself.)

LIMITATIONS OF THE JDS AND CAUTIONS IN ITS USE

Since originally published (Hackman and Oldham, 1974; 1975), the Job Diagnostic Survey has been used in numerous organizations and subjected to a variety of empirical tests (e.g., Cathcart, Goddard, and Youngblood, 1978; Dunham, 1976; Dunham, Aldag, and Brief, 1977; Oldham, Hackman, and Stepina, 1979; Pierce and Dunham, 1978; Stone, Ganster, Woodman, and Fusilier, in press; Stone and Porter, 1977; for a review of studies of the section of the JDS that assesses job characteristics, see Barr, Brief, and Aldag, 1978).

Experience with the JDS, and studies of its properties, have highlighted a number of limitations and suggest several cautions in using the instrument.

1. Job characteristics, as measured by the JDS, are not independent of one another. When a job is high on one characteristic (such as skill variety) it also tends to be high on one or more others (such as autonomy and/or feedback). The positive intercorrelations among the job characteristics may reflect problems in how they are measured in the JDS. Or it may be that most "good" jobs really are good in many ways, and jobs that are poorly designed tend to be low on most or all of the job characteristics (see Chapter 4). At present, we do not know whether we have an instrument problem or an ecological phenomenon on our hands. Yet we do know that it would be better statistically if the job characteristics were independent of one another; because they are not, we should be careful not to overinterpret JDS scores for any single job characteristic considered alone.

2. It is just as good empirically—and usually better—simply to add up the scores of the five motivating job characteristics to get an overall estimate of the motivating potential of a job, rather than to use the more complex formula for the motivating potential score (MPS) suggested in Chapter 4. The advantage of the MPS score is that it derives directly from the motivational theory on which the Job Diagnostic Survey was based. The disadvantage is that computation of the score involves multiplying the job characteristics, which is generally a dubious proposition with measures that are less than perfectly reliable, and especially so when those measures tend to be intercorrelated.

3. The validity of some JDS scales remains unestablished. While it is to the credit of the instrument that it discriminates well between jobs (and families of jobs: see Appendix E), it takes many research studies relating a concept to other variables to firmly establish the meaning of that concept. Far more validity studies are needed before we can be sure that the JDS in fact measures what it is supposed to be measuring. In the meantime, it is especially important to gather information about jobs and people's reactions to them using more than one methodology, and to check for consistency among those measures before using them in planning for change. Of special concern

are the JDS measures of the context satisfactions and individual growth need strength. The context satisfactions are tapped by relatively few items and are intended to provide only a quick check of how satisfied people are with selected aspects of their work environment. When highly trustworthy measures of satisfaction are needed, it is advisable to use the Job Descriptive Index (Smith, Kendall, and Hulin, 1969) rather than the JDS.

The concept of growth need strength is key in the theory of work motivation underlying the JDS, and many items are devoted to assessing the strength of respondents' desires for growth. At present, however, evidence regarding the validity of the growth need strength measure is scattered and inconsistent. Some studies find that the concept, as measured by the JDS, does operate as specified in the theory; others do not. And it is unclear whether the negative findings reflect a fault of the theory (e.g., growth need strength does not really make a difference in how people respond to their jobs), an inadequacy of the measure (e.g., growth needs may be important, but the JDS does not assess them well), or problems in research methodology (e.g., insufficient variation in job characteristics or individual differences exists to provide a good test). Until these ambiguities are resolved—which they may never be—measures of employee growth need strength should be used quite cautiously in planning for work redesign.

4. The Job Diagnostic Survey is easily faked and results may be distorted by tendencies of respondents to present themselves as being consistent in how they respond to various sections of the questionnaire. Because the instrument is fakable, the JDS should not be used for selection or placement unless an extraordinary level of trust exists between the respondents and those who will be using the results. Indeed, even when used for its intended purposes, special care should be taken to ensure that respondents believe that their own best interests will be served if the data they provide *accurately* reflect the objective characteristics of the jobs and their personal reactions to them.

Moreover, if employees feel that it is good to be internally consistent, and if they describe their jobs as being particularly high (or low) on the job characteristics, then they may also tend to report that they are highly satisfied (or dissatisfied) later in the questionnaire. Again, the only way to protect against this possibility is to check JDS results against other data that are collected independently and (when possible) in a way that minimizes self-presentation and consistency biases.

5. Finally, the instrument is not appropriate for use in diagnosing the jobs of single individuals. For one thing, it is preferable for respondents to take the JDS under conditions of anonymity, which obviously is impossible if the person knows that only his or her job is being diagnosed. Beyond that, the instrument was constructed so that the reliabilities of the job characteristic measures would be fully satisfactory when the responses of five or more

individuals who work on the same job are averaged. For data collected from single individuals, scale reliabilities are only marginally acceptable. This means that the JDS scores of single individuals are probably not stable enough to warrant the redesign of individual jobs based solely on those scores.[2]

---

2   An exception is the measure of individual growth need strength. This scale was designed to be a measure of an individual characteristic, not a job attribute, and therefore sufficient items were used to achieve high reliability for single respondents.

APPENDIX E
JOB DIAGNOSTIC SURVEY NORMATIVE DATA
FOR SEVERAL JOB FAMILIES

In this appendix average Job Diagnostic Survey (JDS) scale scores for a number of job categories are presented. These data were obtained from 6930 employees who worked on a wide variety of jobs in 56 organizations throughout the United States. JDS data were collected from individuals who worked on several specific jobs within each job family. The scores of the respondents who worked on the specific jobs within the category were averaged and the means and standard deviations calculated (Oldham, Hackman, and Stepina, 1979).

These means and standard deviations can be used by practitioners to determine if a target job's characteristics are out of line with the appropriate norms. All that is required is that the investigator obtain scores for the target job's characteristics by averaging the JDS scores for all job incumbents. These scores are then compared with the appropriate norms provided in the following table. If the target job's scores are less than one standard deviation away from the normative mean, this suggests that there is an insignificant difference between the two scores. If the target score is (plus or minus) two or more standard deviations from the focal norm, it suggests that the target job is quite discrepant from the normative base. For example, assume that a target clerical job has a task significance score of 2.10. The table shows that this score is more than two standard deviations away from the reported mean, suggesting that action to improve the task significance of the job might be appropriate.

Job Diagnostic Survey Means and Standard Deviations for Several Job Families

Variable	Professional or Technical X	S.D.	Managerial X	S.D.	Clerical X	S.D.	Sales X	S.D.	Service X	S.D.	Processing X	S.D.	Machine Trades X	S.D.	Bench Work X	S.D.	Structural Work X	S.D.
Skill variety	5.4	1.0	5.6	.94	4.0	1.3	4.8	1.2	5.0	1.4	4.2	1.2	5.1	1.2	4.2	1.2	5.2	1.1
Task identity	5.1	1.2	4.7	1.1	4.7	1.2	4.4	1.4	4.7	1.2	4.3	1.3	4.9	1.3	4.5	1.3	5.1	1.2
Task significance	5.6	.95	5.8	.85	5.3	1.2	5.5	1.2	5.7	1.0	5.3	1.2	5.6	1.2	5.8	1.2	5.5	1.2
Autonomy	5.4	1.0	5.4	.92	4.5	1.2	4.8	1.4	5.0	1.2	4.5	1.3	4.9	1.3	4.6	1.1	5.0	1.2
Feedback from job	5.1	1.1	5.2	1.0	4.6	1.3	5.4	1.0	5.1	1.2	4.7	1.2	4.9	1.2	4.4	1.3	4.9	1.2
Feedback from agents	4.2	1.4	4.4	1.2	4.0	1.4	3.6	1.2	3.8	1.6	3.6	1.5	3.8	1.4	4.2	1.4	4.5	1.2
Dealing with others	5.8	.96	6.4	.58	5.2	1.1	6.4	.84	6.0	1.0	5.3	1.1	5.3	1.0	5.0	1.2	5.4	1.2
MPS	154	55	156	55	106	59	146	93	152	70	105	57	136	64	110	57	141	63
Experienced meaningfulness	5.4	.87	5.5	.96	4.9	1.0	4.9	1.3	5.2	1.1	5.0	1.0	5.3	.89	5.3	1.0	5.2	1.0
Experienced responsibility	5.8	.72	5.7	.81	5.3	.88	5.5	.73	5.6	.86	5.2	.92	5.4	.94	5.4	.89	5.1	.90
Knowledge of results	5.0	.99	5.0	.97	4.9	1.1	5.0	1.2	5.0	1.1	5.1	1.2	5.3	.99	4.9	1.2	5.2	.96
General satisfaction	4.9	.99	4.9	1.0	4.5	1.1	4.4	1.2	4.6	1.2	4.6	1.2	4.9	1.1	4.7	1.1	4.9	1.2
Internal motivation	5.8	.65	5.8	.64	5.4	.83	5.7	.59	5.7	.76	5.3	.89	5.6	.80	5.5	.91	5.6	.89
Pay satisfaction	4.4	1.5	4.6	1.2	4.0	1.5	4.2	1.2	4.1	1.5	4.5	1.4	4.2	1.4	4.4	1.6	4.5	1.3
Security satisfaction	5.0	1.2	5.2	1.0	4.8	1.3	4.0	1.5	4.9	1.3	4.6	1.3	5.0	1.2	4.7	1.5	5.0	1.3
Social satisfaction	5.5	.85	5.6	.68	5.2	1.0	5.4	.71	5.4	1.0	5.3	.95	5.5	.75	5.1	1.1	5.1	1.0
Supervisory satisfaction	4.9	1.3	5.2	1.1	4.9	1.4	4.6	1.7	4.7	1.6	4.6	1.4	4.6	1.5	4.5	1.5	4.9	1.3
Growth satisfaction	5.1	1.1	5.3	.97	4.6	1.2	4.5	1.4	4.9	1.4	4.7	1.2	4.8	1.0	4.4	1.2	5.0	1.0
Would like GNS	6.1	.82	5.9	.77	5.6	1.1	6.5	.30	6.1	.96	5.3	1.2	5.5	1.2	5.5	1.4	4.9	1.3
Job choice GNS	4.8	.64	4.7	.58	4.2	.67	4.9	.61	4.6	.74	3.9	.71	4.1	.70	4.0	.68	4.2	.68
Total GNS	5.6	.57	5.3	.54	5.0	.74	5.7	.39	5.4	.68	4.6	.79	4.8	.78	4.9	.87	4.5	.81

REFERENCES

Alderfer, C.P. An organizational syndrome. *Administrative Science Quarterly,* 1967, *12,* 440-460.

Alderfer, C.P. Group and intergroup relations. In J.R. Hackman and J.L. Suttle (eds.), *Improving life at work: Behavioral science approaches to organizational change.* Santa Monica, CA: Goodyear, 1977.

Argyris, C. *Personality and organization.* New York: Harper, 1957.

Argyris, C. *Interpersonal competence and organizational effectiveness.* Homewood, IL: Irwin-Dorsey, 1962.

Argyris, C. The incompleteness of social psychological theory: Examples from small group, cognitive consistency, and attribution research. *American Psychologist,* 1969, *24,* 893-908.

Arnold, H.J. Effects of performance feedback and extrinsic reward upon high intrinsic motivation. *Organizational Behavior and Human Performance,* 1976, *17,* 275-288.

Arnold, H.J., and R.J. House. Methodological and substantive extensions to the job characteristics model of motivation. *Organizational Behavior and Human Performance,* in press.

Baron, R.M., and J. Rodin. Personal control as a mediator of crowding. In A. Baum, S. Valins, and J. Singer (eds.), *Advances in environmental psychology.* Hillsdale, NJ: Erlbaum, 1978.

Barr, S.H., A.P. Brief, and R.J. Aldag. Measurement of perceived task characteristics. Working Paper 78-14, College of Business Administration, University of Iowa, 1978.

Bass, B.M., and J.A. Vaughan. *Training in industry*. Monterey, CA: Brooks-Cole, 1966.

Blake, R.R., and J.S. Mouton. Group and organizational team building: A theoretical model for intervening. In C.L. Cooper (ed.), *Theories of group processes*. New York: Wiley, 1975.

Blood, M.R. Organizational control of performance through self rewarding. In B. King, S. Streufert, and F.E. Fiedler (eds.), *Managerial control and organizational democracy*. Washington, D.C.: Winston & Sons, 1978.

Blood, M.R., and C.L. Hulin. Alienation, environmental characteristics, and worker responses. *Journal of Applied Psychology*, 1967, *51*, 284-290.

Bluestone, I. Decision making by workers. *The Personnel Administrator*, July-August 1974, 26-30.

Brehm, J.W. *Responses to loss of freedom: A theory of psychological reactance*. Morristown, NJ: General Learning Press, 1972.

Brief, A.P., M.J. Wallace, and R.J. Aldag. Linear vs. non-linear models of the formation of affective reactions: The case of job enlargement. *Decision Sciences*, 1976, *7*, 1-9.

Brousseau, K.R. Personality and job experience. *Organizational Behavior and Human Performance*, 1978, *22*, 235-252.

Bucklow, M. A new role for the work group. In L.E. Davis and J.C. Taylor (eds.), *Design of jobs*. Middlesex, England: Penguin, 1972.

Bureau of Labor Statistics, U.S. Department of Labor. *Employment and Earnings*, 1976, *22*, 127-131.

Campbell, J.P., and M.D. Dunnette. Effectiveness of T-group experiences in managerial training and development. *Psychological Bulletin*, 1968, *70*, 73-103.

Campbell, J.P., M.D. Dunnette, E.E. Lawler III, and K.E. Weick. *Managerial behavior, performance and effectiveness*. New York: McGraw-Hill. 1970.

Cathcart, J.S., R.G. Goddard, and S.A. Youngblood. Perceived job design constructs: Reliability and validity. Technical Report No. 7, Center for Management and Organizational Research, University of South Carolina, 1978.

Champoux, J.E. A three sample test of some extensions to the job characteristics model of work motivation. *Academy of Management Journal*, in press

Cherns, A. The principles of sociotechnical design. *Human Relations,* 1976, *29,* 783-792.

Clegg, C., and M. Fitter. Information systems: The Achilles heel of job redesign? Memo No. 187, MRC Social and Applied Psychology Unit, University of Sheffield, Sheffield, England, February 1978.

Cohen, A.R., and H. Gadon. *Alternative work schedules: Integrating individual and organizational needs.* Reading, MA: Addison-Wesley, 1978.

Csikszentmihalyi, M. *Beyond boredom and anxiety.* San Francisco: Jossey-Bass, 1975.

Cummings, T.G. Self-regulating work groups: A socio-technical synthesis. *Academy of Management Review,* 1978, *3,* 625-634.

Davis, J.H. *Group performance.* Reading, MA: Addison-Wesley, 1969.

Davis, L.E. Developments in job design. In P.B. Warr (ed.), *Personal goals and work design.* London: Wiley, 1975.

Davis, L.E., R.R. Canter, and J. Hoffman. Current job design criteria. *Journal of Industrial Engineering,* 1955, *6,* 5-11.

Davis, L.E., and E.L. Trist. Improving the quality of work life: Sociotechnical case studies. In J. O'Toole (ed.), *Work and the quality of life.* Cambridge, MA: MIT Press, 1974.

Deci, E.L. *Intrinsic motivation.* New York: Plenum, 1975.

Delbecq, A.L., A.H. Van de Ven, and D.H. Gustafson. *Group techniques for program planning.* Glenview, IL: Scott, Foresman, 1975.

Dunham, R.B. The measurement and dimensionality of job characteristics. *Journal of Applied Psychology,* 1976, *61,* 404-409.

Dunham, R.B., R.J. Aldag, and A.P. Brief. Dimensionality of task design as measured by the Job Diagnostic Survey. *Academy of Management Journal,* 1977, *20,* 209-223.

Dunnette, M.D. *Personnel selection and placement.* Belmont, CA: Wadsworth, 1966.

Dunnette, M.D., J. Campbell, and K. Jaastad. The effect of group participation on brainstorming effectiveness for two industrial samples. *Journal of Applied Psychology,* 1963, *47,* 30-37.

Farris, G.F., and F.G. Lim, Jr. Effects of performance on leadership, cohesiveness, influence, satisfaction, and subsequent performance. *Journal of Applied Psychology,* 1969, *53,* 490-497.

Fayol, H. *Industrial and general administration* London: Sir Isaac Pitman, 1948.

Fein, M. Job enrichment: A reevaluation. *Sloan Management Review,* Winter 1974, 69-88.

Fein, M. Improving productivity by improved productivity sharing. *The Conference Board Record,* July 1976, 44-49. (a)

Fein, M. Motivation for work. In R. Dubin (ed.), *Handbook of work, organization and society.* Chicago: Rand-McNally, 1976. (b)

Fine, S.A., and W.W. Wiley. An introduction to functional job analysis. In E. Fleishman and A. Bass (eds.), *Studies in personnel and industrial psychology.* Homewood, IL: Dorsey, 1974.

Fleishman, E.A. Leadership climate, human relations training, and supervisory behavior. *Personnel Psychology,* 1955, *6,* 205-222.

Florman, S.C. The job-enrichment mistake. *Harper's,* May 1976, 18-22.

Ford, R.N. *Motivation through the work itself.* New York: American Management Associations, 1979.

Frank, L.L., and J.R. Hackman. A failure of job enrichment: The case of the change that wasn't. *Journal of Applied Behavioral Science,* 1975, *11,* 413-436.

Gainor, P. Do blue collar workers really have blues? *Detroit News,* January 5, 1975.

Gardell, B., and E. Dahlstrom. Teorier on anpassning och motivation. In E. Dahlstrom *et al.* (eds.), *Teknisk forandring och arbetsanpassning.* Stockholm: Prisma, 1966.

Garson, B. Luddites in Lordstown. *Harper's,* June 1972, 68-73.

Giles, W.F., and W.H. Holley. Job enrichment versus traditional issues at the bargaining table: What union members want. *Academy of Management Journal,* 1978, *21,* 725-730.

Glaser, E.M. *Improving the quality of worklife . . . And in the process, improving productivity.* Los Angeles: Human Interaction Research Institute, 1975.

Goldmann, R.B. *A work experiment: Six Americans in a Swedish plant.* New York: The Ford Foundation, 1976.

Goldstein, I.L. *Training: Program development and evaluation.* Belmont, CA: Wadsworth, 1974.

Gooding, J. Blue collar blues on the assembly line. *Fortune,* July 1970.

Guion, R.M. Recruitment, selection, and job placement. In M.D. Dunnette (ed.), *Handbook of industrial and organizational psychology.* Chicago: Rand-McNally, 1976.

Gulick, L., and L. Urwick (eds.), *Papers on the science of administration.* New York: Institute of Public Administration, 1937.

Gulowsen, J. A measure of work group autonomy. In L.E. Davis and J.C. Taylor (eds.), *Design of jobs.* Middlesex, England: Penguin, 1972.

Gyllenhammar, P.G. *People at work.* Reading, MA: Addison-Wesley, 1977.

Hackman, J.R. Toward understanding the role of tasks in behavioral research. *Acta Psychologica*, 1969, *31*, 97-128.

Hackman, J.R. On the coming demise of job enrichment. In E.L. Cass and F.G. Zimmer (eds.), *Man and work in society*. New York: Van Nostrand Reinhold, 1975.

Hackman, J.R. The design of self-managing work groups. In B. King, S. Streufert, and F.E. Fiedler (eds.), *Managerial control and organizational democracy*. Washington, D.C.: Winston and Sons, 1978.

Hackman, J.R., K.R. Brousseau, and J.A. Weiss. The interaction of task design and group performance strategies in determining group effectiveness. *Organizational Behavior and Human Performance*, 1976, *16*, 350-365.

Hackman, J.R., and E.E. Lawler III. Employee reactions to job characteristics. *Journal of Applied Psychology Monograph*, 1971, *55*, 259-286.

Hackman, J.R., and C.G. Morris. Group tasks, group interaction process, and group performance effectiveness: A review and proposed integration. In L. Berkowitz (ed.), *Advances in experimental social psychology* (Vol. 8). New York: Academic Press, 1975.

Hackman, J.R., and G.R. Oldham. The Job Diagnostic Survey: An instrument for the diagnosis of jobs and the evaluation of job redesign projects. *JSAS Catalog of Selected Documents in Psychology*, 1974, *4*, 148. (Ms. No. 810) (Available from the National Technical Information Service, U.S. Dept. of Commerce, 5285 Port Royal Rd., Springfield, VA 22161. NTIS Report No. AD779828.)

Hackman, J.R., and G.R. Oldham. Development of the Job Diagnostic Survey. *Journal of Applied Psychology*, 1975, *60*, 159-170.

Hackman, J.R., and G.R. Oldham. Motivation through the design of work: Test of a theory. *Organizational Behavior and Human Performance*, 1976, *16*, 250-279.

Hackman, J.R., G.R. Oldham, R. Janson, and K. Purdy. A new strategy for job enrichment. *California Management Review*, Summer 1975, 57-71.

Hackman, J.R., J.L. Pearce, and J.C. Wolfe. Effects of changes in job characteristics on work attitudes and behaviors: A naturally occurring quasi-experiment. *Organizational Behavior and Human Performance*, 1978, *21*, 289-304.

Hall, D.T. *Careers in organizations*. Santa Monica, CA: Goodyear, 1976.

Hedges, J.N. Absence from work: Measuring the hours lost. *Monthly Labor Review*, 1977, *100* (10), 16-23.

Herman, A.S. Industries studied show productivity declines. *Monthly Labor Review*, 1975, *98* (12), 50-52.

Herold, D.M., and M.M. Greller. Feedback: The definition of a construct. *Academy of Management Journal*, 1977, *20*, 142-147.

Herzberg, F. *Work and the nature of man*. Cleveland: World, 1966.

Herzberg, F. One more time: How do you motivate employees? *Harvard Business Review*, January-February 1968, 53-62.

Herzberg, F. The wise old Turk. *Harvard Business Review*, September-October, 1974, 70-80.

Herzberg, F. *The managerial choice*. Homewood, IL: Dow Jones-Irwin, 1976.

Hinrichs, J.R. Personnel training. In M.D. Dunnette (ed.), *Handbook of industrial and organizational psychology*. Chicago: Rand-McNally, 1976.

House, R.J. and L. Wigdor. Herzberg's dual-factor theory of job satisfaction and motivation: A review of the evidence and a criticism. *Personnel Psychology*, 1967, *20*, 369-389.

Hulin, C.L. Individual differences and job enrichment. In J.R. Maher (ed.), *New perspectives in job enrichment*. New York: Van Nostrand Reinhold: 1971.

Hulin, C.L., and M.R. Blood. Job enlargement, individual differences, and worker responses. *Psychological Bulletin*, 1968, *69*, 41-55.

Hunt, J. McV. Intrinsic motivation and its role in psychological development. *Nebraska Symposium on Motivation*, 1965, *13*, 189-282.

Ilgen, D.R., C.D. Fisher, and M.S. Taylor. Performance feedback: A review of its psychological and behavioral effects. Technical Report No. 1, Dept. of Psychological Sciences, Purdue University, 1977.

Janis, I.L. *Victims of groupthink: A psychological study of foreign-policy decisions and fiascos*. Boston: Houghton Mifflin, 1972.

Jenkins, G.D. Jr., D.A. Nadler, E.E. Lawler III, and C. Cammann. Standardized observations: An approach to measuring the nature of jobs. *Journal of Applied Psychology*, 1975, *60*, 171-181.

Jones, E.E., and R.E. Nisbett. The actor and the observer: Divergent perceptions of the causes of behavior. In E.E. Jones *et al. (eds.)*, *Attribution: Perceiving the causes of behavior*. Morristown, NJ: General Learning Press, 1971.

Kagan, J. Motives and development. *Journal of Personality and Social Psychology*, 1972, *22*, 51-66.

Kanter, R.M. *Men and women of the corporation*. New York: Basic Books, 1977.

Kanter, R.M. Work in a new America. *Daedalus*, Winter 1978, 47-78.

Katz, D., and R.L. Kahn. *The social psychology of organizations* (2nd ed.). New York: Wiley, 1978.

Katzell, R.A., P. Bienstock, and P.H. Faerstein. *A guide to worker productivity experiments in the United States 1971-1975.* New York: New York University Press, 1977.

Kerr, S., C.A. Schriesheim, C.J. Murphy, and R.M. Stogdill. Toward a contingency theory of leadership based upon the consideration and initiating structure literature. *Organizational Behavior and Human Performance,* 1974, *12,* 62-82.

Kochan, T.A., D.B Lipsky, and L. Dyer. Collective bargaining and the quality of work: The views of local union activists. *Proceedings of the 27th Annual Meeting of the Industrial Relations Research Association,* 1974, 150-162.

Kohn, M.L. and C. Schooler. The reciprocal effects of the substantive complexity of work and intellectual flexibility: A longitudinal assessment. *American Journal of Sociology,* 1978, *84,* 24-52.

Kornhauser, A. *Mental health of the industrial worker.* New York: Wiley, 1965.

Lawler, E.E. III. *Pay and organizational effectiveness: A psychological view.* New York: McGraw-Hill, 1971.

Lawler, E.E. III. The individualized organization: Problems and promise. *California Management Review,* Winter 1974, 31-39.

Lawler, E.E. III. Should the quality of work life be legislated? *The Personnel Administrator,* January 1976, 17-21.

Lawler, E.E. III. Reward systems. In J.R. Hackman and J.L. Suttle (eds.), *Improving life at work: Behavioral science approaches to organizational change.* Santa Monica, CA: Goodyear, 1977.

Lawler, E.E. III The new plant revolution. *Organizational Dynamics,* Winter 1978, 2-12.

Lawler, E.E. III., J.R. Hackman, and S. Kaufman. Effects of job redesign: A field experiment. *Journal of Applied Social Psychology,* 1973, *3,* 49-62.

Lawler, E.E. III, and J.G. Rhode. *Information and control in organizations.* Santa Monica, CA: Goodyear, 1976.

Leavitt, H.J. Suppose we took groups seriously . . . In E.L. Cass and F.G. Zimmer (eds.), *Man and work in society.* New York: Van Nostrand Reinhold, 1975.

Locke, E.A. Toward a theory of task motivation. *Organizational Behavior and Human Performance,* 1968, *3,* 157-189.

Locke, E.A. The case against legislating quality of work life. *The Personnel Administrator,* May 1976, 19-21.

Locke, E.A., D. Sirota, and A.D. Wolfson. An experimental case study of the successes and failures of job enrichment in a government agency. *Journal of Applied Psychology*, 1976, *61*, 701-711.

Lowin, A. and J.R. Craig. The influence of level of performance on managerial style: An experimental object-lesson in the ambiguity of correlational data. *Organiztional Behavior and Human Performance*, 1968, *3*, 440-458.

Lupton, T. Efficiency and the quality of worklife: The technology of reconciliation. *Organizational Dynamics*, Autumn 1975, 68-80.

Luthans, F., and R. Kreitner, *Organizational behavior modification*. Glenview, IL: Scott, Foresman, 1975.

Luthans, F., and D.D. White, Jr. Behavior modification: Application to manpower management. In J.R. Hackman, E.E. Lawler, and L.W. Porter (eds.), *Perspectives on behavior in organizations*. New York: McGraw-Hill, 1977.

MacKinnon, D.W. An overview of assessment centers. Technical Report No. 1, Center for Creative Leadership (Greensboro, NC), 1975.

Macy, B.A., and P.H. Mirvis. Measuring the quality of work and organizational effectiveness in behavioral-economic terms. *Administrative Science Quarterly*, 1976, *21*, 212-226.

Mayo, E. *The human problems of an industrial civilization*. New York: Macmillan, 1933.

McCormick, E.J. Job and task analysis. In M.D. Dunnette (ed.), *Handbook of industrial and organizational psychology*. Chicago: Rand-McNally, 1976.

McGrath, J.E. Stress and behavior in organizations. In M.D. Dunnette (ed.), *Handbook of industrial and organizational psychology*. Chicago: Rand-McNally, 1976.

Meadow, A., S.J. Parnes, and H. Reese. Influence of brainstorming instructions and problem sequence on a creative problem solving test. *Journal of Applied Psychology*, 1959, *43*, 413-416.

Meister, O., and D. Sullivan. Human factors: Engineering's blind spot. *Electro-Technology*, 1968, *82*, 39-47.

Mooney, J.D. *The principles of organization*. New York: Harper, 1947.

Nadler, D.A. *Feedback and organization development: Using data-based methods*. Reading, MA: Addison-Wesley, 1977.

Nadler, D.A. Consulting with labor and management: Some learnings from quality of worklife projects. In W. Burke (ed.), *The cutting edge: Current theory and practice in organization development*. La Jolla, CA: University Associates 1978.

Oldham, G.R. Job characteristics and internal motivation: The moderating effect of interpersonal and individual variables. *Human Relations.* 1976, *29,* 559-569. (a)

Oldham, G.R. The motivational strategies used by supervisors: Relationships to effectiveness indicators. *Organizational Behavior and Human Performance.* 1976, *15,* 66-86. (b)

Oldham, G.R., and J.R. Hackman, Work design in the organizational context. In B.M. Staw and L.L. Cummings (eds.), *Research in organizational behavior* (Vol. 2). Greenwich, CT: JAI Press, 1980.

Oldham, G.R., J.R. Hackman, and J.L. Pearce, Conditions under which employees respond positively to enriched work *Journal of Applied Psychology.* 1976, *61,* 395-403.

Oldham, G.R., J.R. Hackman, and L.P. Stepina. Norms for the Job Diagnostic Survey. *JSAS Catalog of Selected Documents in Psychology,* 1979, *9,* 14. (Ms. No. 1819) (Available from Journal Supplement Abstract Service, American Psychological Association, 1200 Seventeenth St., N.W. Washington, D.C. 20036.)

Oldham, G.R., and H.E. Miller. The effect of significant other's job complexity on employee reactions to work. *Human Relations,* 1979, *32,* 247-260.

Orpen, C. The effects of job enrichment on employee satisfaction, motivation, involvement, and performance: A field experiment. *Human Relations,* 1979, *32,* 189-217.

Osborn, A.F. *Applied imagination* (Rev. ed.). New York: Scribner, 1957.

O'Toole, J. The reserve army of the underemployed: I—The world of work, *Change,* May 1975. II—The role of education. *Change,* June 1975.

O'Toole, J. *Work, learning and the American future.* San Francisco: Jossey-Bass, 1977.

Paul, W.J. Jr., K.B. Robertson, and F. Herzberg. Job enrichment pays off. *Harvard Business Review,* March-April 1969, 61-78.

Perlmuter, L.C., and R.A. Monty. The importance of perceived control: Fact or fantasy? *American Scientist,* 1977, *65,* 759-765.

Perrow, C. *Complex organizations: A critical essay* (2nd ed.). Glenview, IL: Scott, Foresman, 1979.

Pierce, J.L., and R.B. Dunham, Task design: A literature review. *Academy of Management Review,* 1976, *1,* 83-97.

Pierce, J.L., and R.B. Dunham, The measurement of perceived job characteristics: The Job Diagnostic Survey versus the Job Characteristics Inventory. *Academy of Management Journal,* 1978, *21,* 123-128.

Porter, L.W., E.E. Lawler III, and J.R. Hackman. *Behavior in organizations.* New York: McGraw-Hill, 1975.

Quinn, R.P., G.L. Staines, and M.R. McCullough. *Job satisfaction: Is there a trend?* Washington, D.C.: Manpower Research Monograph No. 30, U.S. Dept. of Labor, 1974.

Reeves, T., and J. Woodward. The study of managerial controls. In J. Woodward (ed.), *Industrial organization: Behavior and control.* London: Oxford, 1970.

Rice, A.K. *Productivity and social organization: The Ahmedabad experiment.* London: Tavistock, 1958.

Rodin, J. and E.J. Langer. Long term effects of a control-relevant intervention with the institutionalized aged. *Journal of Personality and Social Psychology,* 1977, *35,* 897-902.

Roethlisberger, F.J., and W.J. Dickson. *Management and the worker.* Cambridge, MA: Harvard University Press, 1939.

Rousseau, D.M. Characteristics of departments, positions, and individuals: Contexts for attitudes and behavior. *Administrative Science Quarterly,* 1978, *23,* 521-540.

Salancik, G.R., and J. Pfeffer. An examination of need satisfaction models of job attitudes. *Administrative Science Quarterly,* 1977, *22,* 427-456.

Sales, S.M. Some effects of role overload and role underload. *Organizational Behavior and Human Performance,* 1970, *5,* 592-608.

Sarason, S.B. *Work, aging, and social change.* New York: Free Press, 1977.

Schein, E.H. *Process consultation.* Reading, MA: Addison-Wesley, 1969.

Schein, E.H. *Career dynamics: Matching individual and organizational needs.* Reading, MA: Addison-Wesley, 1978.

Schwab, D.P., and L.L. Cummings. A theoretical analysis of the impact of task scope on employee performance. *Academy of Management Review,* 1976, *1,* 23-35.

Scott, W.E. Activation theory and task design. *Organizational Behavior and Human Performance,* 1966, *1,* 3-30.

Scott, W.G., and T.R. Mitchell, *Organization theory* (3rd ed.). Homewood, IL: Irwin, 1976.

Seashore, S.E., E.E. Lawler III, P.H. Mirvis, and C. Cammann. *Observing and measuring organizational change: A guide to field practice.* New York: Wiley-Interscience, in press.

Seeborg, I.S. The influence of employee participation in job redesign. *Journal of Applied Behavioral Science,* 1978, *14,* 87-98.

Seligman, M.E.P. *Helplessness.* San Francisco: Freeman, 1975.

Shaw, M.E. *Group dynamics* (2nd ed.). New York: McGraw-Hill, 1976.

Shea, G.P. Work design committees: The wave of the future. *Journal of Applied Management.* March-April 1979, 6-11.

Sheppard, H.L., and N.Q. Herrick. *Where have all the robots gone?* New York: Free Press, 1972.

Siassi, I., G. Crocetti, and H.R. Spiro. Loneliness and dissatisfaction in a blue collar population. *Archives of General Psychiatry.* 1974, *30*, 261-265.

Sims, H.P., A.D. Szilagyi, and R.T. Keller. The measurement of job characteristics. *Academy of Management Journal.* 1976, *19*, 195-224.

Sirota, D., and A.D. Wolfson. Job enrichment: What are the obstacles? *Personnel.* May-June 1972, 8-17.

Sirota, D., and A.D. Wolfson. Job enrichment: Surmounting the obstacles. *Personnel.* July-August 1972, 8-19.

Slocum, J.W., and H.P. Sims. A typology of technology and job redesign. Unpublished manuscript, Pennsylvania State University, 1978.

Smith, A. *Wealth of nations.* Edinburgh: Adam and Charles Black, 1850.

Smith, P.C., L.M. Kendall, and C.L. Hulin. *The measurement of satisfaction in work and retirement.* Chicago: Rand-McNally, 1969.

Sogin, S.R., and M.S. Pallak. Bad decisions, responsibility, and attitude change: Effects of volition, foreseeability, and locus of causality of negative consequences. *Journal of Personality and Social Psychology.* 1976, *33*, 300-306.

Staines, G.L., and R.P. Quinn. American workers evaluate the quality of their jobs. *Monthly Labor Review.* January 1979, 3-11.

Staw, B.M. *Intrinsic and extrinsic motivation.* Morristown, NJ: General Learning Press, 1976.

Staw, B.M., and G.R. Oldham. Reconsidering our dependent variables: A critique and empirical study. *Academy of Management Journal.* 1978, *21*, 539-559.

Stein, M.I. *Stimulating creativity.* (Vol. 2). New York: Academic Press, 1975.

Steiner, I.D. *Group process and productivity.* New York: Academic Press, 1972.

Stone, E.F., D.C. Ganster, R.W. Woodman, and M.R. Fusilier. Relationships between growth need strength and selected individual difference measures employed in job design research. *Journal of Vocational Behavior,* in press.

Stone, E.F., and L.W. Porter. On the use of incumbent-supplied job characteristics data. Paper No. 635, Institute for Research in the Behavioral, Economic, and Management Sciences, Purdue University, 1977.

Strauss, G. Is there a blue-collar revolt against work? In J. O'Toole (ed.), *Work and the quality of life.* Cambridge, MA: MIT Press, 1974.

Taylor, J.C., and D.G. Bowers, *Survey of organizations*. Ann Arbor, MI: Institute for Social Research, 1972.

Taylor, F.W. *The principles of scientific management*. New York: Harper, 1911.

Terkel, S. *Working*. New York: Pantheon, 1974.

Thayer, R.E., Measurement of activation through self-report. *Psychological Reports*, 1967, *20*, 663-678.

Tichy, N.M., and J.N. Nisberg. When does work restructuring work? *Organizational Dynamics*, Summer 1976, 63-80.

Trist, E.L., G.W. Higgin, H.Murray, and A.B. Pollock. *Organizational choice*. London: Tavistock, 1963.

Trist, E.L., G.I. Susman, and G.R. Brown. An experiment in autonomous working in an American underground coal mine. *Human Relations*, 1977, *30*, 201-236.

Turner, A.N., and P.R. Lawrence. *Industrial jobs and the worker*. Boston: Harvard Graduate School of Business Administration, 1965.

Umstot, D.D. MBO plus job enrichment: How to have your cake and eat it too. *Management Review*, February 1977, 21-26.

Umstot, D.D., C.H. Bell, and T.R. Mitchell. Effects of job enrichment and task goals on satisfaction and productivity. *Journal of Applied Psychology*, 1976, *61*, 379-394.

Van de Ven, A.H., and D.L. Ferry. *Measuring and assessing organizations*. New York: Wiley-Interscience, in press.

Van der Zwaan, A.H. The sociotechnical systems approach: A critical evaluation. *International Journal of Production Research*, 1975, *13*, 149-163.

Van Maanen, J., and E.H. Schein. Career development. In J.R. Hackman and J.L. Suttle (eds.), *Improving life at work*. Santa Monica, CA: Goodyear, 1977.

Vernon, H.M. *On the extent and effects of variety in repetitive work*. Industrial Fatigue Research Board Report No. 26. London: H.M. Stationary Office, 1924.

Vroom, V.H. *Work and motivation*. New York: Wiley, 1964.

Vroom, V.H. Leadership. In M.D. Dunnette (ed.), *Handbook of industrial and organizational psychology*. Chicago: Rand-McNally, 1976.

Vroom, V.H., and P. Yetton. *Leadership and decision-making*. Pittsburgh: University of Pittsburgh Press, 1973.

Walker, C.R. and R.H. Guest. *The man on the assembly line*. Cambridge, MA: Harvard University Press, 1952.

Wall, T.D., C.W. Clegg, and P.R. Jackson. An evaluation of the job characteristics model. *Journal of Occupational Psychology*, 1978, *51*, 183-196.

Walters, R.W. and Associates. *Job enrichment for results*. Reading, MA: Addison-Wesley, 1975.

Walton, R.E. How to counter alienation in the plant. *Harvard Business Review*, November-December 1972, *50*, 70-81.

Walton, R.E. From Hawthorne to Topeka and Kalmar. In E.L. Cass and F.G. Zimmer (eds.), *Man and work in society*. New York: Van Nostrand Reinhold, 1975. (a)

Walton, R.E. The diffusion of new work structures: Explaining why success didn't take. *Organizational Dynamics*, Winter 1975, 3-22. (b)

Walton, R.E. Successful strategies for diffusing work innovations. *Journal of Contemporary Business*, 1977, *6*, 1-22.(a)

Walton, R.E. Work innovations at Topeka: After six years. *Journal of Applied Behavioral Science*, 1977, *13*, 422-433. (b)

Walton, R.E., and L.S. Schlesinger. Do supervisors thrive in participative work systems? *Organizational Dynamics*, Winter 1979, 24-38.

Wanous, J.P. Individual differences and reactions to job characteristics. *Journal of Applied Psychology*, 1974, *59*, 616-622.

Weiss, H.M., and J.B. Shaw. Social influences on judgments about tasks. *Organizational Behavior and Human Performance*, 1979, *24*, 126-140.

White, B.J. Innovations in job design: The union perspective. *Journal of Contemporary Business*, 1977, *6*, 23-35.

White, R.W. Motivation reconsidered: The concept of competence. *Psychological Review*, 1959, *66*, 297-333.

Whyte, W.F. Human relations theory: A progress report. *Harvard Business Review*, 1956, *34* (5), 125-132.

Whyte, W.F. Skinnerian theory in organizations. In J.R. Hackman, E.E. Lawler III, and L.W. Porter (eds.), *Perspectives on behavior in organizations*. New York: McGraw-Hill, 1977.

Winpisinger, W.W. Job enrichment: A union view. *Monthly Labor Review*, April 1973, 54-56.

Work in America. Cambridge, MA: MIT Press, 1973.

Wortman, C.B. Causal attributions and personal control. In J. Harvey, W. Ickes, and R. Kidd (eds.), *New directions in attribution research*. Hillsdale, NJ: Erlbaum, 1976.

Wortman, C.B., and J.W. Brehm. Responses to uncontrollable outcomes. In L. Berkowitz (ed.), *Advances in experimental social psychology* (Vol. 8). New York: Academic Press, 1975.

Zajonc, R.B. Social facilitation. *Science*, 1965, *149*, 269-274.

Zander, A. *Motives and goals in groups*. New York: Academic Press, 1971.